DUCHESS OF CORK STREET

Lillian Browse was brought up in South Africa, and she returned to England in the mid-1920s to study ballet with Margaret Craske, joining the Dolin-Nemtchimova Ballet Company in 1930. She became ballet critic to the *Spectator* for four years in the early 1950s. She worked at the Leger Galleries from 1931 to 1939; then, during the war, she organized exhibitions at the National Gallery and for CEMA, the precursor of the Arts Council. She was a founder partner of the art gallery Roland, Browse & Delbanco in 1945, and also of Browse & Darby in 1977. It was Lillian Browse's neighbour Rex Nan Kivell, the founder of the Redfern Gallery and a close friend, who christened her 'duchess of Cork Street'. She organized the Sickert centenary exhibition at the Tate in 1960, later exhibiting her own private collection at the Courtauld Institute Galleries in 1983. Among her many books have been volumes on Augustus John's drawings, Sickert, Degas' dancers, William Nicholson (catalogue raisonné) and Forain's paintings.

Dedication

Above all to Sidney

then to my Godchildren

Jill
Mathieu
Tamasin
Susanna
Justine
and
Catherine

Duchess of Cork Street

THE AUTOBIOGRAPHY OF AN ART DEALER

LILLIAN BROWSE

CBE

dlm

First published in 1999
by Giles de la Mare Publishers Limited
3 Queen Square, London WC1N 3AU

Typeset by Tom Knott
Printed in Great Britain by
Hillman Printers (Frome) Limited
All rights reserved

A CIP record of this book is available
from the British Library

ISBN 1-900357-14-3

Contents

Illustrations

LINE DRAWINGS

All works illustrated in the book were sold by Roland, Browse & Delbanco

Acknowledgments

In the beginning it was Josef Herman who encouraged me to continue with the writing of this book; it was Douglas Hall who was my wise and patient editor; and finally it was Nicholas Stewart whose erudition and taste helped in so many ways. I am most grateful to Mariegold Heron for allowing me to quote her very personal view of the 'triumvirate' which she had formed over the years; and also to Matt Pia for the photograph of the Mané Katz portrait for the front of the cover, and to Lyn Fuss for the photograph of me on the back of the cover; and to Barney Perkins of the National Art Library and to Peter Bassett of the Laban Centre for help in tracking down artists' and dancers' dates.

Preface

My late partner, Gustave Delbanco, used to say that to write one's own autobiography was the most arrogant form of conceit and, because I have the greatest respect for most of his values, I have now to confess myself guilty of committing this act of self-aggrandisement. In my own defence, I must say that I do not believe I would ever have dreamed of doing any such thing had I been more tolerant and patient; but, sadly lacking the latter attribute in certain spheres, I got either irritated or bored by so frequently being asked to recount how and why I made the transition from ballet to art and how I came to join two German-born art-dealers in partnership – on the surface so unlikely a trio. With my tongue in my cheek, I even thought how convenient it would be if I had had made a record of these answers, but *au fond* I was puzzled by such curiosity for I could not regard myself or my background as of any particular interest and certainly not remarkable.

When I retired from Browse & Darby, having had just over fifty years of gallery life, it seemed that, although I was busily keeping the records of my published artists up to date, it would be interesting to tell of the revolution that had taken place in the commercial art scene (quite apart from the aesthetic one) in the comparatively short thirty-two years of Roland, Browse & Delbanco's existence. It was difficult to know when to stop looking backwards, for with the logic – I would call it the Divine Plan – which informs our lives, one happening led to another, and then there was no stopping until all had been told.

LILLIAN BROWSE
February 1998

Pablo Picasso, *Half-length of Seated Girl in Profile*. Melbourne Art Gallery, Felton Bequest

Part One
South Africa

My family

On the deck of a Union Castle liner a small girl was sitting playing with a toy tin bathroom. This is my first conscious memory and I do not remember one other thing about that three weeks' voyage from Southampton to Cape Town. My brother Jack and I had been born in London and I was three years old before we sailed to join my father, Michael Browse, who had already settled in Johannesburg.

My mother's upper-class Jewish family had lived in London for several generations. Her father and uncles all seem to have been on the Stock Exchange. Their patronym was Moses but four changed their names. It became a family joke that on occasions my grandfather would introduce his four brothers with: 'May I present my brother Mr Moses, my brother Mr Murray, my brother Mr Maynard and my brother Mr Moseley.' He himself was called Meredith.

The Merediths had had three daughters, of whom my mother, Gladys, was the youngest, and an only son, Hubert, who became a brilliant 'prima donna' in the City. It was said he could also have made a career on the stage, instead of which he exploited his histrionic talents by taking a leading part in the Stock Exchange Dramatic Society. Their shows were presented annually at the Scala Theatre, and were reputed to be the best of all amateur productions in Britain. I once devised, and also danced, a ballet number for one of their rare musical comedies. Uncle Hubert scored a great success playing in *Trilby*, which I can well imagine, for I always saw him as having some Svengali-like characteristics in his own personality, and with his compelling dark eyes, bushy black eyebrows and wealth of hair, he would have needed little of the conventional make-up for the role.

Hubert and my mother adored each other, and he never forgave my father for taking her so far away and for being, in his eyes, quite unworthy of her. In later years and during his periods of displeasure, the most cutting insult he could hurl at me was: 'Anyone can see that you are your father's daughter.' His own father Meredith had died early, leaving his widow with slender means, so that Hubert had left St Paul's before he had had time to complete his education. At a tender age he became the patriarch of the family and, in order to start earning, got a job as office boy in a firm of stockbrokers. While still in his thirties he was the manager of an important European bank, and he was lured away by Fleet Street to be Financial Editor of the *Daily Mirror*, in which capacity he so impressed Lord Rothermere that he was made Financial Editor to all the Rothermere papers. Finally he was 'bought' from Rothermere by Philip Hill, ending his highly successful career as Managing Director of Philip Hill & Partners.

Hubert made an unsuccessful marriage and had no children, so there was never anyone to say him nay – a most unsalutary situation for any human being. As was only to be expected, this powerful City man was flattered and fawned upon until he came to believe that he was only wanted because of the favours it was imagined he might bestow. He found it almost impossible to believe that there were those who appreciated him for his very real qualities of kindness and generosity and, therefore, while as a careerist he was enormously successful, as a family man he was impossible.

Of the three sisters it was the middle one, Gertrude, who most closely resembled her brother. She too had a compelling personality and a first-class intellect, which, had she been born a generation later, might well have led her into a professional career.

The change that has taken place in the status of women since I was a girl now appears unbelievable. Devoted though my aunt was to me, and proud of what she considered to be my achievement, she must have been a tiny bit envious that by sheer accident of date I had the opportunities denied to her. She was one of the most attractive women it was possible to encounter, a wonderfully warm-hearted human being, interested in everyone but fastidious in her morals and tastes to a degree that would be dismissed as ridiculously old-fashioned by today's impoverished standards. Her children clustered round her, reluctant to leave home, while any acquaintance who once visited her house in Cookham would invent the slightest excuse to return again and again. Hers was a beautifully run household where good news was welcomed and troubles could be shared. She had made a marriage, not of love but of duty, with one of three brothers all of whom had served in the Guards, an unusual circumstance for a Jewish family. It was regarded as a good marriage into a family of substance, and Aunt Gertie felt she should embark upon it in order to relieve some of the financial pressure on her widowed mother.

The other two daughters had no special talents or interests outside their husbands and children, but they too were wonderful home-makers. My mother, Junoesque in figure and with huge china-blue eyes, was one of those unremarked heroines whom infatuation had uprooted from the protective soil of a family background and transplanted into the infertile earth of a distant, strange and undeveloped land. Johannesburg, in the first decade of this century, was a harsh place for a girl nurtured in London, and for a wife whose husband could not afford the comforts available to the wealthy. With no family or friends, with in-laws who resented her, and without experience of the black races, she fortunately had the guts of a pioneer. Being young and selfish, I did not realize her problems until too late. 'Home' in our family meant only London, and although she never put it into words – probably because she feared it would never happen – I know that her dearest ambition was to return with a prosperous (and therefore vindicated) husband and two well-brought-up children.

My father's meeting with my mother had all the flavour of a Victorian novel. Two of my great aunts on my mother's side ran an 'establishment for young ladies', I believe in the Hampstead area. What qualifications they may have had is dubious but in those days few would have been necessary. In a genteel family a girl's future lay in marriage and children and, if she was moderately literate and could practise the feminine skills of sewing, tinkling on the piano and perhaps painting a few timid watercolours, no more was expected. To learn how to cook was not contemplated, since there would always be servants to do it – and to attend to the household chores. Even a family of modest means like the Merediths could afford Swiss or French governesses for their daughters, so that my mother's first tongue was French. Sadly she forgot it and could say only one phrase: *Bonne nuit.*

The great aunts counted among their pupils two of my father's sisters, and it was when he was visiting them that he saw and fell in love with my mother. To the dismay of her family, she also fell head over heels for him. Dismay it certainly was, for the young man was totally impecunious and had no firm professional or business prospects. Worse still, it was clear he would settle abroad and was considering Argentina or South Africa.

After the fateful meeting with my mother, and upon his return from an abortive trip to Argentina, father sailed for South Africa to try to establish himself and make some sort of home in which he hoped to receive a young wife. Her parents must have prayed she would forget him, but this was far from the case. Instead she lived from one Friday to the next – the day when the Union Castle liners carrying the Royal Mail docked in Southampton waters. Each week she would unfailingly receive a letter. In after years father was a notoriously bad correspondent and through long separations

I grew accustomed to not hearing from him, although I knew it was not because of lack of devotion.

My father was one of the most endearing of men with a charm that could not be resisted. He came from a large family but, in his case, it was his mother who had died while he was still very young. My paternal grand-father was a White Russian in the ostrich-feather trade in Port Elizabeth. By the time I knew him he was retired: an impeccably dressed and correct old man of great dignity, with a gleaming head of white hair and matching moustache. As children of eight and ten my brother Jack and I spent a holiday with him and our step-grandmother, our first seaside holiday. Throughout our lives, and despite long separations, my relationship with my brother was wonderfully close. A year and a half older, even at that age he was very much the man looking after his sister. On this memorable journey to Port Elizabeth we not only dined on the train, Jack ordering from the menu with great aplomb, but at the conclusion of the meal, and much to the astonishment of the steward, he grandly ordered a green Chartreuse for each of us. After that I imagine we slept soundly.

Being a child in South Africa

We spent two weeks of unimaginable happiness on this seaside holiday, and although I know Port Elizabeth is now very different, I hold it in my memory as some kind of heaven. It is difficult to describe the sensations of wonder left by that first glorious morning we ever spent on a beach; they come flooding back with astonishing vividness as if it had been yesterday. Breathing an air filled with ozone was so novel and intoxicating that I felt wild with joy. Discarding my shoes to walk on the sand, I found myself sinking into its warmth as its softness caressed my toes. Towards the tide's edge, where it was cooler and firmer, I watched the imprint my feet had made until I had reached and splashed in the water. As if such delights were not enough in themselves, there was the rhythmic thunder of breakers as, having reached their peak, they turned themselves over to crash into foam and run up the sands until they were a trickle. Then they quietly retreated into unfathomable depths – the whole a duet of power and gentleness. Sight, smell and sound were so fully charged that I did not know how to respond; then, like a foal released in a meadow, I tore over the sand with the excitement of living until I was quite out of breath.

Father could do almost anything with his hands – a trait which to some extent I have inherited, so that it was I and not Jack who was invariably his mate. Together we made all the tack, except only the saddles, for the many racehorses he was training. Leather is stitched with two needles threaded with waxed yarn, and I would take one needle and he the other; we would start from the raw skins and cut them to make bridles, surcingles and all the rest. We even cut his monogram out of the leather and stitched it onto the horses' felt body-cloths, which were also home-made by us. I loved all the tools which gave our work a professional finish – the punches for making buckle holes; the edging tools for use on both sides of a strap; the hard balls of wax with which we rubbed and polished till the leather was like shining gold. With a little tuition and some more equipment we could have set up in business as saddlers. During the years that I worked in Cork Street, I often stopped to admire (as I still do) the fine horse equipment in W. & H. Giddens' window in Clifford Street and savour the good familiar smell of leather. I must have been very much of a tomboy for I loved helping my father, with the aid of some stable-boys, to construct a hard tennis court and make a duckpond, concrete lined, in which we children used to paddle.

In his youth my father became the Champion Cyclist over a course that extended from Johannesburg to Salisbury – or Harare as it now is – and back, a distance each way of some 1,200 miles. I think that after this marathon he lost all interest in cycling for we never saw him on a bicycle and I, at least, was not taught to ride one, though Jack, being a boy, had his own. Father could have stayed in Argentina to work for the great Raleigh bicycle company. I think, however, that he would have felt too alien to settle in any country outside the Empire; for better or worse he refused the position and chose instead to make his life among horses. It was the Boer War that had introduced him to the world of horses in which he felt more at home. Horses meant racing, and he was by no means a gambler, but they represented the opposite to an office routine, to which he could never have submitted. He had not the slightest sense of business or of the value of money. When he had it, he spent it and only the best was good enough. He would lend freely to all those in need and it became known that he was 'easy to tap'. Naturally, he expected reciprocal treatment but more often than not he did not receive it. My brother Jack knew far more than I did about our father's eccentric behaviour and loved listening to his stories, but one that eluded him did not come to light until father was into his eighties. Jack, a lawyer, discovered that our father had never been officially discharged after the Boer War. He had simply walked out of his own accord as soon as hostilities were over! He was a law unto himself and was lucky that nothing worse than a small pension was forfeited.

The Union Castle Line seemed as permanent and inevitable as the Bank of England: who could have thought that it would disappear and we should all be travelling by air? But the days of sea travel were not without their own poignant moments, the worst of which was the long drawn-out agony of standing on the quayside watching a loved one slowly moving out of one's life, knowing it could be for ever. I have never yet found the anguish of parting to be 'sweet sorrow'. But sea travel also prolonged and heightened the anticipation of meeting again, as it must have done when my mother and her children were reunited with my father. When the family arrived in Johannesburg, we stayed for a while at Long's Hotel at the bottom of Eloff Street, a modest hotel which disappeared many years ago. I have some faded snapshots of Jack and myself taken on the iron veranda; he on a tricycle with a mop of curly hair and I in a frilly dress, bestarched and beribboned, topped by a large floppy hat.

During the years I lived in Johannesburg we occupied two different homes: these had to be near the main race-course in the socially downmarket neighbourhood called Turfontein. All our friends lived on the 'right' side of the city, where we eventually went to school. I can still see the front of our first mean bungalow but do not remember its interior. It was on a main road, very dusty indeed, with a front garden that was merely a patch separated from the sand pavement beyond by a few rows of bricks. In the backyard was the usual hovel of corrugated iron – the room for a servant – and also a lavatory, the only one we possessed. We were brought up to refer to this convenience with circumspection, a habit I have not lost to this day. Even when we moved to a much larger house in four acres of ground, we still did not have indoor sanitation or hot water laid on. Bath water was heated in four-gallon petrol cans on the coal range in the kitchen and was carried to the bathroom on Friday nights for our special ablutions.

On my last visit to Johannesburg several years ago, I went to see a friend in her charming new house, very luxurious with its own little swimming pool and all the comforts one could imagine. I was shocked to find that a servant's room could still be little more than an outside dog kennel, and although it had been improved as much as possible, the space was too confined to have any effect. In Johannesburg suburbs where old houses exist, blacks may be seen squatting outside on the pavements, laughing and talking together. The reason is that their quarters are stifling and when they are not working there is nowhere airy to meet except under the shade of the trees in the street.

One afternoon, when I was about six and we were still living in our first little house, there was a knock on the door and a very attractive, beautifully dressed young woman was standing on the threshhold. She apologized for her intrusion and explained to my mother that she had started a dancing class, just at the top of our street. I never understood why she had chosen so unlikely a neighbourhood when she already held classes in wealthier parts of the town. She said she had seen me playing in the garden and was asking my mother whether she would allow me to become one of her pupils. My mother replied that much as she would like it, we could not possibly afford such a luxury, while I stood and listened breathless with excitement and fearful that such a wonderful thing might never happen. I immediately adored this young Englishwoman whose name was Madge Mann. I had never yet seen her like and from that moment on I quite lost my heart to her.

Madge Mann would not be thwarted by my mother's reply and said that she would teach me for nothing. Whether this offer was accepted or not, henceforth this charming creature called to collect me once a week, and my dancing lessons began. Now it was I and not my mother who lived from one week to another. As I walked beside my teacher on my way to the classes I exaggeratedly tried to turn out my toes; I thought this was the way that all dancers walked and was determined to emulate them.

Jack and I started our education by having a governess at home. This was Miss Herbert, who lived near us and ran her own private school in the hall where my dancing classes were held. She must have been in her thirties, quiet, dignified and very correct; years later I discovered that the gossip was that she was having an affair with the local chemist. She used to call me her 'bundle of charm', which I thought was a funny expression, and she came to us in the afternoons after her own school had closed. Her discipline wavered when I was put in a corner and made to stand with my face to the wall; my father came in when this was happening and, with straight face, took his place beside me. Miss Herbert took this in good part and all ended in laughter.

When we were ready, we progressed to the school where my best friend was the one coloured pupil, whose name was Vera. Looking back it was remarkable that she was there at all and it said a great deal for Miss Herbert's open-mindedness. My mother also showed her good sense by not taking exception to the friendship; on the contrary I was allowed to ask Vera home for tea, after which we generally played our favourite game of hopscotch in the spacious stable yard. After a time Jack went to St John's College, the foremost of the boys' private schools; but he was enrolled only as a day boy, for my parents did not believe in boarding. They said they wanted to enjoy their children and would not contemplate sending us away. I in my turn duly left Miss Herbert's to go to Miss Rudd's private school, to which I travelled with Jack. I hated the trams which rocked sickeningly in the heat. It was a comfort that our dog, Widgey, who was half a black poodle, used to see us off and meet us at the tram stop. Years later, in London, I paid homage to Widgey by acquiring a black poodle and later a white one, and I have never lost the feeling that a dog is part of my life.

For a while I was contented with my new school but eventually I realized how casual it was; there seemed to be so little method that it must follow the standards were low. I may have resented that such care was taken when it came to educating a boy, while a girl did not matter at all. It mattered to me and I was resolved to show it, but not in a spirit of revolt. I was by this time in the Junior Certificate class and wanted to take the exam, but Miss Rudd, a tall, parched-looking lady with rabbit teeth, as the French like to caricature the typical English spinster, pronounced me too young. Although she was sure I would not get through, I sat it all the same with a handful of other pupils, and was the only one to pass. I believe it was determination that brought me success for I was no more intelligent than the others. Fortified by having passed the exam, I was able to persuade my mother and father to send me to a better school. Funds would not stretch to an expensive education for me as well as for Jack, so I entered a huge public (free) school where, after two years, I completed my education.

I cannot speak too highly of the free education then given to pupils in South Africa – white ones of course. There were some 1,200 pupils in our Upper School and, as each of the forms in which I worked comprised between fifty and sixty pupils, they were divided into three sections to allow more individual attention. The strictest discipline was brought to bear and those who flouted it were immediately expelled. One girl I knew was punished in this way for a mere prank. She had pulled out the pins which held the 'drawing horse', so that when the mistress sat down to make a correction it collapsed and she fell flat on the floor. But I am sure that the young respect, even demand, some kind of discipline both in their homes and at school, and I have never remarked that it cramps the development of personality – nowadays the argument against it.

In my second year at the Girls' High I was made a prefect, much to my amazement and that of my friends who had been at the school longer than I. Prefects were allowed to enter the school through the main doorway, while lesser mortals had to use the side doors, and because I felt it incumbent on me to exercise my rights I would, after the lunch break, deliberately leave my pals in the grounds to take the much longer walk into the building. This was an early example of the snobbery of which, in some form or other, we are all guilty. Prefects also enjoyed the privacy of their own recreation room and had to wear badges to show their authority. But I am afraid my elevation was a pure case of favouritism on the part of the acting headmistress.

Miss Buckland, who had started the school, was an old lady and had assigned most of her duties to the deputy headmistress, who was also our French teacher. So famed was Miss Friquet for her severity that many pupils, terrified of her reputation, would not even enrol at the school, while others had left on her account. We had French lessons every day of the week. Miss Friquet would sail into the classroom wearing her dark brown wig from which a few wisps of grey hair usually escaped, while we stood to attention not daring to giggle at this hirsute truancy. '*Asseyez-vou*s', she commanded and we chorused '*Je m'assieds*'. Then it was '*A qui le tour, aujourd'hui?*' '*C'est à moi, Mademoiselle*' came from the appropriate girl and the lesson began. It is not any exaggeration to say that for the first few weeks I was so frightened that each morning, during the French period, my knees positively knocked together under the narrow, upright school bench. Also I was far below the general standard and had to work extra hard to catch up and thus avoid the sarcastic tongue that could suddenly lash out like the whip of a snake. Unwittingly, and because of my application, I evidently won my way into Miss Friquet's heart and it was she who had rewarded me by making me a prefect. Nevertheless, to the end of my schooldays, I felt awe and respect for this admirable French woman, none of whose pupils, over her many years of teaching, ever dared fail an examination in French.

Our larger house was a great improvement and I even thought it quite grand; like most in the neighbourhood it was a bungalow, with rooms leading off on either side of the passage and a nice wide veranda on two sides. The windows and swing doors were fitted with mosquito wire and the roof, as also on the stables and buildings, was again made of corrugated iron. For the first time Jack and I had our own bedrooms. We also had a schoolroom where we did our homework and in which we secretly smoked Three Castles. After one cigarette we would open the window, flapping the curtains to get rid of the smell. Jack also caused some minor explosions through the chemical experiments he practised; he thought of becoming an analytical chemist and on leaving school began preparations for a degree.

The property was hemmed in by four or five rows of tall, gaunt pine trees which gave it a somewhat gloomy appearance, and which took so much out of the soil and allowed so little sunlight to penetrate, that only a few straggly roses were able to survive. Every now and then I would buy a packet of seeds, scatter them upon the dry impoverished ground and feel puzzled and sad at the lack of results. Our large peppercorn tree was some consolation, with its hanging bundles of tiny red fruit and the 'room' we had built far up in its branches.

Behind the house was a long row of stables, flanked on each side by a wing; one wing comprised half a dozen stalls, the saddle-room, accommodation for a resident jockey and a room for the cook. On top of the other was a large loft where the fodder and bedding straw were stored. We also used it for our theatricals or as a playroom on a rainy day. We were able to stable about thirty horses, some of which belonged to my father; the others were in training for individual owners who usually came to inspect them on

Sundays. Jack and I knew each of the horses intimately but we had our particular favourites, and always there was one that we called our own. One of these was a filly who showed much promise but I suppose would have been termed a rogue, for she did not allow anyone to enter her box excepting Jack and me and her stable-boy; not even my father. Another horse that we loved had been with us for so long that he was practically retired; he had come to know that he could open his box by putting his head over the stable door and, reaching the bolt, nosing it aside. When he was free he would take himself for a walk either in the paddocks or in the grounds, but as the property was safely enclosed nothing was done to restrain him.

Such were the intimacies between us and our horses that the memory has remained over the years; but I am sure we all wished, especially my mother, that our livelihood could have depended on almost anything but racing. It involved too much anxiety of which, even as children, we could not fail to be aware. On Saturday evenings, when my father and mother – for she always went with him – returned from a race meeting, we had to do no more than glance at their faces to know what the day had brought forth. A good one was celebrated, usually by going to a box at the theatre, while the bad ones, which seemed to be in the majority, plunged the four of us into gloom. Our stable was not a rich man's hobby – something which my grandmother in London could not understand – but a risky and unpredictable way in which to try to earn a living.

I learnt to ride on a Transvaal farm on one of those huge, gentle creatures, a Clydesdale. With its broad back like a comfortable chair, and its cumbersome pace, it felt as safe as a rocking-horse and I think it is ideal for a child to start on. How lovely was the freshness of those early morning rides when the dew was still glistening on the grass and the bushes, and the air was still fragrant as it softly blew on one's face before it became contaminated by the heat and dust of the day. The rise to the trot, when I had learnt how to manage it, had a lovely sense of rightness; it spelled a rapport between horse and rider – a feeling of inherent harmony. Unlike Jack, I never owned a real hacking pony. I should very much have liked to become a good rider but this was hardly possible on a racehorse.

I suppose we had ten to twelve stable-boys always living on the premises, and although there was a sprinkling of different black tribes, the majority of them were coloured. On the whole they were honest and well behaved, and the only recurring problem with which my father was faced was their habit of smoking dagga (marijuana). They had a curious and, to my mind, uncomfortable method which was so familiar a sight that we took it for granted. We thought nothing strange about seeing a 'boy' kneeling on the ground, his chin on the earth, inhaling as one would at a pipe or a hookah, only with the smoke emerging from under the soil at a distance of a couple of yards. An underground channel had been stuffed with the dry marijuana leaves which were then lit and the broken-off top of a glass mineral-water bottle, pushed into the opening, served as the smoker's mouthpiece. The boys would take it in turns to have a few puffs and after a session they often looked muzzy, with glazed eyes and a tottering stance. This Dagga smoking was illegal, and whenever my father discovered a run he would dig it up with a spade. But it was impossible to put a permanent stop to such a long-established habit and so the channel would appear in some other spot and its destruction would be repeated.

The most unusual character we ever had in the stables was of the almost extinct Bushman race, whose sad story has been so movingly highlighted by Sir Laurens van der Post. Bokkie was pale in colour, tiny of stature and as wizened as a very, very old man – he had no idea whatever how old he was. We were all very fond of this little person with the most ancient genealogy, who looked just like a monkey when crouched upon the back of a horse from which no bucking or shying could dislodge him. From time to time, in a mysterious way, he would get hold of a bottle of methylated spirits which he drank neat in its entirety, then with the fire inside him he would go almost berserk and leap with great ease over our main gates which were very much higher than he was. He did quite as well as the Olympic champions but without the aid of a pole. My father put up with all sorts of tantrums from him which would not have been tolerated from any of the others, for Bokkie was different: child-like, always happy and never malicious, he remained with us over the years.

I have deliberately left to the last the black man who was no less than a pillar of our establishment, and who helped stamp a pattern of good be-haviour on Jack and myself, one which I hope we never betrayed. Albert, our cook, was a Zulu chieftain who, typical of his tribe, was tall, handsome and dignified, with a presence that was both quiet and imposing. Always impeccably dressed in European style, he was a man of some property with sugar plantations in Natal where his family lived – whom he only visited at two or three yearly intervals. Albert would work for no other than an 'English gentleman' and so he regarded my father. He and his tribe hated the Boers, whose insolent treatment of this proud and once powerful race gave them full reason to do so. In place of the spear and assegai, Albert now wielded a sharp kitchen knife, but there was no trace of servility in the man whose ancestors were wont to command. Like other Zulus I have known, he was a natural cook; I can still see him rolling the *lokshen* quite thin and cutting it into the finest of strands for the soup that was traditional to Sundays. His domain was the kitchen and we were not allowed in except as a special treat, neither could we enter his spick-and-span room unless he invited us to do so. There we were fascinated by his collection of razors, a different one for each day of the week; even our father owned nothing so grand.

Albert was very strict about discipline and we were careful not to arouse his displeasure; when he thought we were behaving badly we were told in strong terms and never did he have to repeat himself. He came to regard us as his own children and wrote to us when we were on holiday – even to the time when I came back to London.

He never demeaned himself by mixing with the stable-boys but would visit his friends in different parts of the town. We could never understand why he had to walk this distance of two-and-a-half miles, but in those days no blacks were allowed on the trams and there was no alternative transport. Whenever he went out he had to carry a pass, on which scrap of paper my father would write: 'Please pass boy Albert until (say) 10 pm.' Once in the streets he could frequently be challenged and if by five minutes he had overstayed his pass he would immediately be taken to jail. His absence next morning made it clear what had happened and my father would then bail him out. We were outraged that our own dear Albert could be treated like a common criminal when in reality he was so fine a man. We were witness to many such indignities suffered by the black people in general – being kicked off the pavements to walk in the gutters and other mortifications too numerous to mention.

While nobody with any real knowledge of South Africa would have minimized the enormous problems that confronted any government trying to rule a population that comprised some 17 million blacks and 3½ million coloured and Asians, against only 4½ million whites – and on top of these problems the inherent tribal feuds – I firmly believe that the petty indignities imposed on the non-whites, which robbed them of personal pride, inflicted as deep, and perhaps more incurable, wounds as all the severe political and social restrictions together.

Only in retrospect and after an absence of years did my buried awareness of the beauty and variety of the South African landscape come to the surface. There is a compelling attraction about the veldt which, because we lived in the Transvaal, was the area I knew far the best. As children we were bored by this flat, arid vastness stretching mile upon mile into the horizon and, like visitors who never had time to get the 'feel', we much preferred – and I still do – the luscious fertility of Natal and the grandeur of the mountainous Cape.

From the time we could afford to take family holidays, we went to Natal each July; my father sent horses to the winter (July) meetings, and thus we combined business with pleasure. We motored the 400 miles down to Durban, not on the fine motorways enjoyed by travellers today, but on bumpy hard roads full of pot-holes and furrows which often deteriorated into little more than dust tracks. A heavy storm would turn the surface to mud when the car would skid round to face the opposite way; we wondered why this made my mother so nervous for Jack and I welcomed it with glee.

Our holiday was an adventure right from the start and we were always on the road by five in the morning; as the darkness dispersed and the sun rose in the heavens, so we became ravenously hungry. We would draw to a halt in the middle of nowhere to set about preparations for breakfast; I am sure that the penchant I still have for picnics goes back to these delectable meals. Large stones were collected to serve as a grate and with whatever sticks or branches were found Father would expertly kindle a fire over which he then grilled our steaks. Such meals were the precursors of the fashionable barbecues – *braaivleis* in the Afrikaans language. When we used to light log fires in the huge open fireplace of our Tudor cottage in Sussex, my husband said that anyone could see I was a Brownie. In fact I owe my successful kindling to my *Vortrekker* experiences on these journeys and not to the Girl Guide organization to which I never belonged.

We crossed the great Vaal river, the only important one in the whole of the Transvaal, at Standerton, and continued south-east until we reached Volksrust in the late afternoon. There we spent the night with my father's eldest sister and her husband, who owned the only store in the dorp. These stores were like Aladdin's caves for, apart from containing all the necessary provisions, they also kept the brightly coloured blankets worn by the Africans, beads of every hue threaded into articles for use or decoration, and finely woven baskets for carrying or storage as well as for the lamp-shade hats which the Basutos, especially, weave with much skill and delicacy. It was exciting to have the freedom of such a treasure house and to be given all sorts of artefacts, since our aunt was always overjoyed to see us and lavishly plied us with presents.

When we reached Pietermaritzburg the following day, the most beautiful and coolest part of the drive lay ahead. Down the long winding road, woody and steep – the Valley of a Thousand Hills – innumerable little monkeys chattered and swung in the branches just over our heads. The Indian Ocean was now visible in the far distance, a glimpse that was ever exciting, and gradually we dropped down to its level to enter the charming Natal port of Durban. It was thrilling enough to be by the sea after the dusty Transvaal, but one of the attractions I always anticipated was the sight of the rickshaws – only to be found at the coast.

Each colourful vehicle was drawn by a 'boy', scantily clad in gaudy war-paint; on his head he wore ox-horns and long feathers which waved about in the winds, while his ankles and wrists were encircled by bells, tinkling with the slightest move. Having lifted the shafts of the rickshaw he would leap in the air with a resonant whoop and set off at a run. All these men were apparently the picture of health but their appearance was sadly deceptive for, like the thousands of blacks who work down the mines, the toll on their health was inevitable. As they panted their loads up the numerous hills, their lungs gave way through the strain; they shortened their lives for a miserable pittance – strong and fine men, beasts of burden. At the time I loved going on these novel rides, too young to appreciate the cost; but later I longed for the law to step in and put a stop to this lamentable practice.

There were only three big hotels in Durban and we were lucky enough to stay at the King Edward, the only one right on the sea. It faced the long beach which curved round the bay, and a deep veranda terrace served as its foyer, stretching the whole of its considerable width. In front of this terrace Indian traders would squat to display the contents of their bundles: cottons and silks in those magical colours that only their own people dare juxtapose. Behind the veranda was a spacious 'palm court' and beyond that the big dining room; all were exposed to the breeze of the ocean, for classical columns replaced solid walls. This openness gave a wonderful feeling of freedom in which mingled a curious aroma – a mixture of curry and ozone.

The King Edward was owned by Errol Hay, a masculine Friquet who managed his hotel in martinet fashion. When first we stayed there he informed my parents that Jack and I would eat apart from the adults in the dining room set aside for children. My father adamantly refused this ruling and told Hay that if we did not behave just as well as the adults, then and only then would he give his consent. I can only assume that our manners were impeccable for the matter was not broached again.

Once we were unpacked we could not wait to change into bathing costumes and get into the surf. The icy cold of the ocean on bodies warmed by the sun at first made one gasp but was quickly dispelled by the force of the waves' pounding; they were so strong as to tumble one over as if in a washing machine. Later we learned to dive deeply beneath them and wait for the next breaker to follow. Along the coast were also those lovely, solitary resorts of Umhlanga Rocks, Karridene, Isipingo and others, each of which had but one hotel. Although, unlike Durban, they did not have nets, no sharks intruded and it was quite safe to go into the sea and, by catching the surf at the precise moment, be carried right up into the mouth of the river.

I was often invited to spend the weekend with a poor little rich girl called Lulu Freedman, who lived in Parktown, Johannesburg's superior suburb. We were both pupils at the same dancing class and she, the only child of elderly parents, was delicate and suffered from phobias from an early age.

I believe I was invited to relieve her loneliness because I was thought to be a suitable friend – one who, though a child, might have a salutary effect. Ours was indeed a curious friendship which, although we lived far apart and our meetings were rare, endured to the end of her sad life. In adulthood we instinctively agreed to differ on spiritual and philosophical matters, and were only at one in our love of the arts – she of literature and music, I of the pictorial arts and ballet. Lulu published translations of the best Zulu poems and had the temerity to try yet another *Fleurs du Mal*, but her only nearly serene moments were at her piano, to which she retreated for solace. A highly intelligent, unhappy woman, Lulu died in her seventies. Throughout her life, she never found a glimmer of hope nor any reason why one should be born into a world of such misery.

My first holiday on a South African farm came through an invitation from an aunt of Lulu's. Her farm was situated just outside Standerton and the Vaal ran through its land. We arrived in the dark at the spreading bungalow and I was longing to know what I would see when I awoke the next morning. An astonishing sight greeted my eyes: by this time the portulacas had opened theirs also, had unfolded their petals to the blazing sun so that before me was spread a dazzling patchwork of colour. They, and only they, constituted the garden in this pale and sandy soil. Like the flora of the desert they chose the gaudiest colours for their flowering, as if trying to compensate for the aridity of their surroundings. When darkness fell, like most of their species, they closed up again and disappeared into nothingness as rapidly as the southern sun sinks into the horizon, so that it was difficult to believe in the Pointillist painting that had been covering the ground.

When we went for walks along the banks of the Vaal I drank in the sight of the river; I could have spent hour upon hour just gazing at the deep, flowing water. At the side of the dam where, with baskets of food, we spent glorious days on a raft moored to the bank, we would lazily let our fingers and toes dip into the green coolness. Lying on our backs we basked in the heat as we listened to the cooing of wood pigeons. I still cannot hear this familiar sound without reliving those days.

My second farm holiday came when I was sixteen, and it was much more primitive. My beloved dancing teacher, Madge Mann, had forsaken her teaching to marry an easy-going, warm-natured but not over-intelligent Englishman who was familiarly known as 'Mealie' Baker – despite being much fêted and sought after in Johannesburg. Without money of his own, Baker was probably given an '1820 Settlers Grant' with which to start a small farm in an area that needed development. There they tried to live from one crop to another but with no capital put by to sustain the exigencies of farming – and this in a place where drought or locusts could destroy a year's toil completely – they were inevitably fighting a losing battle.

The farm was situated in the Northern Transvaal in an area known as Bandolier Kop, the name of a railway halt with a small general store on its platform. It was an overnight journey from Johannesburg to Bandolier Kop, which was reached quite early the following morning. The railway line ran through the Bakers' farm, so it was arranged with the guard that on my subsequent visits the train would come to stop on their land to cut a few miles off my journey. I felt rather important on these occasions when the train halted in the middle of nowhere, and passengers' heads popped out of the windows to see what was wrong – just a young girl alighting!

Miss Mann – as she was always to remain to me – met me on my first visit in an ox-wagon, which at the time was their sole means of transport. Riding in this was a fascinating but uncomfortable experience. The solid wheels ground harshly over each stone and rut, grating on the ears and shaking the passengers spitefully, while the dust rose in clouds to settle like a rough glaze on our skin damp with sweat. The pace was slow, for the animals were impervious alike to the driver's behests and the crack of his *sjambok*; but at last we arrived at the Bakers' farm. When first I saw it, the Bakers' home consisted of one room, their bedroom. Onto it they intended to add the rest of the house as soon as they could afford it. Seemingly dropped into a great treeless expanse, this tiny square edifice with its sloping tin roof, expectantly awaiting a further attachment, looked very lonely, also bizarre, reminiscent of a canvas by Dali. The rest of the farmstead consisted of *rondavels* – mud walls, thatched roof unlined, and with cow dung thickly layering the floors. The latter, despite its unhygienic implications, made a clean and splendid ground cover. I used to watch the natives adding fresh layers, pouring the liquid dung from their buckets and smoothing it over to make a good surface. The heat quickly made it dry and harden and as cattle are not carnivorous it did not smell – an excellent and cheap mode of continuous recarpeting. The bedroom and the *rondavels* were about forty feet apart and were arranged in a triangle. The kitchen and living room together formed one point while my 'bedroom' constituted the other. In the distance was the *kraal* where the farmhands all lived and at night, because I felt and indeed was rather physically detached, it was comforting to hear them beating their drums and making their own kind of music and song in a somewhat unusual lullaby.

There was no lock and key, nor even a latch on the rough wooden door of my bedroom, but only a tape with which to tie it inside. But there was never any fear of an intruder for the natives had no desire to leave their own quarters and always kept at a respectful distance. The only danger I ever encountered was from a tarantula which crept into my room through the space between the ground and the door. On stormy nights the rain poured in torrents through the thatching, but an umbrella was at hand for this particular purpose and I would sleep with it clutched in my hands. Once I was awakened by a loud hissing noise so close that it seemed to come from the thatch directly above where I lay. I immediately thought it must be a snake – perhaps it was even with me in the 'room'. To be petrified with fright is no idle saying. I simply froze, hardly daring to breathe. The hissing probably continued for no more than seconds but it was an eternity to me; then blessed relief, it faded into the distance until it was faint enough for me to recognize the call of a bird to whose curious notes my attention had been drawn only a few days before.

This holiday was made memorable by several 'firsts', the funniest of which was my first proposal of marriage. The little store on the siding from which all bought their provisions, was owned by a young, plump, mid-European Jewish man whom everyone knew just as Hymie. He could not have seen me more than three or four times when on horseback we called to buy household provisions, but one day he appeared at the Bakers' farm on an unheralded visit. His purpose was to ask my hostess whether he might offer me his hand in marriage. Utterly taken aback by such an unexpected request, she managed to keep a straight face while with courtesy she thanked him for his tribute, telling him that my parents would never consent and that, in any case, I was far too young to contemplate marriage to anybody. I can scarcely imagine any position more foreign to my temperament and tastes than being the wife of a storekeeper in the siding of Bandolier Kop.

Another 'first' was my participation in a Protestant church service. It was on Christmas Day and a local parson – from where he came I have no idea – arrived near the farmstead to conduct the service held under a small cluster of bushes. A handful of farmers, mostly settlers from England, together with their wives and families, gathered from miles around for the celebration and I automatically went with my hosts. I had not yet begun to appreciate the true meaning of a religious ceremony, and although I had been a few times to a synagogue, I did not understand anything of the services, which were conducted in Hebrew. Moreover, in the orthodox manner, the women sat upstairs apart from the men down below, and with the possible exception of my mother who tried to listen devoutly, it seemed to me that most of the others were discussing their fine clothes or revelling in the latest bit of gossip. But the simple Christian ceremony out in the wilds was obviously totally different; I could relate it to the prayers we said each night although it was strange to be celebrating the birth of Jesus Christ, who was not to be mentioned in our teachings. This small congregation was truly united in prayer and looking back over the years I can easily believe that this was where the seeds of my subsequent non-denominational faith were sown.

When the service was over we had Christmas lunch under the shade of a solitary tree; despite the hot sun of a midsummer day, we ate hot roast turkey and plum pudding, all brought to the spot in containers.

Amongst plagues in the Bible I had read about locusts but had never seen one until I went to this farm. 'Mealie' Baker was trying to establish tobacco and his first crop of plants, young, green and tender, were growing well and had reached about twelve inches in height. Success seemed most likely and everybody was hopeful until one afternoon the disaster occurred when a heavy dark cloud like an approaching rain storm suddenly appeared in the sky. The natives started shouting and wildly gesticulating for they all recognized what it meant; then they rushed to gather brushwood and sticks which they set alight in each of the four corners of the field. Pieces of cloth were also collected to wave about on the perimeter, for the cloud was in fact a swarm of locusts and once they had settled the crop would be lost. Neither the waving of cloths nor the smoke from the fires proved to be of any avail and we stood watching helplessly as the creatures ate their way through the field. When they were satisfied and indolent, resting after their meal, the natives would fry them as they were considered a delicacy; cooked crisp they looked like succulent whitebait, but I never had the courage to try one.

Later I had a second experience of locusts when, by a fatal misjudgement of its leaders, a swarm was guided into the centre of Johannesburg. I was driving into the town to do some shopping when, to my astonishment, two or three locusts hurled themselves at the windscreen and, as they are the size of large grasshoppers, even these few made a squashy mess on the glass. Quickly I closed all the car windows, only just in time for I found myself in the middle of a swarm, with the insects thudding the windows around me. I could no longer see where I was going and the car was skidding all over the place on the slippery yellow mush of their bodies, so I drew to a halt and waited until what was left of the swarm had flown off.

Jack and I had a cousin who was married to a mining engineer. He had had the temerity to try to start his own mine on the outskirts of Bulawayo and was still in the process of testing its worth. Gold there was, but how much could only be ascertained by digging. The potential mine was christened Leonora after the family's elder daughter. We were let down the shaft in a primitive hoist to watch the natives at work, as well as being allowed to take part in the panning. Our cousin's house lay under the shadow of a longer established gold mine to whose roar of machinery one became so accustomed that if for some reason it was brought to a stop it seemed as if the world had come to a standstill. We watched all the mine's external working procedures but by far the most exciting was the sight of its precious finished product. These golden nuggets were casually loaded on barrows like so many piles of ordinary bricks, but as they were wheeled to the trains, they were carefully guarded every inch of the way by men with rifles. In comparison with these glittering bricks, the few grains of gold left in our basins were as nothing; but we could not toss real gold powder away so we meticulously wrapped it all in our handkerchiefs to keep as a treasured momento. We lost touch with our cousins in later life but heard, with much sadness, that 'Leonora' had failed.

Such are my memories of southern Africa. In Rhodesia, as it then was, we were taken to see the Cecil Rhodes monument which, as he had wished, was a simple stone set in the rocks on the summit of the Matopo Hills. Majestic and lonely, it commanded a view of the whole countryside so that the stone's isolation and its very chasteness imparted a grandeur that was far more impressive than any more elaborate mausoleum. After so long a period of event-filled years its picture still remains with me vividly, as does the image of the ruins of the Great Zimbabwe.

The most famed sight of all was the one that we actually missed – the Victoria Falls, although I had not the courage in after years to admit not having seen them, and would give graphic accounts of their size and beauty gleaned from photographs. In recompense I have since been to the Iguacu Falls, the 'star' role in the film *The Missionary*: this valley of falls on the Parana river, which lies at the point where Uruguay, Paraguay and Brazil meet, must be one of the world's greatest unacclaimed wonders. Unlike Niagara with its awful coloured lights and its uninteresting setting, Iguacu is surrounded by exotic growth and has mercifully remained in its primordial state.

Dancing days

When I moved to my new school on the other side of Johannesburg, I also graduated to the dancing classes at the smart Carlton Hotel; these were held on Saturday morning and were in fact like dancing displays with only a smattering of serious training. Leading out of the splendid, old-fashioned Palm Court, a popular meeting place before Saturday racing, was a large ballroom in which our classes were held. The mothers sat at tables around the floor keenly, often jealously, watching their hopefuls, just like the Degas mothers watching their *rats*, while visitors wandered in to be entertained by the pupils – there were about fifty, mostly under twelve years of age – who were dressed in the prettiest frilly frocks. I was considered to be one of the most talented and was often singled out to display my gifts; my great role was that of an abandoned Pierrot whose Columbine had deserted him for another. The little number ended by my tearing off my tall hat, bursting into tears, and hurling myself face downwards on the floor in a paroxysm of cruel despair. I obviously did this with such vehemence that it always brought forth a heady applause. This was the only occasion in my ballet career when I felt any power over my audience and enjoyed a really good 'show-off'.

The important events of the year were our dancing displays held in one of Johannesburg's theatres when, if they happened to be in the city, we danced to the accompaniment of the newly formed Cape Town Orchestra, the first professional concert orchestra of the Union. After the uninspiring tinkle of a piano it was tremendously uplifting to have a full orchestra, and I am sure that our performances were enhanced. For many years after I said goodbye to my *pointe* shoes, I could not sit still while listening to music but found myself translating it into movements of ballet and quietly swaying in my seat to the mood and the tempo.

For these dancing displays many costumes were needed and their provision always worried my mother: not only were they an unnecessary expense but, although she was a beautiful needlewoman as far as stitchery was concerned, she dared not cut into a virgin length of cloth, and she lacked the necessary inventiveness. Happily I was able to suggest how this or that effect might be obtained, for there is nothing like necessity to foster resourcefulness when theatrical paraphernalia are not to be found. I was always very bold with my scissors and never used patterns, believing that mistakes could be turned to good account. Now when I am gardening I am equally bold with my secateurs, very often to my husband's alarm.

One of the proudest press notices I ever received was the *Rand Daily Mail*'s praise of the dress that I wore when I went to my first grown-up dance, to which I was escorted by the young man with whom I was madly in love. Although his father was an old family friend, I was not allowed to go without a chaperone, but luckily Jack was always willing to take his own partner and therefore to accompany me. By this time I was sixteen and making all my own ballet costumes, even applying myself to the hard task of covering my *pointe* shoes in satin: in South Africa it was only possible to buy them in black canvas. For a recent display I had needed a crinoline, so I had made one in white crêpe-de-chine with a silver lace bertha. For my 'coming-out' dance I just removed the cane hoop and there was a very pretty evening dress. The surprising press approval so encouraged me that little by little I began to make all my own clothes, so that, by the time of my first marriage, I was able to make my entire trousseau – evening and day wear, top-coats and all. I flatter myself that they did not look home-made.

The first professional dancers I ever saw were members of the well-known Espinosa family. Espinosa was accompanied by his wife Eve Kelland – a musical comedy actress, his son, a dancer though only in his teens, and his younger daughter, Yvonne. But the person who really opened my eyes was Espinosa's sister, known as Ravodna. I suspect that she was middle-aged at the time and I have since realized that she was by no means outstanding, but she had the professional dancer's command and her dancing was as far removed from ours as our tennis was from Wimbledon. Espinosa produced two musical comedies in which his wife starred and in which he inserted irrelevant numbers for Ravodna; he also gave a few dancing lessons and for a while I enjoyed the kind of tuition I never thought to receive in Johannesburg.

For the second of his musical comedies Espinosa required a child dancer; to my joy and excitement I was the one chosen and surprisingly my parents gave their consent. The role I danced was that of 'Midnight' and for one glorious moment I was a 'star', making my entrance through the dial of a clock placed centre back-stage, and with the entire cast turning towards me and watching whilst I performed my solo. My mother, while secretly proud, was at the same time anxious, for I had to dress in the chorus girls' room and she feared for my innocence. The girls, however, petted and spoiled me and carefully guarded their talk, and although I learned a few titbits about which I had hitherto been unaware, I emerged from their company unsullied. This first taste of the footlights enhanced my desire eventually to go on the stage and like most young dancers I dreamed of a glittering career, preferably in London but certainly somewhere overseas.

My second professional engagement, far less spectacular but also more serious, came when I was in my teens. An Italian trio – father, mother and son – whose names I have now completely forgotten although I remember what they looked like, were paying a professional visit to Johannesburg and dancing some numbers during a break in a cinema programme at the Orpheum. They required three girls to perform with them and I was selected as one of the trio on a run which only lasted three weeks. By this time I was old enough to benefit and learn from this more adult experience.

I was just about to leave school when the blow fell: without warning Miss Mann announced that she was going to be married and had sold her teaching practice to someone called Pearl Adler. I was devastated. Pearl was already an established teacher of ballet and, because she had studied overseas under Lydia Kyasht, the famous Russian ballerina, her tuition was on quite a different level from the amateurish methods of Madge Mann. Physically they were quite dissimilar: Pearl was small, plump and of spotty complexion, and obviously thought it was not worthwhile to try to improve her appearance. Had she been Juno herself, it would not have predisposed me in her favour, for she was usurping the place of my idol since childhood. However, as I was part of the practice's goodwill and Miss Mann had made me promise to continue my studies and be an assistant to Pearl, I grudgingly and broken-heartedly agreed. Being full of resentment, sullen and uncooperative, I behaved in such a bloody-minded fashion that I was not surprised when, after a few months, I was summoned to have a talk with my teacher. I expected to be asked to leave, which my sense of fairness told me would be fully justified.

I was wholly mistaken. Without preamble, for she was a straight talker, Pearl told me that she wanted to make me her partner and give me a half share in her now considerable practice, for which I knew that her wealthy father had paid several thousand pounds. For a moment I was speechless, taken aback, but when I recovered I stammered the question: why had she made such an undeserved offer, one that was generous in the extreme? She answered with her usual self-conscious giggle. It appeared that her senior students had been telling her unpleasant tales about me whereas I, un-suspectingly, had remained aloof and never uttered a word against any of them. Well aware of the ill feelings I harboured against her, she understood and made allowances; she needed a partner to share her work and responsi-bilities and I was the one she trusted. From that moment on my attitude changed. Pearl had taught me a lesson in human values and although I was always alive to her unprepossessing appearance (for I have always loved beauty in women) I learned to appreciate something more real – her many sterling qualities.

My relatively short teaching career had begun. To look older and more responsible, I doubled my plait into a large bow at the neck, changed my black stockings for adult flesh-coloured ones, and lowered my skirt by inches. Immensely flattered at being a partner in a large dancing school, and delighted by my first steady earnings, I worked with enthusiasm, though I am not a born teacher and never gave up hope of becoming a performer. For a couple of years we were enormously busy, holding classes each day of the week. We travelled to the outer districts in Pearl's Austin coupé which was finally discarded when it burst a tyre and somersaulted with both of us inside. Astonishingly we sustained nothing but scratches from the glass that had shattered about us, and when the next passers-by stopped to render help to the injured – if there were people still alive in the mangled heap – we were standing there laughing from the shock, having crawled out from under the wreckage.

It was not long after this that a miracle occurred, a dream at last come true. Pearl announced that she thought we should both go to London to take the esteemed Cecchetti exams, the passing of which would, in Johannesburg, greatly enhance our reputation as teachers.

Pearl's plan was that we should go to London the following November, which would give us two to three months' study under Miss Margaret Craske, the leading Cecchetti teacher, in preparation for the intermediate examination which was scheduled for the beginning of the new year. Thoughtfully saving me any embarrassment, for she knew that my family could not afford so expensive a journey, Pearl had already asked her father to put up a loan for my fare. My mother wrote to ask her sisters and brother whether one of them could have us to stay, and it was Uncle Hubert who agreed to her request. He had plenty of space in his roomy flat in Maida Vale, whereas both of my aunts were living out of London and in any case their homes were too small to take us both.

My mother was unselfishly delighted for me and never spoke of her own longings but I knew she continued to have bouts of homesickness when she badly missed her family and friends. Lily Hanbury, the actress, was her heroine (just as Madge Mann had been mine), and when I was born she became one of my godmothers, whom sadly I was never to meet. To me she remained no more than a myth for she died giving birth to her first child, but I knew that she came from the acting family of Terrys and that she was chiefly famed for her beauty. Robin Fox, the well-known theatrical agent, was one of her nephews and all of his sons have carried on the family tradition by making names for themselves in theatre and films. I was therefore acquainted with the Fox family long before I actually met them, so that when many years later they came into my life, not through my mother but through my profession, I felt that events had neatly described a full circle.

For my trip to London my mother set about gathering what amounted to a beautiful trousseau. I am sure we could have ill afforded the expense but like most teenagers I gave little thought to the sacrifice. It is amusing to think back to the clothes that were thought necessary, especially as Mother must have been at great pains to show that her family lacked nothing. My luggage included several evening dresses as well as an evening coat, and *thé-dansant* frocks, which most intrigued me, but which Uncle Hubert had impressed on us that I would need because these occasions were an accepted part of privileged London life. I had to have at least one tailored costume: heavy clothing to withstand an English winter of a kind which was never worn in South Africa; and just as important as anything else, there were hats to go with each outfit. Travelling by train and ship the weight of our luggage was in those days of no consequence and Father, who had a passion for leather – as might have been expected as we two were saddlers – bought me one of those large wardrobe trunks which, acting like a piece of furniture in the cabin, eliminated the chore of unpacking.

Preparations for London comprised other matters just as important as clothing. My mother briefed me haphazardly in minutiae ranging from social etiquette to the weather. I was not to be surprised by the darkness that fell, in the northern winters, as early as mid-afternoon; nor by London's fabled 'pea-soup' fogs during which it was impossible to see one's own hand if it was stretched out before one. When less intense, like a silver grey mist, the fog could transform any ordinary urban scene into one of ethereal beauty, while the snow, which the traffic ground to a dirty brown slosh on the roads, also etched each branch and twig in loving delineation and laid a dazzling white blanket upon every roof-top. This unfamiliar snow imparted an uncanny, hushed silence as if the entire universe were holding its breath, while the gentle drizzle could only be seen but seldom heard. I was so accustomed to hearing rain whose drops, as huge as in a tropical storm, hit with loud and staccato sounds upon corrugated iron roofs, that I could not imagine it might be almost inaudible falling lightly upon London's tiles. If this was so, how was one aware that it was raining?

As to the proper behaviour in private houses where, my mother reminded me, 'you will see that the staff has only white faces', I was not to forget to tip the maid who, after a dinner party, would be there to help me with my coat. I was shocked at the idea that anyone should be kept up so late in order to perform so simple a function. When the time came I was even more shocked by the sight of a white woman, often not young, kneeling with a pail and brush at her side, scrubbing the steps from the pavement to the door. It seemed as ignominious as scrubbing the street itself, and for a long time the scene continued to affront me. In this as in other matters no briefing could be complete enough to cover every eventuality, or save a young girl unfamiliar with London society from embarrassing *faux pas*.

Thus I was told that it was more thoughtful to send flowers to one's hostess before, instead of after, a dinner party, but not told to be sparing with the grapes at dinner because they were a luxury and were probably grown in a hot-house. So my first social *faux pas* was that I took the whole bunch of grapes, which was not all that big by South African standards! Neither did anyone tell me how to eat whitebait. A sophisticated young cousin with one of his men friends took Pearl and myself to my first London restaurant before the theatre. Whitebait was ordered as our first course and when the plates were put before us the two men waited, as good manners demanded, for the ladies to start eating. Pearl, like me, was unused to these little fish, neither of us knew how to tackle them, and although I glanced surreptitiously at the others for guidance, none was forthcoming and we sat looking at each other in silence. I was not allowed to forget this for many a day. Such seemingly trivial embarrassments would not be worth mentioning had they not slowly intensified themselves within me out of all proportion to their importance. Later they made me careful of the sensibilities of others so that, when the war brought many refugees to London, I like to think that I was alive to their predicament and vulnerability, however different the circumstances.

The day for departure on this longed-for trip drew near and I greeted it for reasons both joyous and painful. The young man with whom I was desperately in love and who romantically filled my adolescent thoughts, had made no secret of his own passion for a very lovely girl who lived in Durban and with whose looks I could not possibly compete. He possessed what I believe to be an exclusively masculine trait, the ability to care for two women at the same time, but as one of them was removed by distance while I was at hand, I persisted in hoping that he might gradually forget her and turn all his affections towards me. But it was not to be. Two weeks before I was due to sail for England he announced his engagement and my world crumbled about me: I would never in my life love anyone else – the same but always poignant story of unrequited love. Despite my longing to see him each and every day, reason told me that my going overseas was the best thing that could happen in the circumstances and that, at the very least, I would be spared the agony of having to be present at his wedding. I could not have envisaged what was subsequently to happen, for the marriage ended in total disaster and when at the end of the war I was visiting my father and Jack in Johannesburg and we met again, he begged me to stay and marry him – a proposal I would earlier have given years of my life to receive. It was too late; too much had happened to each of us in the interim and fate had decreed that my working holiday was transformed into a permanent stay, so that I had become a passionate Londoner.

I have often pondered as to whether the land of one's birth does not send down its deepest and most meaningful roots into the human psyche with only the laterals remaining on a superficial level. It seems to me that man, like a plant uprooted out of its native soil and planted in a foreign environment, either withers and dies or struggles to exist until the years have acclimatized it, not only to new physical conditions but overridingly to that absolute existence upon which I feel sure all living bodies depend. How otherwise can one account for the profound love most people have for their native land, whatever its drawbacks and hardships? Patriotism is no explanation for this phenomenon: the word is simply descriptive of the state, not an elucidation of it.

The natural beauties of the country, the startling changes of magnificent scenery from one province to another, the free open-air life which a splendid climate affords and which so greatly adds to the strength of the body and its physical bearing: all this was insufficient to quell the restlessness which, in my inherent being, I had vaguely felt during my years in

South Africa. Looking back on my life in Johannesburg, I realized that I was a square peg in a round hole. In London I found my rightful ambience. It was all I had imagined and hoped it would be.

Edgar Degas, *'A Good Plié Makes a Good Dancer'*. Private collection

Part Two

London in the Thirties:
Ballet and Art Dealing

'The most austere of disciplines'

The day for departure finally arrived. The boat-train for Cape Town left in the evening and when dusk had fallen we drove to the station. In order to keep as close to them as possible before this, my first extended parting, I sat crushed between my mother and father on the front seat of the car, clinging to my mother's hand and growing more and more desolate and apprehensive. As we drew near to our destination the realization that I was about to be separated from my loved ones became increasingly unbearable; that aching lump in the throat inseparable from physical pain refused to be swallowed and the tears rolled uncontrollably down my cheeks. If only my father would turn the car around and return home... Did I have a premonition that I was never again to see my mother; that this was to be no three months' parting but a final farewell? Had I known 'the end of this day's business ere it come' I would never have embarked upon this journey, nor been able to look back, as now I can, upon a life so truly blessed as mine has been.

During the course of the years I have been shown many times how everything comes to pass just at the right moment; that the most stringent trials all have their rightful place in the development of one's growth, and although it may be well nigh impossible to accept at the time, all is ordained for our highest good.

I do not have travelling by sea in my veins and although life on board was an interesting experience, on subsequent sailings I came to dislike the same old passenger-ship routine of deck games, fancy-dress dances, and the like. But the short break at Madeira was full of delight – my very first flavour of southern Europe, though placed in the rough Bay of Biscay. After the clipped intonations of English-speaking South Africans, the melodious Mediterranean tongue seemed to caress my ear. I loved the quaint four-poster sleighs that conveyed us bumpily down the hillside, gaily adorned, like the women, in yards of brightly coloured chintz. The women also wore jockey-like boots made of red leather as soft as kid. I could not resist buying a pair, which occasionally I dared to wear in London; they drew many a stare for I was anticipating the fashion for coloured footwear by something like twenty years.

Aunt Gertie had come to Southampton to meet me and as the liner docked at the quayside she instinctively knew who I was, as I stood with Pearl, and called out with the kind of spontaneous but nonsensical utterance one is apt to make on such occasions. This meeting was the beginning of a mutual devotion which was to last throughout her long life; she and 'Dardoo' became second mothers to me and I tried, not always successfully, to live up to her high esteem and even loftier standards.

Until that journey from Southampton to London, I had not realized how small England was compared with South Africa. When the boat train had been travelling for some fifteen minutes, I began to wonder when we would get into the country. I could hardly believe we were already in it, for this was not country as I knew it. These lush little meadows delineated by hedges and peppered with cottages, never far from a village, all seemed much more like a series of gardens with their beautiful trees and patches of flower beds, even though these were past their best and preparing for winter. The straight-furrowed ploughed fields appeared so tiny that I could not reconcile them with those of my past, uninhabited expanses that were apt to stretch as far as the human eye could see. Here was a landscape cosy and gentle; no wonder that Americans often call England 'that darling country' and almost immediately I, too, came to regard it as such.

London's domestic architecture was equally strange. In South African towns, where space is not limited, the majority of people lived in their own houses, modest or grand by local standards, but always placed in some kind of garden. When I was a child there were few blocks of flats and although they were increasing in number when I left the country, hardly any of our friends chose to live in them. I had never seen a terrace of tall and, as it seemed to me, forbidding buildings like the one in Maida Vale where Uncle Hubert resided. Although, admittedly, his flat was spacious and comfortable I felt very confined, for one could not step out into one's own ground but had to go to a park to find greenery.

When my uncle returned from the City on the evening of my arrival, he greeted me with a great open-armed gesture and there were even tears in his eyes. Being emotional by nature and uninhibitedly dramatic, he was moved by this meeting with his favourite sister's daughter whom he had not seen since she was little more than a baby. My visit with Pearl called for a celebration, which took the form of a grand family dinner of several courses with their appropriate wines; for he never did anything by halves. This was my first experience of something like a banquet. The welcome I received was touchingly warm and I met two new cousins and an uncle, but 'Dardoo' and her husband were missing. They had been living in Hong Kong for years and Ivan, their son, was at boarding school. Nevertheless I was back in my mother's family circle.

Pearl had already arranged the date when we would start our ballet studies with Margaret Craske, the leading exponent of the Cecchetti method. Enrico Cecchetti was in his late sixties when in 1918 he settled in London and opened a school. As a teacher of genius under whom the greatest had studied, he had been *maître de ballet* to the Diaghilev company and one of its most distinguished character dancers. But he had grown tired of incessant travelling and only worked with the company when it visited London, where his studio in Shaftesbury Avenue became the Mecca for all famous dancers, in those days mainly from Europe. By the time he retired, in 1923, to return to his home in Italy, he had appointed Margaret Craske to take over his school and the Cecchetti Society came into being. It was important for posterity to record his famed method and Cyril Beaumont's *Manual of the Theory and Practice of Classical Theatrical Dancing (Méthode Cecchetti)* admirably fulfilled this task, while the Society's function was to preserve its practice by supervising the training of dancers and teachers – for the latter, examinations were inaugurated.

Margaret Craske had been a member of Diaghilev's company. She trained under Cecchetti until he went back to Italy, when he gave her a certificate indicating that she was qualified to carry on his teaching traditions – a rare honour. Miss Craske, as we all called her, for although we respected and loved her dearly she invited no intimacies, became the leading Cecchetti teacher and the acknowledged world authority on his method, to the continuation of which, in its purest form, she was totally committed.

As well as studying ballet with Miss Craske, Pearl was intent on bringing herself up to date on the latest methods and steps in ballroom dancing, which she also taught in Johannesburg. In those days ballroom dancing was not just a jogging with each doing their own thing irrespective of partner and attempting a rhythm only innate to black people, but was a necessary social art for every well-brought-up young person and had to be mastered as such. For her refresher course, Pearl's choice of teacher was Santos Casani, one of the most expert and well-known exhibition dancers in London, who also coached professional pupils. His studio was in Cork Street where Pearl had an appointment, and it was there that we ventured upon our earliest pilgrimage.

I could not possibly have guessed what an important role this little West End street was to play in my life and in a profession which I hardly realized existed. How could I know, on this initial visit, that over a period of some forty years my work would take me daily to this very street and that jokingly I would become known by some of my colleagues as 'the Duchess of Cork Street'?

Margaret Craske held her classes in a building in West Street, just off Shaftesbury Avenue in the heart of theatre land. As I nourished the hope that I would make my career on the stage, the situation itself was important to me. The street, as today, was rather dismal but, in compensation, there was opposite our building a famous little shop where toe-shoes were made – not only in canvas but also in satin. Round the corner was Charing Cross Road lined on each side by bookshops, from which old and second-hand books spilled onto the pavement where they were displayed on stalls. Among them was that treasure house for all works on ballet, Cyril Beaumont's tiny emporium. In this minute shop he and his wife, always courteous and smiling, sat squeezed among ballet books and bric-à-brac, so that there was hardly room for a client. It was, nevertheless, *the* meeting place for all renowned dancers from home and abroad whenever they had engagements in London.

No. 26 West Street was shabby and dirty; Margaret Craske's studio was on the ground floor with Mme Judith Espinosa teaching above. As snooty as the pupils of some expensive girls' school, we were scornful of Mme Judith's method. We were certain that our system, evolved by the world-famous Enrico, was by far the superior of the two. We used to joke about the manner in which the Espinosa dancers held their fingers – the thumb pressing down on the first finger thus enclosing the hand and giving it an impression of nervousness – while we, superior, held our hands open so as to carry the feeling through to the tips of the fingers.

Our studio was in a building, originally a chapel, where John and Charles Wesley had preached and which later was leased to the Methodists. I assume that we worked in what was the church hall, an unusual environment for a ballet school, but then one of London's greatest charms is that it is full of such surprises. The *barre* ran the length of the longest wall opposite which, in front of a large mirror, was placed a chair for Miss Craske. Adjoining this room was a small one for changing, equally dusty and shabby and eternally pervaded by the smell from our tunics, which after the strenuous classes were always soaked in sweat. There is no glamour about a ballet school; it demands a hard and relentless grind rewarded by occasional little triumphs when some *pas* or *enchaînement* seems to come right, but more often by despair when all is imperfect and one is convinced that one will never, never make a dancer. Without complete dedication it is not possible to continue – but this is by no means exclusive to ballet and extends over the whole range of serious achievement.

From both floors of the building came the same familiar sounds as the bored accompanists banged out the eternal tunes suitable to the individual exercises of *pliés*, *battements*, *ronds-de-jambes*, *port-de-bras*, etc. No music could have been less inspiring for them or for us – it sounded as mechanical as a pianola – yet its familiarity was somehow comforting and we would have been put out had it been changed.

Thanks to my preliminary training with Pearl I did not feel as strange in Miss Craske's classes as I feared I might. I was already acquainted with most of the classical ballet steps, together with their French names. I knew the order in which exercises were practised and which always began at the *barre*, first with *pliés* in all five positions, then the *battements*, *ronds-de-jambes*, etc; each was completed by a half turn so as to train and strengthen right and left equally. These exercises were repeated away from the *barre* to obtain the necessary good balance; the *centre* was followed by an arrangement of *pas* composed by the teacher and known as *enchaînements*. It was then that I appreciated the old adage that 'a good *plié* makes a good dancer', which taken at its face value is an enormous simplification, but which nevertheless contains a basic truth. For the first time in my life, I had the exhilarating experience of working among a group of professionals who were training to be either performers or teachers, and as I do not remember any sense of embarrassment I can only conclude I was able, at least, to keep up with the rest of the class.

At the end of three months Pearl and I and some others took and passed the Intermediate Cecchetti exam, after which, having completed our mission, we were due to return to South Africa. Miss Craske, however, suggested to me that I remain in London for another few months in order to try for the inaugural Advanced. My parents agreed to this prolongation, not primarily on account of my studies but because my mother wanted me to experience the particular glories of an English spring. Pearl, therefore, unselfishly set sail on her own in order to resume our South African classes, whose students had already had a rather long holiday.

The Cecchetti method, evolved by the Maestro over long years of devoted application, left nothing whatsoever to chance; every part of the body from the toes to the fingers had to be felt and imbued with meaning. This meant that each muscle must be strengthened and disciplined, yet the whole body should appear supple and light; only with the achievement of such apparently contradictory qualities could aesthetic demands be fully met.

It goes without saying that technique is crucial and that only when mastered may it be forgotten, even refuted, should artistry deem this necessary. Anna Pavlova, arguably the most famous of all Cecchetti's pupils, came to Johannesburg on one of her world tours when I was still a child. It was not necessary to be an experienced balletomane to be captivated by her extraordinary magnetism which cast a spell over everyone. I, too, was bewitched and delightedly shocked at seeing her break an elementary ballet rule, that of keeping the knees as straight as possible during a run on the *pointes* – a movement of which her famed *Dying Swan* was almost entirely composed. All the way through she ignored the old canon by letting her knees bend at their will. Only many years later did I really appreciate the significance of her calculated departure; her interpretation was paramount, her identification with and her love and understanding of natural phenomena were so complete that technical considerations could be thrown to the winds so as to attain translations of perfection.

It could not have defined it at the time but from my very first meeting with Margaret Craske I felt she was somebody out of the ordinary: an aura of serene insubstantiality hovered about her as if she were living partly on the astral plane. When suddenly she left her classes in charge of her friend, Mabel Ryan, to follow to India a *guru* who by this time had decided not to utter a word, we in our ignorance thought it a joke. Since then my own experiences have opened my mind to the understanding of one whose visible air of unearthliness I came to recognize as an outward manifestation of deep mysticism; I also learnt that her abrupt but temporary departure was caused by a summons from Meier Baba to one of his few chosen English disciples.

Margaret Craske looked exactly like a Romantic ballerina and might well have stepped out of the celebrated engraving showing Taglioni, Ellsler and Carlotta Cerito in the celebrated *pas de trois*, in which each vied with the other for primacy. The image of the classical dancer they created persists to this day. Miss Craske possessed a lithe slender body upon whose graceful neck was poised the ideally small head with a finely structured forehead and tightly drawn hair. The remote expression of her deeply set eyes belied the keenness with which she spotted the slightest error of technique; she had a quiet air of authority which kept everybody on their toes so that her praise was a gift to be treasured. When she demonstrated a movement it was imbued with the quality of Markova's ethereal beauty. I had a longing to see her perform but sadly this was no longer possible. The onset of tuberculosis affecting the Achilles tendon had brought an end to her dancing career, but if she regarded this as a tragedy, she gave not the slightest indication; instead she turned her misfortune to brilliant account and hundreds of students have benefited from her teaching. Her attitude was in harmony with her spiritual thinking – what seemed evil was transformed into a blessing without thought of self.

In so conscientious an upholder of Cecchetti's system of training as Miss Craske, I now feel that his method became somewhat imprisoned – not able to grow as if he had still been teaching. The regular routine for each day of the week, when emphasis would be laid upon one technical aspect, was so rigidly adhered to that, if absent from class, one could be certain what the students were practising at that very day and hour. *Batterie*, *élévation*, *pirouettes* and *adagio* all had their attention in turn, and only at the end of a class of two hours were we allowed a short period of freedom. Then we performed a few interesting *enchaînements* which Miss Craske devised on the spot; they were verbally dictated in the language of ballet as she remained on her chair. Sometimes, almost subconsciously, she would illustrate her words by 'dancing' a sequence with her fingers; this is a habit not unknown among teachers of ballet and even choreographers. These ten or fifteen minutes were extremely precious for at the end of a class the body is warm and therefore supple and responsive. Then we could release any personal expression and, temporarily forgetting about 'turning out' and all the other stringent rules of technique, indulge in the enormous pleasure of untrammelled movement. I do not believe that we chafed at the discipline, since we were aware that in both the creative and interpretive arts the student must submit to the most rigorous training, and that in the meantime individuality must, so to speak, be kept in cold storage. If at the end it is dulled, even dead, then it was too slender to mourn its loss.

Among the pupils at Margaret Craske's were some very good and quite well-known dancers who went on to make contributions of value, not necessarily on the stage but in other ways. Among them was Ailne (Babs) Phillips, a former student of Lydia Kyasht, who had been the principal dancer with the Carl Rosa Opera Company. After dancing for six years with the Sadler's Wells Ballet she became a senior production teacher at their school and personal assistant to Dame Ninette de Valois. Another co-student was Mary Skeaping who, like Babs Phillips, had had the advantage of working under such famous dancers as Novikoff, Trefilova and Egorova; she had made her début with Pavlova's company but did not continue her theatrical career. It was Mary to whom I most warmly responded; her approach to her dancing was matter-of-fact and workmanlike but tinged with a wry bump of humour, a combination which I found attractive. Each member of her family was involved in the arts: one of her brothers was a violinist, while John, another, was the well-known sculptor and first husband of Barbara Hepworth. They all swam about in the artistic pond as naturally as ducks in water and I felt a little envious of Mary's background and lifestyle, so very foreign to my own.

Thanks to my schooling and its subsequent influence I had become tolerably well read, but otherwise I was so absorbed in the ballet that, for me, the other arts did not exist. I had only been to one concert, when the newly founded Cape Town Orchestra – the only one in the Union – gave their first performance in Johannesburg. That was an occasion, an important event, but it did not instil a desire to hear more, for I thought of music as merely an accompaniment to ballet. Going to the theatre was a special treat, but the majority of shows were musical comedies with any 'straight' play a rarity. I had never visited the Johannesburg Art Gallery. Thanks to the bounty of Lady Phillips (William Nicholson's mother-in-law by his second marriage), who was advised by Sir Hugh Lane, it contained some really good pictures, mainly of the Barbizon school. I had never seen a contemporary painting and the only living artist of whom I had heard was the son of the dressmaker who made my clothes as a child. Mrs Wolfe talked with pride about her son Teddy who was making a name as a painter in London – a profession considered rather more than bizarre.

Many years were to pass before I entered an art gallery and saw my first exhibition. Six of Craske's students, myself among them, were dancing in Amsterdam – but this comes later. As Mary Skeaping was with us she insisted on our seeing a Van Gogh exhibition in the Rijksmuseum. I was totally overawed by this large, serious edifice in whose numerous galleries hung so many pictures, all incomprehensible to me. I saw that the exhibition was full of colour but otherwise it left not the slightest impression. Mary said these pictures were by a great artist – but why were they great? To me they seemed daubs.

Mary's career was to develop successfully in her twin roles as teacher and producer. After serving as ballet mistress to the Sadler's Wells company she first went to Canada and then on to Cuba, in both of which countries she produced classical ballets. But her greatest achievement was with the Royal Swedish Ballet whose standards had sunk surprisingly low; under her guidance it regained its quality with a repertoire including, among the known classics, her own reconstruction of Swedish Court ballets. After I had abandoned ballet for some forty years, Mary and I met again only briefly. I had gone to the private view of John Skeaping's memorial exhibition, hoping to see her and there indeed she was, looking, I thought, very ill. She was leaving next day for France, so we arranged to meet upon her return. Sadly this meeting never took place, for while in France she died.

Sometimes towards the end of our classes that remarkable woman, Marie Rambert, would come to practise with us. Quite old by this time she was still enthusiastic and bubbling and never failed to inject a note of merriment into a class somewhat jaded by a morning's hard work. She only exercised to keep in trim, thus enabling her to continue her inestimable work of running her own ballet company.

Looking back on those years, and even more forcibly since reading Robert Medley's memoirs,* one of my greatest regrets is that I never really

* Robert Medley, *Drawn from the Life: A Memoir*, Faber & Faber, 1983.

got to know and therefore appreciate the only male student among us. Rupert Doone was slight but beautifully built, with the face and shaped head of a Botticelli. With a dreamy expression and a Renaissance air he mingled among us with a touch of disdain like a Greek god descended into the world of mortals. I was attracted to him, but from a distance, being completely intimidated by his sophistication and elegance which made me feel gauche and clumsy; and I was grateful that he never chose me when bestowing the favour of practising 'lifts' with one of the more advanced students.

Rupert had also studied under great Russian dancers and made his youthful début as understudy to Espinosa; then he partnered such ballerinas as Ludmilla, Trefilova and Phyllis Bedells, dancing in many Western countries with them. As a soloist he joined Diaghilev's *Ballets Russes* in what turned out to be its final season, and as no further opportunities were open to him – or indeed to most other dancers – he settled in London and was installed with Craske by the time I, too, joined the classes. Considering his background no wonder he felt thwarted for, apart from being a very fine dancer with a once hopeful future, he was also a dedicated man of the theatre – actor, producer and choreographer. But as Robert Medley points out, the existence of Margaret Craske's school was crucial for him. With her insight she was one of the few who understood and encouraged him in every possible way, allowing her students to try out his revolutionary conceptions although there was slender hope, or none at all, of their being realized in a production.

I was one of those privileged to experiment with Rupert though I fear I did not profit from the opportunity, for I had not the foggiest idea what he was driving at. Still struggling to improve the classical technique, I was amazed and discomforted by the strange, ungainly movements he demonstrated in quick and varying succession. Above all I could not comprehend his deliberately meaningful use of the floor. In classical ballet it played no more important a role than that of a platform upon which to dance. The floor was never embraced as an entity in its own right and far from being anchored to it, the endeavour when in movement was to skim across it with the flowing ease of a skater, or to use it in *élévation* as a springboard from which to leap as lightly and as high as the combat between muscle and gravity would allow. Now Rupert was giving it a fresh dimension, acknowledging it in its archaic form as the earth from which our bodies sprang and to which they will finally return.

It was not until later when I went to Paris expressly to see Maurice Béjart's masterpiece, *Le Sacre du Printemps*, that my eyes were opened and I began to appreciate the vibrant new field of modern dance; and when Martha Graham gave her first London season I was completely won over.

Both these outstanding modern choreographers were using the floor as Rupert had envisaged. If I had been unable to accept his innovations, Mary Skeaping, on the contrary, understood them exactly and was in complete harmony with his aims. Robert Medley quotes from a conversation with her whilst in the process of writing his book: 'I had been working with Rupert at West Street and he had been picking up all sorts of ideas ... ideas so modern, so interesting, that I was keen to do them. He was full of ideas – they would come chasing out, I had to grasp these ideas and try to bring them to life ... I could see the value of what he was trying to do, many dancers couldn't...'* To my loss I was of their number.

As already mentioned, Mary and Rupert had enjoyed years of training in the Classical tradition under some of its greatest exponents, whilst by this time I had had barely three years with Miss Craske. These strange innovations were too soon for me; I was not yet ready and never would be since, in the capacity of performer, I was shortly to leave the world of ballet for ever.

The death of my mother

I had duly taken and failed the Advanced Cecchetti exam, which did not surprise me at all. My natural and therefore preferred tempo is slow; I love doing things at a leisurely pace which enables me to savour and enjoy every moment. *Adagio* was therefore my strongest suit and, although I worked hard, I could not attain the speed and brilliance demanded of *batterie* and of all *pizzicato* movements. Neither am I creative – certainly not in the choreographic sense – so that towards the end of the examination when unexpectedly called to invent a sequence indicating 'Night', my mind became an absolute blank; not a glimmer of inspiration came to my aid and I moved about in a meaningless way as if I were a zombie.

My failure was fully deserved and although it naturally disappointed me it seemed to satisfy both of my aunts who agreed that 'it would do me good to fail at something'. How they arrived at this particular verdict I could not fathom, for during the time I had been back in England I had achieved next to nothing. It got to my ears that one aunt had remarked she did not mind my feeling superior so long as I did not look it as well. Her reported judgement came as an unwelcome shock for I thought I was on my best behaviour and I was certainly painfully aware of my inadequacies in my chosen profession of ballet. In retrospect I see that, without my realizing it, I was drifting away from the family background and tastes as my interest in

* Robert Medley, *op cit*, p.86.

the arts was being gradually born. Less and less did I enjoy their pursuits and pleasures, and apparently I did not put up a good show of pretence.

There was no question of my remaining any longer in London in order to have a second shot at the Advanced. My mother and father were longing to see me, while I had a duty to Pearl who was carrying the whole weight of our teaching practice upon her own shoulders. I was just about to book my return passage home when I was faced with the first tragic experience of my life. A cable arrived one fateful evening telling me that my beloved mother was seriously ill; the very next morning she died. She was only forty-two. She had contracted pneumonia which, in the days before penicillin, all too often proved fatal. My persistent childhood fear had been that Mummy might die before me – the kind of irrational obsession to which perhaps women, more often than men, are prone. It was not until I was well into my forties and had gone through other very painful experiences that I came to the conviction that our very fears draw these potentially threatening experiences towards us, and that they continue to repeat themselves until, by grace, we are able to work through them and emerge with greater courage and hope.

Terribly immature as I was, and behaving like a very spoilt child, I was determined not to let those around me forget for one moment the depth of my sorrow. During the whole of the following year I wore my grief for everyone to see, not caring how I looked or dressed and even abstaining from using make-up. I felt myself imprisoned in a wall of despair – how was I to face a future without that warm, unselfish and loving mother? All I knew was that I could never go back to Johannesburg to a home which was henceforth to be deprived of her presence.

In an effort to cheer me up Uncle Hubert decided to take me to Paris. We stayed in one of the finest hotels; dined in the beautiful restaurants in the Bois; went to the Opéra, which bored my Uncle stiff, but which he dutifully endured as he did our visits to the Louvre and other places of historical interest. He did everything possible to make me happier, including giving me some beautiful clothes, but I refused to be distracted and would not make the effort even to raise an appreciative smile. I must have been a pain in the neck, for in my grief I thought of no one but myself. Later my conscience was to reproach me bitterly; not only did I desert my father at a time when he needed me most and leave my brother Jack the burden of supporting him, but I also broke my professional contract with Pearl – this in repayment of her goodness and trust. In terms of human behaviour I believe this to have been the most shameful period of my life, but evidently I was fulfilling a benevolent destiny. Whatever I have achieved in life stems from the inglorious decision to ignore the voice of my responsibilities and remain in the London I had come to love so much.

And so I never returned to my life in Johannesburg. My uncle and aunts might well have decided to get rid of the burden I had become to them by sending me back to South Africa. But they did nothing of the sort. Instead they seemed to take it for granted that henceforth my life was to be spent among them and, as they had little regard for my father, whom they scarcely knew, they could hardly have been expected to worry about the sacrifice he was being called upon to make. He, on his side, never reproached me for my desertion nor hinted in one of his rare letters that he thought it my duty to return. I thus went to live in Cookham where both my aunts with their families had made their homes. Aunt Gertie did not have any room for me but 'Dardoo' treated me as if I were the daughter she had always longed for but never had; her only child was a son named Ivan who was to become my first husband.

For a while we lived in the old Church Gate House, originally occupied by the clergy; my bedroom window looked down on the churchyard, and more specifically on Stanley Spencer's *Angel* – a bonus of which I was unaware. It must have been my own good angel who had decreed that I should find refuge in this then unspoilt little riverside village whose peace gradually soothed the ache in my heart and also restored those quiet delights which I thought had forsaken me for ever.

Church Gate House is within a stone's throw of the Thames at a point where the river is spanned by a bridge on which tolls had formerly been charged. To live in a real Tudor house was something I had never thought to do. I had not even seen one at close quarters until I went to Cookham and only knew what they looked like from photographs. I loved the sturdy oak beams which against the whitewashed wattle and daub of the walls made such fantastic and irregular patterns that no other decoration was necessary. How welcoming was the huge open fireplace where logs flamed high and emitted their own pungent yet fragrant smell. I did not even mind the draughts that blew in from under the ill-fitting doors, nor the noises made by the small latticed windows as they rattled in the slightest of winds. It was rumoured that Church Gate had its own ghost but I was intrigued rather than fearful, even though Ivan said he had seen it when ill in bed with mumps. The aura of centuries pervades all such homes and those who have lived in modern cities with little or no history behind them, find themselves more than ordinarily sensitive to such ineluctable spells. On Sundays there was also the ringing of church bells, sonorous and loud because so close to us. I who was unaccustomed to them found their summons imperious, while the locals – half-hearing – took them for granted.

In my new life I was living near water which played not a small part in my recovery, and I was also learning to punt, though the river at Cookham was not ideal. But there was a choice between the stretches that led to

Bourne End, Marlow and Henley, where annually we punted to the regattas. Or we could go downstream through the Cliveden reach to Maidenhead, negotiating the famous Boulter's Lock on the way. For less energetic days there was the peaceful millstream brought to a halt by the weir; in it one could moor under the shade of the beeches, eat a picnic lunch and take a quiet nap while the water lapped softly against the side of the craft.

The river's chief boatman was established at Cookham where he had his punt-hiring business. Mr Turk was the master of the King's Swans and it was his duty, in full regalia, to preside over the ceremony of Swan Upping. He owned many punts which were gaily bedecked in summer with brightly coloured cushions. Moored side by side all ready for clients, they gently knocked on each other in the wake of larger boats. They were as fabulous to me as the gondolas of Venice but mournfully most have now disappeared.

Through the tutoring of an expert friend, I became a proficient punter. The movement of changing the weight of the body while throwing the pole into the air and letting it fall until it reached bottom, when a thrust sent the craft through the water, had a rhythm I felt was closely allied to dancing. Although I played all the usual games I was never a keen sportswoman. Punting was something quite different. Near balletic, uncompetitive, which I liked, its success depended also on volatile conditions, a challenge I enjoyed. If the pole happened to lodge in the mud it could only be freed by a sharp turn of the wrist; when this ploy failed, the pole had to go else one came to resemble the subject of many a caricature of the novice punter hanging on to his pole in midstream while his craft drifted slowly away. A sudden gust of wind could send the punt spinning or tacking from side to side like a yacht, but on a calm day and upon shallow water the crunch of the pole on the underlying shingle meant that the boat would dart swiftly ahead, a response that was eminently fulfilling. Those summer evenings and days on the Thames are amongst the most benign of my memories, and on leaving Cookham I promised myself I would one day return to go on the river. But this promise has never been realized. Together with the few punts left on these beautiful reaches, there are now smart motor craft, and the lapping of water and song of the birds have been drowned by the noise of incessant pop music.

New movements in ballet

Travelling up to London each day I continued my classes with Margaret Craske, still hoping, but with ever-increasing doubts, that I might yet become a really fine dancer. Ballet had been the chief love of my life; there was nothing else I could or would do. If I had estimated my situation with enough courage and objectivity, I should have come to the conclusion that, like most of the professionals in Margaret Craske's classes, I would never be more than proficient; one whom the Opéra would have classified as being in the *second quadrille*, a useful member of some company or other. This modest niche was not to my taste – it had to be all or nothing. The years when I was still dancing were extremely precarious in all ballet circles. To the élite in London, ballet was synonymous with the name of Diaghilev, while to the general public it meant Pavlova. She was revered throughout most of the world because she had travelled incessantly, but she had died early, in 1931, and her troupe was therefore dispersed. Diaghilev's death had come two years before and his company was likewise scattered, so all of these dancers, some of whom were among the best in the world, were suddenly deprived of their background. They wandered about like a lot of lost children wondering how and where to anchor themselves, for Diaghilev's loss was a major tragedy and there were no other companies for them to join.

Later de Basil appeared on the scene, which brought some compensation. He had been a colonel in a Cossack division but, growing ever more in-terested in the art of the theatre, he decided to start his own agency. With-out the great impresario's imcomparable flair or his determination to seek perfection, de Basil's feet were more firmly on the ground and he sensed it might be possible to popularize ballet. Moreover, there was the vacuum left by Diaghilev, so why not take advantage and form a new company? With Balanchine as choreographer, Grigorieff as stage-director and a nucleus of very experienced dancers, he and René Blum launched out with a troupe which in 1932 made its début in Monte Carlo.

De Basil had chosen as his stars three unknown child prodigies. In Paris each had trained under Maryinsky ballerinas, themselves refugees from the Russian Revolution. The extraordinary virtuosity of these 'baby ballerinas' astonished and enthralled their audiences and, after critical acclaim and various vicissitudes, the company opened at the Alhambra in London where the season scored an immediate success. The baby ballerinas became all the rage. The ballet boom in England had started.

Outwardly the period between 1929 and 1931 gave the impresssion of hopeless sterility, but those behind the scenes knew to the contrary that this was a time of steady gestation out of which British ballet would finally be born. It was Marie Rambert who became the new baby's nurse. Having first trained in Dalcroze she grew passionate about ballet when she joined Diaghilev as a eurhythmics teacher, and it was her own miniature theatre at Notting Hill Gate that became the first permanent home of a British ballet company. Not only did Rambert spot the potential in young and untried performers who were allowed to retain their English names instead of adopting Russian ones, but she also promoted designers and choreographers in the pioneering productions at her Ballet Club.

The time had to come, however, when the children would need to leave home, and Rambert, like nannies of past generations, had to step aside and watch the young people who had taken their first steps under her guidance, come to maturity, and sometimes to fame, under the aegis of another. This other was Ninette de Valois. Her achievements are legendary and need no repetition, for, unlike the once underestimated Rambert, she was soon acclaimed for her feat of promoting and establishing our National Ballet Company.

But in the interim, before this happened, the prospects for the dancer were negligible indeed. Just as musicians need an orchestra to enfold them, so dancers require their own setting. But there were no possibilities, no companies to join. Even the 'stars', both men and women, were in this sorry plight; some had recourse to performing as an act in one of the still extant music halls. In this way I saw the great Spessivtseva, described as the Classical ballerina *par excellence*, in wonderful *pas seuls* from *Giselle* which she danced – as far as I recall – at the Empire. This was and still remains one of the most memorable performances I have been privileged to watch. To my mind Spessivtseva was of Pavlova's calibre but of a greater purity of line, more aloof and more private. She was a 'dancer's dancer' just as an artist may be a 'painter's painter'.

Other 'stars' formed temporary troupes of their own, taking engagements wherever they found them; such a one was the little company formed by Anton Dolin with Vera Nemtchimova as his ballerina, which I and my co-students joined. Prior to that the only engagement that Margaret Craske had been able to find for her regular pupils was one that could adequately have been fulfilled by amateurs. But at least it was a job and therefore not to be scorned. A film of *The Bondman*, based on the novel of that title by the then popular writer, Hall Caine, was being shot on the Isle of Man. Several dancers were needed to perform a hay-making dance on location and I was one of the chosen. My only experience of film-making had been as an extra in one of Michael Balcon's productions; this had come about through my close friendship with his wife Aileen, who knew how badly I wanted some kind of work. When *The Bondman* was offered, I jumped at the prospect, however lowly, though it did not turn out to be a very enjoyable experience. The crossings, as often, were horribly rough and I am a notoriously bad sailor. On the island we spent the best part of a week, for it would not stop raining and we needed the sun which finally appeared for just long enough to enable us to perform our short, simple dance. With a certain amount of amused curiosity we went to see our début on the screen; hardly had the words 'there we are' passed our lips than we simultaneously had disappeared.

The Dolin/Nemtchimova engagement, however, promised to be something more in our line. One morning in the summer of 1930 I went to class in the usual way, not expecting anything of import to happen. All of a sudden Anton Dolin appeared. He never came to practise as did Marie Rambert, so we were all in a twitter to know why he was there. He told Miss Craske that with Vera Nemtchimova he had been invited to present a season in Holland and as he wished to do excerpts from the Classics he needed another six dancers to augment those he had already chosen. I was greatly excited to be among the selected, who included Mary Skeaping, Babs Phillips, and Elizabeth Hepworth, Barbara's young sister, who subsequently married John Summerson. Only two days of rehearsals were necessary, as we already knew the Classics. As we gathered on the station platform a few days later, I noticed a chattering among our group and found they were discussing the latest scandal in the art world: Barbara Hepworth had just left her husband, John Skeaping – both I was told were well-known sculptors – to go off with the painter Ben Nicholson, the son of the distinguished artist, William. I would not have been particulary interested in this news, had it not been for the fact that the sisters of both the 'culprits' were members of our party. One of the reasons given for the elopement was that Barbara Hepworth had grown tired of domesticity. If this were so she was to fall out of the frying pan into the fire for, in due course, she gave birth to triplets!

We were to appear in Amsterdam for a couple of weeks and then go on to Haarlem. In those days the Netherlands did not possess its own national ballet company and, as it was the year of the Olympic Games in the city, all kinds of artistic events were being organized. I well remember the attractive dressing-room assigned to us in the Amsterdam theatre. Unlike most drab and workaday dressing-rooms, this one was charmingly decorated and cheerful with its red-lacquered furniture and its window overlooking a canal.

To me Amsterdam was an enchantment, only the second continental city I had seen. It seemed like a miracle that all these legendary towns should be so close at hand, just across the Channel, and that within the space of a few hours the boat and train could whisk one there. I had heard about Amsterdam's canals but had not imagined them to be so numerous and so beautiful. Even the smells from the water, which to others were unpleasant, I found not distasteful but actually agreeable. I watched the ever-changing pictures created by reflections of the trees in their full summer glory, and by the typical seventeenth-century Dutch houses. They changed continuously through the play of clouds above and shimmered as the tranquil surface of the water was disturbed.

Once settled down in our modest quarters we went off to buy the traditional clogs and found them exceedingly difficult to wear; they could only be held on by contracting the toes and the hard wood, unrelenting, made my feet very sore. Oblivious to the fact that few passers-by were similarly clad, we went clattering upon the cobbles believing that we were conforming. On the corners of the street there were stalls selling sweet pickled cucumbers, soused herrings and shrimps, whose freshness smelled so temptingly of the sea that we had to stop and buy, and eat them on the spot. As our pay was minimal we could just afford to indulge in these cheap everyday temptations but I promised myself that if and when I ever visited Amsterdam again, I would stay in one of the finest hotels and eat in the grand restaurants whose appetizing odours, wafting into the streets, were so very tantalizing to the impecunious.

Some years later I was able to fulfil this wish and learned at the same time the potency of Holland gin, so that the city of Amsterdam is linked in my mind with the one and only time I have ever been really drunk. I had been in Paris with Taubie Kushlick, the doyenne of South African theatrical producers, in order to be present at the marriage of a much younger friend whose first child, Mathieu Rossano, is my only godson. After the wedding we took it into our heads to go on to Amsterdam instead of returning directly to London. Taubie was always game for a jaunt and her legendary high spirits infected me to such an extent that when we were dining – this time in one of the expensive hotels – we allowed ourselves to be picked up by a good-looking fellow-diner, who turned out to be a university lecturer. As we had never seen the Dutch equivalent of a pub he took us to one in the vicinity where he said we should try the famous *oude genever*, which he warned was extremely potent. This drink, served in thimble-size glasses filled to the brim, we found so delicious that we tossed down three or four before going back to our hotel. We were in the jolliest of moods, so much so that by the time we had walked down the corridor and reached our room, neither of us were able to put our key in the keyhole for the paroxysms of drunken laughter which made our hands shake uncontrollably. Fortunately for us we did not have a hangover and were able to lunch the next day with our host of the previous evening. Alas, on future visits to Amsterdam I came to the conclusion that Dutch cuisine was stodgy and dull, and could not hold a candle to that of the Latin countries.

Besides being acknowledged as the most reliable and best mannered partner any ballerina could wish to have, Anton Dolin was also known as a fine athletic dancer, interested in all forms of sport. He was therefore in his element to be in Amsterdam when the Olympic Games were being held in that city and very thoughtfully organized seats for us. The historic background behind the Olympics was, like so much else, unknown to me, so I did not realize how lucky we were to be present at the legendary gathering. I confess that I was more impressed by the spectacle of the immense stadium packed with its huge number of excited spectators than by the games themselves; so much was happening all over the arena that I found it impossible to focus attention on any one event. It was an experience I am never likely to repeat, but now, when I watch the Games on television and from close quarters can marvel at the prowess of the athletes, I am able to recapture the atmosphere they generate as if I were actually on the spot.

Our programme in Holland consisted of excerpts from *Les Sylphides*, *Le Lac des Cygnes* and *Giselle*. Although Nemtchimova was not the type of ballerina I most admired, it was an extremely valuable experience to be on the same stage as a dancer of her quality and to be able to study, on consecutive nights, the strength and accomplishment of her technique. Contrary to what I had expected, and despite my enjoyment of the modest performances I had already experienced, this time I felt ill at ease and inadequate. As the season progressed my conviction increased that everyone else, even the most junior, was dancing far better than myself. It may seem arrogant, but I also dared to criticize aspects of the choreography. I thought, and still do, that *Le Lac* contains arrangements for the *corps de ballet* that are unsympathetic and over-regimented – more evocative of the Trooping of the Colour than of a flock of graceful swans. This opinion was shared by the critic, Fernau Hall, who wrote in the *Daily Telegraph* that '... the *corps de ballet* manoeuvre like soldiers in geometrical evolutions...'* There are also *pas* I find discordant and awkward, even when they are beautifully executed; one in particular can best be described, in non-balletic terms, as hopping across the stage with the raised leg in *arabesque* (*sauté en arabesque en demi-plié* perhaps). Danced in straight and precisely intersecting lines to and fro across the stage, this arrangement seems far removed from a flock of elegant swans or from an apparition of ethereal *Willis*. Also when the *corps de ballet* are wearing newly blocked shoes which clatter upon landing with every regular hop, the effect is embarrassing not only for the performers but for the audience as well.

Apart from the dissatisfaction I felt with myself, there was also a kind of *affaire Dreyfus* going on between my uncle and aunts in England. The bone of contention was that I had not asked permission before accepting the engagement, for Hubert now regarded himself as my guardian. It did not

---

* Fernau Hall, *Modern English Ballet: An Interpretation*, Andrew Melrose, 1950, p.44.

occur to me to do so; moreover he had already gone on holiday. But he was convinced that I had been deceitful and had deliberately waited until he had left before taking what he regarded as my first steps towards perdition. Ridiculous as it now sounds, he truly believed that there was little to choose between a ballet dancer and a belly dancer, or an Edwardian chorus girl, with all the loose morals their professions implied. Not only did he involve my aunts in the *affaire* but sought their backing to take his side against me for my unspeakable crime, which, being more broad-minded and knowing me better, they were reluctant to do. Nevertheless Uncle Hubert continually sent telegrams to Amsterdam ordering me home. When the contract was over and I did come back to England, it was to be greeted by a family feud, each member hardly speaking to the other and reproaching me for having been the cause. If I had felt that in my own terms I had scored some success, had advanced even one step up the theatrical ladder, I would have continued despite these family quarrels. But this was not so. I was fed up with everything and everyone, so I stood back and took stock of the situation. I entered into one of those conversations with myself which ran something like this: 'You know, my girl, you have become very spoilt; Uncle Hubert has introduced you to a luxurious kind of life to which you are not fully accustomed. It seems it has turned your head. You have travelled first-class and stayed in the best of hotels; been given costly presents and generally pampered. You have to admit that you resented not receiving the same treatment in Holland. You did not like going third-class on the trains, living on the cheap and being in fact a nobody. As a member of a *corps de ballet*, how could you have expected otherwise? If you are to continue being a dancer you might have to tolerate far worse conditions, so is it not proof that now is the time to put all thoughts of ballet out of your head and turn your attention to something else? A theatrical career can mean incessant travel, continual uprooting. You are essentially a home-bird and although you like travelling, you do not relish the idea of the life of a nomad.'

But way and above these lesser considerations my earlier qualms as to my ability had been confirmed without a shadow of doubt. I accepted the bitter fact that I did not have it in me to be any more than an average good technician, and these were in plentiful supply. Unless technique is mastered the performer is helpless, but alone it is far from sufficient – artistry and magnetism must also be present before the dancer may rise to be an absolute 'star'. Among recent dancers Nureyev, in his heyday, was such a one; he had to do no more than walk across stage for all eyes to be riveted upon him, irrespective of the feats those around him were achieving. Self-deception was folly – I knew I was not born an exceptional being but was cast in an ordinary mould. So once and for all I relinquished my hopes and decided to stop dancing for ever.

It was not all that hard to abandon thoughts of the theatre, but to accept that I would not dance again was almost unbearable; never more to experience that lovely feeling when the body, obedient to many of one's demands, combines its suppleness and its strength to move in accord with the music. I might easily have become a perpetual student at work in the classroom without any goal but my circumstances made this self-indulgence unacceptable. It would have meant continuing to live with my relatives until I might have married, dependent upon my uncle for day-to-day wants; a situation which I could not have tolerated. For a very long while I was so homesick for West Street that I dared not go near its vicinity; nor could I discard my toe-shoes or tights but kept them tucked safely away in a drawer. I had kicked the planks, however fragile, from under my feet and now had nothing to stand on. Being sufficiently versed in the Cecchetti system – I had once substituted for an absentee examiner – I again turned my thoughts towards teaching. This would be *faute de mieux* certainly, not a vocation; but what *was* my vocation? I had no idea – perhaps I did not have one at all. Ballet embraced both design and music, but to neither had I paid much attention; I was fascinated by the costumes, while Tchaikovsky or Chopin were lovely to dance to. But to me all were just reinforcements of ballet.

I did not know how to start a class for adults, but with the help of some friends I gathered a few children, and so resumed the profession I had practised as a teenager. My most active supporter was my pal Aileen, the wife of Sir Michael Balcon, whose small daughter Jill, the future wife of Cecil Day-Lewis, became my first pupil; Aileen also recruited some children of friends and acted as pianist on the old tinpot instrument already installed in the room I had hired. Our efforts to gather more pupils were in vain, so after a few months, and not too reluctantly, I decided to call it a day. Then I was offered a post to teach at a dance school, the most fashionable one for children in London. I did not accept because I had heard that they put the poor mites on *pointes*. At this stage of life the foot muscles are not strong enough to bear the whole weight of the body, even the slender one of a child, so, though desperate for work, my conscience forbade me to be party to a practice I thought was almost criminal.

My introduction to art and artists

During these few abortive months, however, a new vista opened up for me through a friendship I had formed with Amy Greenwood, another of London's leading ballroom teachers in whose rooms I had also held classes. A petite dainty figure with lovely auburn hair and fastidious personal dress sense, her skin, her eyes, and even lashes were as blonde as her personality was sunny. She introduced me to a new enthralling side of life away from the background against which I had grown. In her studio flat in Bloomsbury Street, where the fine eighteenth-century houses were then still privately occupied, I spent many enlightening evenings when we would sit on the floor, smoke long Russian cigarettes and drink Turkish coffee – delightfully unconventional and therefore 'very modern' – as we listened to classical records and talked of books and the arts. Most of the talk was hers for I had little to contribute. I drank in her words, as if my parched throat longed for water. This was the life that I had unknowingly missed, first in Johannesburg and subsequently in London. I felt I had stepped into another world whose atmosphere suited me exactly. I further discovered the surprising fact that there were arts other than ballet.

Amy in her quietly authoritative way was an unusual person. In 1934 she visited Russia as one of the earliest visitors after the Revolution, having been commissioned to give a display of up-to-date Western ballroom dancing. I can still picture her in her dark velvet jacket with which – long before trousers came into fashion – she habitually wore matching knicker-bockers. Amy had two most eligible suitors but was uncertain as to which she would marry. One was the erudite amateur painter, James Wood, who having his own income was able to indulge in his love of art without the need to earn money. He was a close friend of Stanley Spencer and an excellent portrait of him among others is to be seen in one of Stanley's most notable pictures, the *Resurrection in Cookham Churchyard*. His rival in love was the handsome James Shand, the obsessive typographer and creative director of the family firm, the Shenval Press. One of the idealistic ventures financed by him personally was the splendid but short-lived periodical to which he gave the title of *Alphabet and Image*. Amy and I spent one glorious summer's day in a punt on the river at Cookham. In this tranquil setting we discussed her great problem, weighing the pros and cons of her two would-be husbands. She finally decided to marry 'Hamish' Shand.

In the summer of 1937 Amy and I spent a holiday together at Menton, after which we went on to Paris to visit the International Exhibition as we particularly wanted to see Picasso's *Guernica* in the Spanish pavilion. In Amy's studio hung the first picture ever to attract my attention. It did not matter that it was only a reproduction, and of a drawing without colour, nor that I had never heard the name of the artist. The essential truth to the subject held me quite spell-bound – it was *A Young Dancer* by Edgar Degas.

A certain restlessness among better educated upper- or upper-middle-class young women was surfacing more and more in the 1930s: they felt that they wanted some occupation instead of remaining at home. Most hardly dreamed of careers; they wondered what they could do, what pursuit they could follow until they might marry. The possibilities upon which their parents would not frown were limited in the extreme; they devolved upon antiques or interior decorating – each was fashionable, almost *de rigueur*. Modelling was tantamount to being a showgirl. Both occupations extended implicit invitations to men and therefore should never enter the mind of a lady.

I believe that my uncle Hubert had a mistress among the models who showed the fine furs at Bradley's – this was the store for the best ladies' tailoring, the most beautiful furs and, not least attractive, the female assistants employed. His attitude towards women was still Edwardian, for that was the generation in which he had been reared; moreover, he was far too busy, too wrapped in his own highly successful career, to notice how women were changing. Their independence having been fired by their replacement of men during the war of 1914–18, some had begun to realize their own potential and swelled the handful of feminists whom men found ridiculous. For most men, a decent woman's place was at home with her children; most other women were thought to be sexually suspect, either mistresses of those who could afford it, or otherwise 'no better than they should be'. Uncle Hubert went so far as to hold me at arm's length whenever I met him at a restaurant or theatre. Innocently I would approach to give the customary embrace but, being well known, he was not to be seen kissing a young woman in public. 'Niece' was the euphemism habitually used by men-of-affairs when they could not avoid introducing their mistresses, and he was not going to risk this stigma. I was more than surprised at this extraordinary treatment which at first I could not comprehend, but when the reason finally dawned it left a nasty taste in my mouth.

We were no longer living in the much loved Church Gate House, for my uncle and aunt had bought a small modern villa on the other side of the railway at Cookham Dean, the newer and less attractive part of Cookham. So added to the fact that I so missed my dancing, not even my surroundings were as happy as formerly. On the other hand Aunt Gertie had moved with her family to one of the most picturesque cottages in the village where it was not unusual to see the odd stranger wandering about in her garden. It was so attractive, especially to American visitors, that they could not resist entering through the ever open gates, for here was the perfect Tudor cottage, its lovely old barns around which grew shrub roses whose fragrance filled the air on warm summer days. This may conjure up the vision of some nauseating chocolate-box painting but the reality of such places cannot be impaired. Ovey's Farm lies near to the notorious pub Baal and the Dragon – the name now changed to Bel and the Dragon – and whenever

My mother, Gladys Meredith, and my father, Michael Browse, at the time of their engagement, *c.*1902

My father, champion cyclist, Johannesburg to Salisbury and back, *c.*1890

Facing page: Myself, just back from Paris, *c.* 1946

Above: My brother Jack, officer in the 'lost army' in Malaya

Left: My husband, Sidney Lines, director of Wiggins Teape, *c.* 1964

Bernard Dunstan, *The 'Triumvirate' in the Gallery at 19 Cork Street*, c.1966

The gallery, exterior view, *c.*1973

Joan Eardley, *c.*1960 (*above*) and Philip Sutton, *c.*1973 (*below*)

Emilio Greco, Rome, 1972

Robin Philipson, *c.*1989

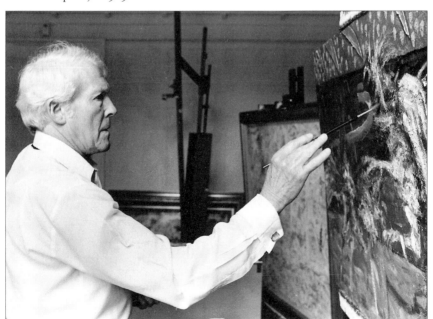

William Nicholson, *Pink Still Life with Jug*. Birmingham Museums and Art Gallery

I visited my aunt in the village I had to walk across the moor to reach her home. Here on this moor I first saw Stanley Spencer.

Having never met any artists at all, my picture of them had been gleaned from odd books, but he did not look as I had naïvely imagined. Surely in the fashion of *La Bohème* he should have been wearing a large black felt hat, a flowing cloak and a beard. Instead he looked like a scarecrow. His shabby clothes hung about his small person as if they were made for a man twice his size; to recompense for this they were generally held up with safety-pins. Obviously caring little about hygiene, such a prosaic matter being of minimum importance to him, his unshaven face gave the impression of being as soiled as his tattered garments. A young woman devotee was once heard to remark: 'How Stanley stinks, but God how I love it.'

He wore a look of piercing concentration and his eyes would light up when in conversation as if a fire of excitement burned behind them. Conversation perhaps is the wrong word to use – monologue would be far more appropriate, for Stanley's discourse gave little chance of interruption, and being well versed in the Old and New Testaments, he dealt discursively with these subjects. Despite this obsessive theme in his speech and his painting, I never felt him to be of deep spiritual belief, but rather one who was engaged in an intellectual exercise in which he saw Christ as one of the villagers with whom he was intimate and had often painted. More out of curiosity than true interest, when I met him crossing the moor I sometimes asked to see what he was painting. Landscapes of Cookham were one of his alternatives to controversial religious themes. He wheeled them about with the rest of his equipment in an old broken-down pram; an incongruous if convenient mode of transport.

Without any preliminary drawing or sketching upon his prepared white canvas, he would start from one corner and work diagonally across it, finishing it in all its Pre-Raphaelite detail as he went along. This seemed to me an amazing feat, not of virtuosity in the sense of the brilliant handling of pigment, but of the foresight which enabled him to visualize the completed picture, with all its intricacies, before he had put brush to canvas. Had he subsequently wished to repaint any part of it, which his certainty seemed to render unlikely, the painting would have been carried to such a pitch of finality as to make the slightest alteration quite out of the question.

Stanley Spencer was born in Cookham of humble, though far from unenlightened, stock; I also came to know his brother, Gilbert, who was then teaching at the Royal College of Art. Stanley was one of those eccentric painters who have regularly enlivened the British scene, while Gilbert was an accomplished landscapist in a more traditional manner. Another brother was an amazing conjuror whom I saw from time to time at the Baal and the Dragon; he fascinated the regulars with his card tricks, performed standing at the bar in such close proximity to other customers that it was impossible to imagine how he practised his deceptions. Drink is said to have prevented him from making a career on the stage. An elderly woman occasionally seen on the moor was thought to have been an aunt of Stanley's; she used to sit astride an old chair, so sadly deluded that she believed she was riding the winds on a horse.

I could not have found any work for myself had I remained all day in Cookham. Aunt Gertie made small artefacts for an annual exhibition each Christmas from which Uncle Hubert habitually bought presents. But although I enjoyed helping her, there was obviously no future for me in that. So I began to take the train up to London with the idea of perhaps entering one of the accepted professions.

In the West End I went into any likely looking antique shop or interior decorator, timidly asking whether by chance they might have a vacancy. Business was slow and as only the largest of firms employed a few assistants, it was not surprising that none gave a thought to a young girl who was ignorant of their trade, had no snobbish connections, and could not even type. Tired and depressed by these hopeless sorties, I wondered what I should do next; somehow or other I found myself wandering into the Print Room of the Victoria & Albert Museum. What drew me there I have no notion – here one might speculate about destiny – for I did not even understand its particular function; far less did I know what I could or would see there. I felt lonely and inappropriate, the only outsider among the scholars studiously examining some print or drawing, or the intent writers taking copious notes. I dared not take a seat for fear that a librarian might ask me what I wanted, so there was nothing to do but to leave through the door which a moment before I had entered.

But something impelled me to keep on returning, and one day I watched, open-mouthed, as a parcel was unwrapped and carefully examined by a learned assistant who pronounced it to be Dutch, of the seventeenth century, a canvas in the manner of Cuyp; or it could be of the nineteenth-century French school, perhaps by Eugène-Gabriel Isabey. This was as miraculous as Spencer's card tricks. How was it possible to know so much?

The fascinating atmosphere of this unknown world had immediately seized me; to withdraw from all the bustle and noise into surroundings so utterly peaceful, where nobody talked above a whisper and all moved around like ghosts, was, I imagined, like entering a retreat. Since those days when I too have been preparing a monograph, it has been the research above all that has given me pleasure, to the extent that I am always reluctant to terminate it. As with my *penchant* for the classroom in ballet, it was the desire to equip myself, and the enjoyment of so doing, that meant more to me than the ultimate goal.

My aunts began to wonder what I was up to, why I was journeying to London each day, and at this stage I was wondering also. As I could not give an answer, even to myself, I think they began to feel slightly suspicious. This state of affairs lasted for weeks, until one day a distant relation, knowing my dilemma, said he was acquainted with one of the foremost dealers in tapestries, to whom he would speak about me. An appointment was made to meet Arthur Kotin in his rooms at St James's. He was Russian by birth, chubby and kindly, and put me at ease even though he explained that I could not join him, as his business was too highly specialized. However, he did know a Mr Leger for whom he had occasionally placed an old master when furnishing some grand mansion or other; he would talk to him in the hope that he might take me into his steadily expanding firm. Unlike most dealers in the art trade, and despite the severe recession, Mr Leger was actually spreading his wings. In addition to the gallery he already owned in Duke Street (started by his restorer father) he had recently opened another in Old Bond Street and yet a third in Brussels. When later I grew to know 'Mr Harold' better – the name given him by the original staff to distinguish him from his father – I realized that he was one of the world's greatest optimists – a trait which impelled him to enlarge his business when caution should have prompted him to reduce it.

The day of my appointed interview drew near and I approached it with much apprehension: did Mr Leger know I had no experience and had never seriously looked at a painting? I decided that although time was too short to put up an appearance of genuine knowledge, I must be able to talk about something pertaining to art, however superficially. I had walked down Old Bond Street to look from the outside at the premises in which I was hoping to work, and noticed in the window of Knoedler's beautiful gallery, next door to Leger's, a *Madonna and Child* by Jacob Epstein. I knew the name of this sculptor through all the attention he had received in the press on account of his 'outrageous' work. This was just it. Here was one item I could say I had seen: something which might endorse, however falsely, my interest in the visual arts. I might even find a little to say about this bronze I neither liked nor understood. But Mr Leger's interest lay exclusively in the old masters, a possibility which I had overlooked. To my relief, he brushed aside my attempts to deliver my small dissertation and without further ado came straight to the point. 'If you really want to, you may work in the gallery, but of course I shall not pay you a salary,' he told me without mincing his words. But the words were so welcome – for I had been accepted – that the proviso left me untouched. Moreover, the terms seemed perfectly fair in view of my utter uselessness. And so in the vaguest possible way I entered the world of the visual arts.

The Leger Gallery – old masters

The staff at Leger's comprised four people: the elderly manager Mr Oldham, a secretary and two porter-assistants. The secretary was a young woman from Holland who pointedly warned me not to fall in love with 'Mr Harold'. I assumed that she regarded him as her very own private property, a fact of which he was entirely unaware. As well as the permanent staff, there was a freelance oldish man who specialized in genealogy. Whenever the portrait of a known sitter was bought by the gallery he would delve into the family's history in the hope of adding to the picture's provenance, which would not only endorse its authenticity but also increase its commercial value. Finally, on the top floor of the building, where 'Mr Harold' had his own flat, there was a small room with a splendid skylight in which 'the Baron' restored Leger's pictures. The pungent smell of turpentine pervaded the atmosphere much as grease-paint pervades the back-stage; daily it wafted down to my office on the floor below, and each has become equally nostalgic. Whenever I was free, I bounded upstairs and crept into the room to watch the Baron at work. Sometimes he happened to be actually in the middle of cleaning, which to a novice was the most spellbinding thing of all.

Buying at auction stimulates various emotions: the challenging competition against all others; the excitement of a discovery upon which one inwardly congratulates oneself while hoping at the same time it has been overlooked by rivals; the fear that enthusiasm has led one to pay more than it was worth. But in those days when paintings were invariably offered for sale with all the dirt and discoloration of time still upon them, the greatest of all anticipatory thrills was to watch the restorer as he started to clean; to see the darkened varnish being gradually removed as the solvent dissolves it onto the saturated pad, hopefully revealing the pigment in its original freshness. If lucky, one's 'find' would then be confirmed; if not, it was all in the day's work of a dealer. But even the most experienced cannot remain quite detached while his fortunes are hovering between a flop and a triumph.

Despite refurbishing and small structural changes, the Leger Gallery (now the Spink-Leger Gallery), among the most spacious in London, remains much the same as in my time. Still working well is the small wood-panelled lift which I always found endearing; the gallery walls on the first floor are still covered in red fabric, though lighter than formerly, more friendly than the heavy dark hangings traditional to old masters. There are people still timid about entering a gallery that has a great air of opulence; they believe that only those who can write a big cheque have any right of entry. If the truth be known, only a tiny proportion are ever in a position to buy; the majority go to look out of interest. This is accepted and they are quite welcome.

'Mr Harold' was wonderfully easy to work for, never in a temper and only rarely annoyed; his pale blue eyes danced behind his glasses with the liveliness of an expectant schoolboy. I often suspected him of being an innocent as far as worldly affairs were concerned. Jovial and smiling, his optimism knew no bounds, so that during the times of dire financial distress he never appeared to be too disturbed but, like Micawber, was sure that something would turn up. He was equally optimistic about each new purchase which, once in the gallery, he would eagerly examine and proclaim to be by some big name or other; sometimes he was testing a companion's reaction; sometimes it seemed he was trying to convince himself. Only reluctantly, and when occasion demanded, would the picture be derogated, given to a painter of lesser importance – that is, if it could be attributed at all. But despite the seriousness of these deliberations they were usually accompanied by a twinkle of merriment.

The Dutch secretary need not have worried – my relationship with Mr Harold remained on a strictly professional, formal level; we never addressed each other by Christian name, but, unlike younger generations who so quickly become 'chummy', we continued to use the appropriate title. This formality extended into all other areas. For my first Christmas present Mr Harold gave me a pair of long evening gloves, considered to be an acceptable gift, without any undertones, for a man to present to a young woman.

I was given an office on the second floor of the building overlooking Bond Street. One of its walls was covered with shelves filled from top to bottom with strong cardboard boxes containing reproductions and photographs of old master paintings. They were divided, primarily, into national sections, then subdivided and labelled in alphabetical order according to the names of the artists. Art magazines and sale catalogues, from which the reproductions had to be cut and filed, lay about in piles. For six months I did nothing but filing. I was at a loss to know how to begin for, having hardly known the names of any painters, I was not likely to know from which countries they came. Sometimes the name gave me a clue. Mr Oldham was helpful and did not seem to mind the frequency of my appeals for aid. So was Mr Harold, but he was seldom at hand and in any case I did not like to bother him. Somehow, being interested and determined, I managed to muddle along and gradually came to recognize the different style of a few of the more famous artists.

But I did need to learn something about the history of art and, as academic instruction was out of the question, I went to a school of Adult Education much used by amateurs. Unaware till then that these schools existed, I was amazed at the variety of subjects they covered and the number of students, men and women of all ages and backgrounds who earnestly went from one class to another, from domestic skills to languages, the sciences, literature and the arts.

I settled down with my notebook to learn from the start about the Classical art of Greece but, though totally absorbed, I could not keep alert and as soon as the lecturer put out the lights in order to project his slides on the screen, I fell fast asleep from sheer fatigue. I had had a long day before starting work with a twenty-minute walk at seven o'clock to catch the train up to London; and as all was new and therefore tiring, I found it was more than I could manage. There was no alternative but to educate myself from books. Finding a complete history of European art – nothing as informative as Gombrich's existed – I read in the lunch hour, in bed and on journeys, in fact whenever I could. One day at Bond Street as I had my head buried in my very ponderous volume, Mr Oldham approached and paused to ask me what I was studying so intently. I told him it was a history of art and that I had got as far as Giotto. He gave me a gentle half-mocking smile, saying, 'You will be rather old by the time you have got to Picasso.' The shaft went home and left me shaken by this mortifying prospect. I had come up against a rather serious problem! But I was determined to persevere.

Art books altogether were in short supply, especially those written in English; Mr Harold did have the important *Klassiker der Kunst* series but I did not read German. On making inquiries I heard about someone who might possibly teach me the language, one of two Germans, Rosenbaum and Delbanco, who had set up in partnership as art dealers. They had left their own country because each had believed the possibilities were more promising in London, but being young they had little capital so the former, Rosenbaum, who upon becoming naturalized changed his name to Roland, was giving lessons in German to augment his income. He proved to be an excellent teacher and gave me a sound grounding in his native tongue; I could read simple things and hold some conversation by the time I discontinued my lessons.

My first experience of an auction sale came speedily and unexpectedly. I had only been at Leger's for two to three weeks, and had not yet found my feet, when I was told to go to Sotheby's to try to buy a painting for the gallery. I had never attended an auction and knew nothing about the procedure, so I was scared stiff but dared not admit it as, trembling, I set off for the rooms. If Mr Harold had noticed my anxious expression he would have

Eugène Carrière, *Deep Concentration*. Mrs Doria Block

dismissed it as rather amusing. Who could be frightened of such an every-day event? The lot he wanted was a portrait by Raeburn of a man wearing a red coat – commercially preferred because more decorative – standing full length in a landscape, holding his horse. Mr Harold was anxious to conceal his own interest and, as I was anonymous, no one in the sale room could possibly know me or for whom I was bidding. He would himself be at the auction and all I had to do was to watch for his signal according to which I was to bid or refrain. A pencil in his mouth meant I was to nod; when he removed it I was to abstain. But as it happened it was not so easy for as the auctioneer was drawing near to my lot, Mr Harold was so surrounded that I could hardly see him and had continually to alter my viewpoint. Apart from this problem it was a jittery trick for a novice to keep one eye on the rostrum and the other on her employer, so with my heart pounding I con-tinued to bid until the figure soared to over £1,000, which at that time was a considerable amount. At last and deliberately the pencil was withdrawn and I heaved an enormous sigh of relief. I could breathe freely again. I was not the least concerned that my mission had failed but only that I had done nothing disastrous such as buying a totally wrong picture. As I left the sale room a stranger approached to commiserate with me on my failure; he thought I had been trying to buy an ancestral portrait, else why should a young girl have wanted so large and not very attractive a painting?

A few months went by and our secretary gave notice because, she said, she wished to return home. I never discovered whether the reason was valid or whether she was forced to do so by her unrequited love. Without ever asking it was taken for granted that I would step into her shoes and assume the position of gallery secretary at £2 10s. per week. I had not learned to write shorthand and had not the slightest intention of doing so; neither had I ever tried my hand at a typewriter. But this was a chance too good to be missed; I was about to become a permanent member of staff instead of an unpaid auxiliary. So that I might cope with the daily correspondence, I invented a quick method of taking dictation and laboriously typed with an eraser beside me, a practice upon which I have not much improved. Mr Harold was gloriously unaware of my struggles and continued to dictate at his normal fast speed so that when I was left to get on with the letters I was often at my wits' end to decipher my scribbles. Often I missed my train back to Cookham, which meant a very long wait. Mr Harold lived only up-stairs and would come and dictate just before we were closing, not realizing that I was on tenterhooks to get home.

I did not chafe at my secretarial duties, being far too absorbed in my interesting subject to wonder what the future might hold: they gave me an insight into running a business and I was fascinated to be privy to deals. There was no doubt about it that buying a picture, seeing it presented in its most favourable state and then finally selling it at a good profit was a rewarding affair. The pleasure it gave me was entirely disinterested for I, like the other staff, received no commission – my own modest one came at a much later date. Besides we all knew how tight business was and how urgently we needed deals, so we all worked together for the good of the gallery. Mr Harold inspired much loyalty.

I got to know most of the dealers in London and from the provinces, also those who came – maybe only annually – from Paris, Berlin and Amsterdam. A friendly rivalry, a certain *bonhomie*, existed among the majority, although there was always a clear division between those who were dedicated and trusted *marchands* and those only interested in profit. The whole art trade too had its well-defined boundary in that the sale room catered for dealers, while they in their turn sold to private people and museums, and not infrequently to each other. This was a straightforward and healthy position – everyone knew where they stood.

After a quick sandwich lunch eaten, when fine, on the rooftop of our building, whence one could wander by way of the fire-escapes almost right down to Piccadilly, I would spend the rest of my break looking at the pictures in one or other of the forthcoming sales. Every day of the week a different one would take place with Christie's conducting two separate auctions – Monday for the 'run of the mill' works, and Fridays for all the finer paintings. Sotheby's, who were then the renowned book auctioneers, held their picture sales on Wednesdays, while Phillips, Son & Neale, Robinson & Fisher, together with Bonham's and Foster's, each had their day to fit in with the others, although some had to duplicate. These sales were spread throughout the year with the exception of the holiday month, so there was always something to view. Now the two predominant sale rooms have grouped their auctions into a few concentrated sessions to make it more convenient for overseas buyers, notably from Japan and America. Then, auctions were almost exclusively of old masters with the eighteenth century being the normal limit; only rarely did anything more recent appear, and when it did it was lumped with the rest. There were no such things as Impressionist sales, which now preponderate in the market.

No sooner had I got used to being the secretary than I was elevated to the status of manager. Mr Oldham had decided it was time to retire and once more I automatically inherited a role. I was faced with more new mysteries, this time of bookkeeping. In compensation it became my job to receive visitors who came to the gallery during Mr Harold's frequent absences at country sales. These took place all over England and Romeike & Curtis daily sent lists from which, if any pictures were mentioned at all, catalogues were immediately requested. Today country sales with interesting pictures are almost a thing of the past, for more and more owners, their hopes boosted high by all the publicity of 'record' prices, send their worthy or, mostly, unworthy possessions to London.

It is amusing to reflect on the *faux pas* I made when, as a manager, I tried to talk with authority on a subject about which I knew little. The span of fine arts is so enormous that it is only possible to know a small part in depth and I was only just beginning to scratch its surface. But my pretence in those days caused me so much discomposure, which I was at great pains to hide, that I feel sympathetic towards all those young people who, in the more prominent sale rooms, have been elevated to positions too high and too quickly. Their very youth and lack of experience debars the expertise they must feign to possess; it is only the few brilliant ones who may ignore these provisos. The rest, like myself, must plod along. So I find myself quoting again and again, 'He rides betimes who rides too fast betimes.'

The dealers treated me with amused courtesy when I had reached my 'exalted' position; there were typists in the trade who were of my age but the women dealers, very much older, had not yet come over from Germany and so, apparently, I was something of a novelty, a woman in a world particular to men. Once one of Mr Harold's associates, on concluding a deal to which I had contributed nothing but moral support, wanted to show his appreciation. Not liking to offer me a monetary commission, he presented me with a hat of my choice. I was touched by the interest of the men, by their occasional instruction, as well as by their forbearance when I made a fool of myself. I think my enthusiasm tickled their fancy and encouraged them to take me under their wing. On one occasion I was extolling the virtues of a George Morland that had in stock to one of the trade's most erudite members. He generally handled old masters of high quality and might well have ignored my ill-informed tittle-tattle. Instead he listened patiently and without contradiction, simply leaving me to discover, in my own time, that Morland, although a tolerably good painter, was in reality of small consequence. During the war years we became friends and I gained from knowing this gentle yet shrewd dealer, who was Francis Zatzenstein, later changed to Matthiesen, under which name his son runs his own gallery with a similar degree of fastidiousness.

Meeting painters and critics

After a couple of years in Bond Street, I got to meet a small number of artists, who were then quite well known but who, with the exception of Ginner and Nevinson, and to a lesser degree James Pryde, have almost disappeared from the artistic scene. They gathered round the figure of Pryde as bees encircle their queen; to them he was God, a quasi-Rembrandt. So I too regarded him with awe. Although some were artists working for journals, all, without exception, were passionate about painting; they opened my eyes to something other than the old masters, and taught me to appreciate British painting of the thirties, albeit in its less adventurous aspects.

Ginner was the oldest of those I knew well; a heavily built, modest, courteous man, he moved about slowly with a half-anxious smile which served as his answer to questions unheard. His deafness had removed him from free conversation and given him an air of wistful apartness. This enforced solitude made me feel sad although I well knew he was wrapped in his painting, with its laborious raffia-like brushstrokes.

Others in the circle included 'Jos' Simpson, the etcher; occasionally Nevinson, whose paintings have suddenly emerged in the sale rooms to fetch quite considerable prices; the robust John Flanagan – Gracie Fields was his patron – and Rowley Smart, of whose watercolours his friends thought so highly but who died early of tuberculosis. There was also Adrian Bury, the poet, critic and journalist, who painted some lyrical watercolours, and finally the writer William Gaunt, one-time editor of the *Studio* magazine, himself a very lively cartoonist whose work is still occasionally seen in mixed exhibitions. But beyond all it was Anton Lock who had the greatest influence on me; not through his painting which was very mannered, contaminated, no doubt, by the journalistic *métier* which I believe he despised, but because of his deep feeling for art. His admiration for it was unstinted, his enthusiasm was infectious and his sense of quality opened up new vistas. I owe him a greater debt than perhaps he ever knew.

It was a great occasion when James Pryde himself condescended to come to a private view. He would be escorted from the Savage Club to which most of these artists belonged, in a doubtful condition, having overimbibed, but expecting and receiving the treatment of a grandee. A commanding tall figure with a beautiful head, but obviously well past his prime, he would enter the gallery like a great histrionic actor, aware of his presence and making the most of it. Like Sickert, he had been on the stage and the aura still hung about him. It is generally thought that he could have gone far had it not been for his inherent laziness, coupled with the fact that he had loyal supporters whether he was working or not. By the time I met him he had not painted for years.

Adjacent to my office was a fairly large gallery used for nothing in particular; I thought it a waste and encouraged by the artists, who I must admit were not entirely disinterested, and with Mr Harold's ready acquiescence, I began to organize contemporary exhibitions in which most of the painters were included in turn. They also suggested names of some others whom they admired but were not in their circle; one of the foremost being Jack B. Yeats who had not exhibited in London for years and was therefore

receptive to the idea of a show. Yeats's early paintings were easy. I knew
that I liked them, but the more recent were something quite different: their
wildness was confusing to my eye, then so raw, and one in particular, try as
I might, I dismally failed to understand. Jack Yeats had come from Dublin
to be at his show's opening, as had his brother, the poet, so I could seek
elucidation from the artist who, though very Irish, was on the whole silent.
'Mr Yeats, would you explain this picture to me?' I ventured in front of the
canvas in question. 'Many people are asking what it is about and I do not
know what to answer.' He drew himself up and looked down upon me,
physically and, I assumed, mentally. 'That painting is to be looked at without comment' came the unhelpful reply. Not knowing that I had been
brought up in South Africa and was unversed in the history of Ireland, he
was scornful that I was unaware of the names of the various Irish martyrs.
Some of his work paid homage to them and was titled in accordance with
their names, but I had to ask him for their significance and was once again
put in my place. Nevertheless, we became friends and when I lunched with
him many years later on one of his rare visits to London, he told me of his
surprise at finding the English so much nicer and more polite than they had
been before the war!

One day a man in his middle thirties ambled into the gallery. He reminded me of a good-natured spaniel and shyly asked if he could show me
some drawings from the portfolio under his arm. I was very taken with
what I saw, highly personal comments on lower-class life: men and women
drinking in pubs, chatting in parks, the women scrubbing doorsteps – the
sight of which had originally worried me – the men haranguing at Speakers'
Corner. Their portly bodies supported on short legs were an echo of the
artist's own figure, but there was acute observation in them and they were
highly individual. My only reservation about the drawings was that their
flavour of kindly caricature might make them even less saleable, when to
sell any drawing was difficult enough. Not yet trusting my own shaky
judgement I asked Edward Ardizzone to leave his portfolio so that I could
consider further. In reality I wanted to consult with my painter friends, and
their approval being unanimous, we launched Ardizzone's inaugural show
and he became a gallery artist.

Given the times, the shortage of money and the general lack of interest
from the public, it was not surprising that none of the shows was a commercial success – or that the majority never even paid their way. On the
other hand costs could be kept very low, for printing and postage were
cheap. Despite having regular reviews in all the papers of note, in London
and in the provinces, the number of visitors, whether wealthy or not, was
minimal in the extreme. It was indeed depressing for me and even more for
the artists who, however, took consolation in that their work was at least

being shown as well as gaining reviews. There were substantial critics on the national papers and art magazines with very few shows for them to review, and although we always grumbled at their lack of space, as we do today but with far better reason, each exhibition at least won a notice almost as a matter of course. Leading writers included Clive Bell, Eric Newton and Raymond Mortimer; and among the critics, Charles Marriott of *The Times*, who had published at least one book on art as well as some novels.

On the *Morning Post* was James Greig, on the *Telegraph*, R. R. Tatlock of whose wife, Cicely Hey, Sickert painted some portraits, and on the *Sunday Times* there was P. G. Konody. The provincial papers too had their serious writers with the *Scotsman*, the *Birmingham Post*, the *Manchester Guardian* and the *Yorkshire Herald* all having correspondents in London, while the editors of monthly art periodicals found time to review the exhibitions themselves. It is indeed ironic that now when we are suffering from an epidemic of exhibitions, when public bodies and museums, not to mention dealers, all feel impelled to launch continuous shows among which are some of real significance, the space allowed to art critics in the press has dwindled so much. Apart from the big international names, who certainly do not need publicity, hardly any established or rising painter succeeds in being noticed. Correspondingly more space is now devoted to the sale-room correspondents, part of whose job it is to report on that perennial subject of public interest, the ever-increasing price of works of art.

I once embarked upon a 'learned' discourse which I delivered to an anonymous critic. Only when he had gone did I suddenly realize that I had been lecturing Mr Konody, who was one of the most powerful and respected of writers. Covered in confusion I vowed in the future to be more careful and reticent, but I did repeat the performance once more. This time my victim left his card on departure and upon it was written the awesome title 'The Keeper of the King's Pictures'.

In order to make a change from one-man exhibitions, it seemed a good idea to base a show on a theme. But I cannot imagine how I came to choose *Nudes* as a subject for this innovation. Nudes were always included in Royal Academy annuals but to make an entire show of them was daring; moreover they were notoriously unsaleable. Mothers of young children would never hang pictures of women without any clothes on, however much they might titillate their husbands, and there were men who were equally prudish. When later I owned one of Epstein's nudes, the best drawing of his I have seen, my uncle, not so jokingly, would take out his handkerchief to hide from his eyes the offensive object.

Despite the drawbacks, I went ahead with my nudes and invited various painters to participate. I was particularly pleased with a delectable one by

Wilfrid de Glehn, a well-known Academician, whose speciality it was to paint lightly clad girls against the background of a bright summer setting. A reclining figure with a slender, lithe body, pale golden hair and a sweet vapid face, she was painted with a showy, superficial virtuosity that I have to confess greatly impressed me. Even though its author had exaggerated all the worst traits of a Sargent, I thought him exciting, perhaps even saleable.

It was through this exhibition that I first met William Nicholson. That he was one of the most unlikely painters of the nude was evidence of my slender knowledge but I was searching for names with which to enhance the show and he happened to be on my list. Without telling him the reason I made an appointment to go to Apple Tree Yard, Nicholson's delightful abode which was also his studio. And delightful it was with its Vermeer-like interior, its feeling of calm. The same black and white squares covered the floor and the same kind of light flooded through the tall window lighting the bric-à-brac on the Regency table. This bric-à-brac comprised a top hat in which Nicholson kept all his brushes, worn right down to the ferrule; jugs of all sorts from his large collection; women's long suede evening gloves in a variety of hues; bilboquets; and also a globe of the world. The top hat had once belonged to Max Beerbohm, the window was from a Lutyens' design. The whole imparted a feeling of elegance combined with a true workman's discipline. One glance revealed the fastidiousness of its owner, used to fine quality in all he possessed but without any hint of pretentiousness. Nicholson's working attire has become legendary for he always wore immaculate white trousers, pink-spotted white shirt and butterfly collar, bow tie, lemon socks and patent-leather shoes. I did not see one scrap of paint that had escaped onto his person or for that matter onto anywhere else. Almost immediately I was put at my ease because I was received with such charming courtesy that, instead of a young, novitiate dealer, I felt like a rich client or a museum director.

Years later when I was preparing Nicholson's *catalogue raisonné*, I found he had painted but three nudes in his life. But however surprised he might have been at my request for a nude, his beautiful manners did not allow him to show anything other than serious consideration. As it happened, he did have one painting for me which was brought forth from behind a stack of canvases. It could not have differed more from the seductive girl I had already been promised for it represented a plain woman lying flat on her back, looking as if she had been run over by a steamroller. But it was a Nicholson, he was ready to lend it and I could not have been more thrilled. Whilst I was there a manservant, carrying a tea-tray, appeared from the floor as if by magic: he came through a trap-door from down below with all the solemnity of a professional butler opening the doors of some magnificent salon. This near pantomime act tickled Nicholson's humour, an element of boyishness which he ever retained. No wonder he was loved by all those who knew him and attractive to those who were only acquaint-ances.

Through the next stage of my education Charles Marriott of *The Times* was unwittingly my tutor when he paid his regular visits to our exhibitions. Mr Marriott must then have been in his sixties, some forty years older than myself. A short paunchy figure with the bright look of a bird, his lively small eyes peered through his pince-nez with the look of the proverbial wise owl. Like Nicholson he had old-fashioned good manners and though he did not actually kiss my hand upon greeting, his salute was akin to this chivalrous gesture. I was surprised, but delighted, when this eminent critic asked me to accompany him on one of his walks in Epping Forest. I had never before 'rambled' in England; so belatedly I discovered the childish fun of threading my way through a thick carpet of leaves, dead or dying, and hearing their swish as they scattered about in response to my shuffling feet. I was familiar with the South African flora but knew nothing about the wild flowers of England, and so I listened eagerly when, on future walks, Mr Marriott pointed out the lanes' different species and told me their charming popular names – Lady's Bedstraw, Scarlet Pimpernel and Speedwell. Soon I was walking with a little book in my pocket to enable me to identify the plants for myself.

But it was only natural that our talk should be mainly about art and here Mr Marriott was invaluable to me as only a friend with much knowledge can be: not as a teacher addressing a pupil but as one who is airing his personal views. Having stood for long periods before some of the master-pieces in the National Gallery without knowing what to look for in a painting, I was becoming exasperated by my inability to understand just what it was that made them so great. I felt myself locked in a cell of obscurity whose key it was impossible to find. There must be some mystery which others could fathom but which was hidden from me. I had got over the hump of believing that art should be an imitation of nature, but like all the uninitiated I was primarily seduced by subject and secondly by colour. Mr Marriott talked, among much else, about the formal aims of a painter: the various technical components that make up a picture – line, plane, volume and so on – the esoteric jargon of the language of art, and how subject or colour were merely a part of any painting. By radically changing my visual attitude he had lifted a veil – but only one veil – from my un-seeing eyes. There was no magic button that could be pressed to make understanding immediate and simple, and although from then on I saw a little more clearly, the rest was a question of years of looking, looking and still more looking – and even that is insufficient. Without eyes to recognize that indefinable attribute known as 'quality', all the conscientiousness and all the studying mean little. And 'eyes' are a gift independent of merit: they can be cultivated but not deliberately attained.

Mr Marriott's tuition was given unconsciously, without any connotation, as I have said, of the sage instructing the neophyte. He had a way of talking as if I were his equal in experience and also in years. Many a time he would say when recalling an anecdote about some artist or critic: 'You will remember…' I smiled to myself but did not retort: 'I could not possibly have known him for he died before I was born.' I was frightened of breaking this endearing habit, the way he treated me as a contemporary, for such easy talk was very relaxing and my receptive ears would benefit. With sandwiches in our pockets, and resting wherever we could get a cup of tea, we spent happy days in very different surroundings from those in Bond Street where we had met.

During Charles Marriott's sixteen years on *The Times* he had enjoyed the reputation of writing liberal and unbiased reviews, and I learned how he had disciplined himself to retain his high critical standards. Whenever I asked whether he would like to be introduced to the artist who was presently exhibiting, he always politely but firmly refused: he could be more objective in his assessments if he were not to have any personal contact. It was a practice I tried to follow when I in my turn became a critic of ballet: unless absolutely necessary, I never went back-stage lest I might have been expected to discuss the performance and be prejudiced when writing my review.

The first two French artists with whom I became acquainted were the good-looking, charming Jean de Botton, a lightweight but elegant Vertes-like painter and the Jewish artist Mané Katz whose subjects were mainly his own people. Born in Russia, he had lived in Paris for years and in his early days had been a friend of Picasso. Without any sittings as such, he painted me – one of his rare portraits – as I moved about casually chatting to him. Possibly on account of this informality the canvas, a good likeness, is spontaneous and fresh. Despite the great energy he brought to bear in his efforts to establish himself as a painter, he never really succeeded, even among the Jewish coterie who were keen on pictures. Now that he is dead he has a following and his prices have risen. What a pity that he could not have basked in some fame in his lifetime. His ever-youthful spirit would have enjoyed it more than most.

Other artists tried to paint me in the pre-war years but their attempts were abortive. Ethel Walker once told me, 'If you take that filthy stuff off your face [lipstick] I would like to paint a portrait of you,' but the occasion never seemed to arise. Ethel Walker was then at the height of her fame, which she never regained after the war; she held all her shows at Reid &

Lefevre, then in King Street, St James's, as did Duncan Grant, Vanessa Bell and their close friend Keith Baynes. All sold quite well considering the times and I noted the little red spots with some jealousy, for 'my' artists were hardly selling at all. When I first got to know her, Ethel Walker was in her seventies but still a compact bundle of nervous energy and tension. A minute wiry figure, a presence charged with authority, the finely structured bones of her sharp-featured face were clearly delineated beneath the tightly drawn skin, pallid and foliate lined. Among a company of women she was conspicuous on account of her masculine clothing; she always wore a dark tailored suit, collar and tie, all topped by the severity of a Stetson. When I walked round an exhibition with her and she paused before something that had caught her fancy, she would throw back her head and examine it steadfastly, half closing the lids over her small piercing eyes until she was peering through no more than a slit. In her deep croaking voice she would make the pronouncement: 'You know my dear there is one thing about me, I can always appreciate the work of other artists.' I giggled inwardly for she was quite unaware that the canvas she liked was unfailingly one that most resembled her own.

Ether Walker lived and painted a stone's throw from Wilson Steer's home in Chelsea. Her studio living-room overlooking the river was chaotic and grubby and in it she housed a collection of mongrels looking quite as unkempt as the interior itself. I had some misgivings when I went there to tea, for the animals drank from the same cups as we did and I had the suspicion that they were cursorily washed if at all. As happens too often an honour was bestowed on her when she was too old to enjoy it. At the age of eighty-two she was made a Dame when, like other artists during the war, her fortunes were at their lowest ebb. She died eight years later in 1951 in much poverty and neglect. One of the Polish painters in London, Marian Kratochwil, himself then very poor, helped her at this time. But the neglect of her reputation has not yet been redressed. Despite the fact that she has no less than fourteen paintings in the Tate Gallery, she is not even mentioned in *The Obstacle Race – The Fortunes of Women Painters and their Work*,* an enormous tome by Germaine Greer. Shortly before Roland, Browse & Delbanco's closure, we made an effort to re-establish her, but the show met with only a modicum of success and failed to achieve its real aim. One day in the future, Dame Ethel Walker must take her place as one of the best British Impressionists, not perhaps on account of the flower-filled canvases that were her most popular works, but for her beautifully understated impressions of sand, sea and cliffs at Robin Hood's Bay, which she loved and where she owned a cottage.

* Germaine Greer, *The Obstacle Race*, Secker & Warburg, 1979.

Although I had seen very few of his paintings I had, from the start, been drawn towards Sickert, an attraction that has puzzled me greatly. I do not know why I chose this particular painter whom I generally find is an acquired taste; one who appeals to the sophisticated palette with none of the seduction the novice demands. Soon after I had started as a beginner at Leger's a dull little *Bust of an Elderly Man* was catalogued at Christie's as being by him and offered in one of their old master sales. I thought I might make my own first discovery for it was a picture that would never be noticed. I had no idea if the attribution was right, so I obtained a small photograph which, with the proverbial temerity of an innocent, I posted to Sickert asking him whether he was the author. I had little expectation of receiving an answer and was therefore surprised when back came a telegram which read very much to the point: 'No I did not paint it but I wish that I had.' I thought at the time this was very polite but later I learned that the mode of communication, as well as the contents, were typical of Sickert's careless extravagance and inborn courtesy. It also confirmed his mode of humour for the picture was devoid of any quality whatsoever and he was simply pulling my leg.

This was the only direct contact I was ever to have with my hero. Now that I was working with contemporary art at the same time as old masters, I felt I must get to know as many well-known living artists as possible. And so I decided that I must try to pay him a visit, a venture I approached with the greatest diffidence. Without writing to make an appointment for fear of a refusal, I found the house in Barnsbury Park, took the bull by the horns and knocked on the door, half hoping that I would not find him in. The door was tentatively opened by a tiny, frail woman who was Sickert's third wife, the painter Thérèse Lessore. She told me in a voice whose quietness matched her own little mousy appearance, that she was very sorry but Mr Sickert was not at home – though I was sure that he was. I thanked her and turned away feeling very relieved that I had performed my self-imposed task, which I promised myself never again to repeat.

Paris

The time came when I felt the need to take another step forward. As far as it went, my group of artists was well enough but as the best known were already contracted, mainly to the Leicester Galleries and Reid & Lefevre, I could not hope to establish good exhibitions without some form of expansion. I must go to Paris to see what I could do. Owing to our fortunes, or rather the lack of them, I embarked upon this trip without a penny to spend, even had I had the confidence to buy; nor did I know one single modern dealer upon whom I could possibly call. With the boldness of youth I stepped into the unknown but Mané Katz came to my rescue; I shall always remember with heartfelt gratitude how he put himself out to help me. He was waiting to welcome me at the Gard du Nord, his face alive with his Harpo Marx grin and with a long-stemmed single red rose in his hand. I could easily have flung my arms about his neck with the relief of seeing one face that was familiar. We went together round the Paris museums; he introduced me to all the modern dealers he knew and took me to meet Othon Friesz and Moïse Kisling who were two of his *copains*. Not yet in a position to know whether or not I liked their work, it was sufficient that I was actually in the studios of two acknowledged French painters.

Friesz was welcoming though somewhat reserved. Kisling, an extrovert and full of *bonhomie* allowed me to examine his extraordinary palette around whose perimeter he had built up a veritable wall of oil paint. Each colour was piled into regular cubes as if they were some stack of bricks, while the pigment appeared so hard and so dry that I wondered how it could possibly ever yield to a brush. Both Friesz and Kisling were having a hard time as were the majority of painters and I only wished I could have bought something from them. Kisling could not have guessed that, decades later, he was to be prized by Japanese buyers with all the high prices their interest entailed. Like Mané Katz, success came too late.

I could not imagine how the hundreds of artists who converged upon Paris could possibly manage to exist; even though living was then very cheap and lifestyle modest, art was a luxury and nothing was selling. They seemed unaware that this beautiful city, so long the centre of artistic creation, had, in this role, passed its day. The illusion was far too sweet to relinquish, and so with nostalgia they lingered on in the capital that had nurtured and inspired so many great figures. If underneath the surface the situation was hopeless, outwardly the atmosphere continued lively: the legendary cafés were filled with painters and writers all engaged in animated conversation while they spun out the solitary drink they could afford. It was the last flicker of the Paris that was. But I am glad to have witnessed even that.

I do not remember how I came to know Albert Marquet, much less why he invited me to lunch. He lived in an apartment with Marcelle Marty, his novelist wife, which was situated high above the rue Dauphine. It commanded a beautiful view of the river, a bonus of which he took full advantage, for from the windows of his front rooms he repeatedly painted the Paris below, the canvases for which he is mainly renowned. As the French are notorious for guarding their privacy and generally entertain in their favourite restaurants, I felt very privileged by Marquet's invitation to have lunch with him in his own home. He reminded me of Ginner, and had that same gentle kindness that was so appealing. His slippered feet shuffled in the most homely way while he, quiet and modest, was a noticeable foil to his dominant wife who appeared as the driving force in their ménage.

We sat down to lunch in the light-flooded room, where the generous round table was evocative of Vuillard, to a true family meal irrevocably French – the tureen of hot soup, the long crusty *baguette*, the platter of cheese and *tarte aux fruits* and the inevitable bottle of wine – this in the days when far less wine was drunk in England. All imparted a liberal welcome and one which, ever since, I have tried to emulate. I left with a promise of a Marquet exhibition in the future, the first held in London for many a year. It was just as well that Marquet did not cross over for the opening as the show was a complete flop: out of some thirty paintings not one was sold, although none was over £300–£400. These same pictures would now form a gilt-edged security for any dealer. The failure was embarrassing enough as it was. Had he been present it would have been that much worse.

Not being a gourmet, I find it surprising that this long-ago visit to the city of Paris should have left two repasts so fixedly in my mind. As well as the lunch mentioned above, the second occasion was when Marcel Bernheim invited me to eat at La Reine Pédauque named after Anatole France's novel, *Rôtisserie de la Reine Pédauque*, the restaurant which specialized exclusively in both hot and cold hors-d'oeuvre. Delicious though these *plats* undoubtedly were, the manner of their serving impressed me even more, for the waiters moved about at an incredible speed as they deftly threaded their way between the crowded tables. In the palm of one hand, and high over their heads, they carried entrée dishes piled to a great height. A crash on the way seemed to be certain but no such disaster occurred. I have no idea if the food and the feats of agility remain as they were then, since I prefer to remember La Reine as it was and have never cared to return.

Marcel Bernheim turned out to be by far the most helpful among the Paris dealers I encountered. Without asking if I would buy any, he offered to lend me an exhibition of Boudin watercolours which apparently he had in stock. This was a quite unheard of proposition, for an unwritten law demanded that by way of ensuring a modicum of sales, the borrower should purchase at least a percentage. Impecunious as I was, I could not have managed this, but M. Bernheim's generosity let me off the hook. The exhibition took place some months ahead, and in normal times would have met with a success, for the English, and especially the Scots, are as loyal in their affection for Boudin as they have remained for Fantin-Latour. But times were not normal and although the top price for any one item did not exceed fifty pounds – I even managed to buy one myself – only a mere handful found owners.

The third exhibition I secured in Paris was of the paintings of Pascin. I did not then particularly like his work, but have since grown to appreciate his fine draughtsmanship, which earned him a position on the renowned satirical magazine *Simplicissimus* when he was only eighteen. Pascin has never found favour in England. Behind the mature oils lies a hint of depravity and their delicate colour seems to heighten this trait which to my mind adds a sense of discomfort. However, he was a painter of standing and I was grateful for the opportunity of staging the show. But once again it was a disaster with nothing at all being sold. On the last morning, a random visitor showed some interest in a couple of canvases but he needed a second look before being able to decide which of the two he preferred. Not living in England, he was to leave London by the midday train on the following day, so how was he able to have another inspection? As I could not afford to miss this very last chance, an unorthodox solution presented itself: I would take the paintings to show him again on a platform at Victoria station. It seemed safer, however, to meet under the clock where so many people over the years have made assignations. So on the following day, which was a Saturday, I rushed from the gallery as soon as it closed and joined the mob of weekenders. Unwrapping the nudes of an appreciable size, I propped them against one of the railings and much to the amazement of all those around who were gaping incredulously at the two 'lewd' objects, I delivered the best sales talk I could muster. How naïve I was, how childishly enthusiastic, for later I realized my supposed client never had the slightest intention of buying. His feigned interest was no more than a ploy with which to extricate himself from the gallery. Every art dealer knows this little trick and when I left Victoria I too had learned it.

It was truly a case of fools rushing in when I came to the conclusion that I should not leave Paris before making an attempt to meet Mme Guillaume, the notorious, formidable and extremely rich widow of the well-known collector and dealer. Having heard – maybe exaggerated – scandalous rumours about her dealings and high life, I cannot imagine, in my humble state, what I expected of her. Much overawed by her grand apartment, which I seem to remember was in or near the Bois de Boulogne, I was received by her equally grand assistant/secretary who informed me that while Madame herself was away, she was at my service if I cared to see anything. I was ushered into an enormous salon, expensively furnished in eighteenth-century style with an upholstered easel against one of the walls indicating that this was the holy of holies. The lady herself had evidently summed me up as not being worthy even of her attention, for that was the last I saw of her; she left me to the mercies of a stately butler who, looking as if his face had never encountered a smile, carefully and with exaggerated ceremony placed a series of expensive paintings on the easel before me. There was nothing to do but participate in the charade, so I played my part and examined each canvas, then signalled for the next 'masterpiece' to appear. Each picture was removed at the same careful pace and another was brought in to replace it. Undoubtedly there were some very fine paintings among all those I was shown but by this time I could not even look dispassionately, all I could think of was how to disentangle myself and make my escape. After what seemed an interminable period I finally rose from my luxurious armchair, thanked the supercilious man for the trouble he had taken and left, in what I hoped was a dignified way.

More exhibitions at the Leger Gallery

The Leger Gallery's day-to-day running was working quite well in one pair of hands and the saving of an extra salary was a welcome economy. Although my own load was very much heavier, I was becoming more and more steeped in art dealing and, fascinated by such an interesting career, the added labours and responsibility did not bother me. What did bother me was our financial position for, like many others, Leger's was living a hand-to-mouth existence with even the payment of the weekly salaries being dependent either on a last-minute sale or on the goodwill of the bank manager. By today's standards our overdraft was negligible but one has to realize that in those times pictures were a collateral that no financier would contemplate. Art was no buoyant, international trade with the prices of good and genuine painting inevitably rising with each change of owner; on the contrary, dealing was a most insecure business in which capital could be tied up, sometimes for years, before it showed any return. Collecting old masters was regarded as an élitist indulgence in which only the rich could participate. The art of the nineteenth and twentieth centuries, later to have such an enormous appeal, had not yet become a factor.

My exhibitions continued to run at a loss and did not introduce any new clients; the gap was too wide between the past and the present – old and modern pictures demanded visual adjustment – and still the twain rarely met. Mr Harold might well have put a stop to my shows for although he did not go quite so far as to avert his eyes, as Mr Oldham had done when walking through the gallery in which they were hanging, he was not at all interested in living artists. By permitting me to continue he was giving me my head and for this understanding I owe him everything. Not only did he allow me to exercise my own judgement but by making me more than just an employee he gave me my first taste of professional independence. Although everything I tried seemed to emphasize the fact that there was not room for one more modern gallery to augment the small number already established, failure may make one more determined to succeed, so I still racked my brains for a show so prestigious that it might yet put our modern exhibitions on the map.

I never did hit upon the illustrious exhibition which was to make us renowned; instead the idea came that it might be of interest to gather together as much of the early work of Stanley Spencer as could be locally found. Although his recent paintings were being exhibited I had not seen a collection prior to 1930 and very much doubted if one had been shown. At that time Stanley Spencer had not yet 'arrived': a long time was to pass before his re-election to the Academy from which he had resigned after the rejection of two pictures; neither was he knighted until 1959 – again only two months before he was to die. Now he takes his place as one of the major figures in twentieth-century British painting, but like most others he has no name abroad.

The paintings I sought were few in number and as the majority were in private hands, the exhibits had mostly to be on loan so there was no possibility of a financial coup. This, my first show of purely artistic interest, was, in its lack of commercial concern, to be the forerunner of many of those later to be presented by Roland, Browse & Delbanco.

All the owners agreed to lend and everything was going swimmingly when out of the blue a letter arrived saying that Spencer was opposed to the show and to prevent it from taking place had telegraphed everyone not to collaborate. This was a situation I had not contemplated. The show had already been announced in the press, all the invitations were posted, and I was on tenterhooks as to the outcome. I need not have worried; no one obeyed Stanley's urgent request and the exhibition went ahead as planned. It was many a year before he forgave me and I realized that, ethically, I had not acted correctly but should have observed the normal courtesy of asking in advance for the artist's approval. Perhaps I had a hunch that this would not be granted, or perhaps I was careless enough to believe that once a picture had left the studio its author no longer has any say. But, all this apart, I am fairly sure that there was more than just etiquette involved: no creative artist can possibly agree that the productions of his younger days equal or exceed those upon which he is currently working. Such an admission would be tantamount to failure and henceforth it would be impossible to continue.

Sadly the continuous rise of excellence is the exception rather than the rule; the majority of painters fail to fulfil whatever early promise they might have shown and begin to deteriorate, usually in mid-career. The large number of exhibitions that I have organized have proved the truth of this dictum. I have my own way of measuring genius, a term currently so abused as to have little meaning. It belongs to the artist who rises to his grandest height with the passage of years, sometimes despite the most dire infirmities. His graph, instead of falling during its course, continues to rise, though irregularly, right to the end, and looking back over the centuries I cannot recall any towering figure who has caused me to alter my yardstick. I would also claim that this rule does not only apply to creative artists but also embraces those in the more ordinary walks of life. Some of the finest people that I have known have been in their eighties and have grown with the years in their spiritual awareness, so that their understanding, compassion and liveliness of outlook have been an example to all. Around them, like a magnet, old and young have been drawn, for their presence meant inspiration and comfort. This, I believe, is what life is about; this is the genius of living.

I still consider Spencer, after the thirties, to have channelled his development into more explicit images at the cost of his subtlety and richness. Yet even an artist's most explicit images are often ambiguous. One of Stanley's drawings had once been given to me for sale. It represented two little girls, one handing a bunch of daffodils to the other, over a hedge clipped to the height of their shoulders. I felt rather pleased with myself for I believed I had interpreted the message that Stanley wished to convey, so when I next met him I spoke about it: 'I do so like the idea that prompted your drawing,' I proudly told him, giving myself a little pat on the back for my newly discovered perspicacity, but on seeing the look of inquiry on his face I went on to explain '... you have evidently wished to show that despite any barrier that might separate two people, a gesture of goodwill, such as the giving of flowers, is able to overcome any ill-feeling.' 'What a very nice thought, it never occurred to me,' he replied with a smile. With so much nonsensical jargon expounded about the art of today, I often think of this enlightening retort with the feeling that other artists must likewise be amused – sometimes annoyed – by the explications with which some critics and historians misinterpret their intentions. Whenever, since this episode, I have been asked to clarify the meaning of an enigmatic picture, I chuckle inwardly, for across the distance of years comes the echo of the words: 'What a very nice thought, it never occurred to me.'

At a moment when he could least afford it, Mr Harold suffered a substantial loss at the hands of a trickster. C— seemed to be wealthy, well educated and well connected, in short, the sort of client whose advent at that time was a minor miracle. He said he was intending to open an old master gallery in Paris; he had taken fine premises, and was buying pictures for stock. He bought, and paid for, a considerable number of paintings from Leger's. But what especially attracted me was his suggestion that Winston Churchill, whom he claimed to know, might be persuaded to hold an exhibition with us. Churchill was then in the political wilderness, but an exhibition of his paintings would have drawn great publicity and I was naturally keen on the idea. C— made an appointment to take me to Chartwell for tea – I do not know what reason he gave but I feel sure no exhibition was ever mentioned.

Winston was in working clothes laying the bricks of a garden wall. He greeted us affably but did not seem at all intimate with my companion. I never did fathom the extent of their relationship, but I imagine it to have been slight. We were taken through the garden to Winston's studio where we saw a few paintings about which I made admiring remarks, not with complete honesty I must admit. I was so anxious to secure the show that I would have approved almost anything. It was to no avail – at tea I was too shy to open my mouth and only half heard the conversation. I was fascinated by the sight of a homely milk bottle among the silver on the tray the butler brought; a small impression indeed to have carried away from what should have been a momentous occasion. The exhibition of course never took place – I do not believe that Churchill ever contemplated it, for he was said to have disliked showing his paintings.

Unfortunately this was not the last we heard of C—. Having gained Mr Harold's full confidence, he asked, quite reasonably, that a number of pictures be lent to him on consignment to swell his stock. After the paintings were despatched he departed for Paris. Some weeks of silence followed but Mr Harold did not worry unduly; not being by nature suspicious, he allowed matters to slide for longer than he should. When it was too late he went to Paris but found no gallery at the given address and C— nowhere to be found. There was nothing to do but to write off the loss. Later we heard that C— was in prison but this was never confirmed. It was another experience to contribute to my education, and it put me on my mettle against the plausible rogues I might meet in the future.

One day I was told a young man was to join us on his return from Holland; while he was there he had written to say he had identified a picture of ours, one that had puzzled Mr Harold. He told us it was by Hendrik Goltzius, a painter I had never yet heard of. I was enormously impressed by his ability to identify a minor painter with such a casual degree of assurance. Soon after Eddie Speelman's arrival I appreciated how well versed he was, especially in the Dutch seventeenth-century school, an area he had worked in with the well-known firm of Duits. It was evident he would become one of London's outstanding dealers in the old master field, and that it was only a question of time before he would leave us to start on his own. This early promise Eddie fulfilled, for with his sharp eye and keen business sense he made himself a highly successful career. Only David Carritt, his younger contemporary who after a long illness died an early death, has arguably surpassed his ability.

Eddie Speelman married his attractive wife, Sally, at about the same time that I married my first husband, Ivan. We four became friends and often played bridge in a light-hearted way, a game I learned because it was easier to play cards than to talk to Ivan's business associates. It is strange to remember now that we were able to live in a flat in Sloane Street with a living-in maid on a combined income of no more than seven pounds ten shillings a week. In that respect these times belonged to a vanished world. But there were already signs of the coming changes in the art world. 'Modern Art' was becoming a matter of public controversy.

I had never come into personal contact with any of our more progressive artists and although I saw their work from time to time, mainly at the Leicester, Mayor and Zwemmer galleries, I did not understand their formal aims or notice the ways in which they had deviated from tradition. My introduction to modern art had been through the more traditional painters among whom were those who, at a much delayed date, had been influenced by the Impressionists and Post-Impressionists. I did not even know the names of such men as Gabo, Mondrian, Moholy-Nagy and Kokoschka, much less that they had arrived in our midst – mostly as refugees from the Hitler régime – and that their meeting with artists like Moore, Hepworth and Nicholson had had a telling effect on the course of modern art in Britain.

The modern movements of Vorticism, Constructivism and Surrealism were an enigma to my half-educated eyes, which had originally been opened by the old masters. When I saw London's first Surrealist show I found it as puzzling as did the hordes of visitors who, having been titillated by press headlines, queued down the street to gape at and make fun of this 'outrageous nonsense'. But while they went there simply to mock, I tried, but failed, to understand. The logic behind such visually illogical pictures was quite beyond my comprehension and again I felt thwarted by my apparent stupidity.

The Royal Academy summer exhibitions were at the other extreme, stultified, dull, a haven for unimaginative portraitists. I always went as a matter of course; besides, I wanted to see everything. It is amusing to look back upon those days now, when the status of the Royal Academy has so radically changed. I do not refer to its newly found liberalism, nor to the commercialism imposed on it, in common with other institutions through-out the world, by ever-rising costs; but to its standing in society. For a very long time its private view was one of *the* social events of the year: it represented the opening of the London Season, and an invitation was to be coveted. Anyone who was anyone had to be there, even those who did not give a fig for art. The ladies christened their new season's outfits and wore their fine Easter hats, vying with each other to be the most elegant. The 'arty' women, preferring to look that way, tried to emulate the Dorelia (John) look with its long full skirt and frilled jacket. Eccentric, elderly women whose charms, if such they had been, had long since faded, appeared in their mother's or grandmother's clothes apparently unearthed from trunks. Without the presence of a set of twins, whose names I have forgotten, the private view was not quite complete. Young, beautiful, slightly weird, with long frizzy hair which would now be fashionable, they were well known artists' models. The ladies in fact were far more interesting than the pictures and as they themselves were of the same opinion, they paid more attention to each other's attire than to any of the work upon the walls.

The private view was also an excuse for a binge by the Trustees of provincial museums and galleries. Travelling to London with their individual directors, they would visit the Academy during the morning, as often as not buy a picture or two, then treat themselves to a congenial lunch at which liquor flowed freely. As a matter of course commercial galleries might expect a visit from them during the same afternoon, and being in a jolly mood they not infrequently made further purchases.

Prologue to war

Towards the end of the 1930s I was beginning to get restless: I felt I had outgrown my time at Leger's. But not having any clear idea where to go from there, I was content to stay where I was, with eyes and ears open until the right opportunity should present itself. I had had an offer from one well-known dealer who specialized in flower and still life paintings, mainly of the seventeenth-century Dutch school; he worked by himself and was highly successful, being respected for the quality of all that he handled. Mr S very generously suggested partnership, the second I had been offered though in a different profession. Although we did not get as far as discussing terms, he must have known that I had no capital and could not have bought myself into his firm. My acceptance would have been advantageous to me if only from the financial angle but, though tempted, I decided to decline. I liked Mr S as far as I knew him, but being a partner means a special relationship into which I did not wish to enter.

The solution to the problem of what to do next, when it came, was to bring to a halt, or turn upside down, not just my life but the lives of millions of people. The months before war was finally declared were fraught with rumblings of so menacing a nature that we tried to push them into the background, not having the courage to face them. We knew from our elders of the ghastly bloodshed that the First World War had caused, and the thought of another made us cold with fear for all those we loved who would certainly be in the firing line. That we too would be among them we had little doubt, but to what extent we could not envisage. Chamberlain's treaty that purported to mean 'peace in our time' is now derided, but I, like the majority not in the know, wept tears of relief that the fearsome danger had passed us by while others were already engulfed. For all but a saintly few, self-preservation is the foremost consideration. As history relates, our selfish relief was short-lived. Another country and then another succumbed before Hitler's invading armies, and we knew that we finally must take our stand.

The months that preceded the declaration of war also began one of the most stricken periods of my life: my marriage, through no other fault than my own, was on the verge of breaking up. I had fallen deeply in love with one of our friends and had to face the agonizing decision whether to leave my husband for him. Feeling lost in a jungle of dark vacillation through which it seemed no gleam could penetrate, I wandered one day into a church in whose emptiness I sat down and sobbed. The parson appeared from out of the shadows and seeing me sitting with my head in my arms, came and asked me the cause of my distress. 'Give yourself to Jesus' came the automatic response but, with my background, these were nothing but words; I had not an idea of their meaning. So with an added sense of despair that this advice was all he could offer, I turned away and left his church in greater distress than when I had entered. I felt like a pariah. Our first home, assembled with such care and high hopes, had all of a sudden been abandoned, cast aside like some empty shell, its furniture in store and myself in limbo without even my work as consolation.

Upon mobilization women who did not enlist in the forces were called to report in order to indicate in which civilian branch they would serve. I got a shock when I looked around me at those who were in my age group; heaven help me, did I really look as ancient as that? But then they were mostly what was called 'working women' and their lives had taken a greater toll than had mine. I chose to enter the ambulance service since at least I could drive a car, and although it was far from convenient I asked to be stationed at a Swiss Cottage garage because my friend, Sally, was already there. I was living at Notting Hill Gate with Kate Fielding (later Kate Wilson), who had married a cousin of mine; and as he was away with the forces she invited me to share her studio flat in one of the double-storey houses in Linden Gardens. I thought I would be there just for the duration but, with one short break, it was twenty years before I left.

On that glorious summer's day in 1939, a day when all nature was trembling with joy while man's primary thought was destruction, I reported for duty. The interminable nights in a pitch-black garage growing increasingly cold as winter approached were a continuing torment. Hour after hour there was nothing to do but dwell on the unhappiness I was causing. During the day it was slightly better, for in our steel helmets, and wearing gas masks in order to get used to their feel, we drove in convoy around unfamiliar streets, headed by one of the taxi drivers who were attached to each station. Their knowledge of London being extensive, they showed us the quickest and easiest routes to get to the incidents that were bound to occur. There was no such thing as a proper ambulance. Instead we drove market lorries fitted with primitive iron stretchers, a far too heavy weight for women to lift with a practising 'body' upon it and one which sometimes caused serious injuries either to the 'body' or its bearers. But every experience, however bleak, has some positive lesson to offer. Part of our training was to spend one day with a regular ambulance team which comprised, I suppose, about half a dozen men. During the periods of inactivity their talk was so coarse and embarrassingly lewd that I scarcely knew where to look, especially as on one occasion I was the object of their ribald joke. But once I was with them when called to an accident. A little old woman had fallen or thrown herself from a floor above into the area, and there she was lying and moaning softly in a small crumpled heap. I had never before, and have never since, witnessed such a complete metamorphosis: those foul-mouthed boors became succouring angels as they tenderly put her on the collapsible stretcher which they adroitly managed up the narrow staircase. They spoke words of comfort in an effort to soothe her as she was driven to hospital, while during the journey they administered oxygen whenever they thought it necessary. They were men transformed by their calling and it was an enlightening human experience.

Part Three
The War Years

The National Gallery in wartime: 'Browse's Academy'

One early summer's evening in 1939 I had been invited by a client of Leger's to go to a banquet at the Coventry Art Gallery, of which he was the chief benefactor. The dinner was to celebrate its opening and the guest of honour was Sir Kenneth Clark, then Director of the National Gallery. I had met him on several previous occasions but would not have claimed to know him well. As I was waiting at the junction for Coventry, he came up and suggested we continue our journey together. I had to tell him I was travelling 'hard', to which he disarmingly and with feigned apology replied that he was travelling first but that I should not mind, for he would pay the difference. We were booked into the same hotel and wishing to fortify himself against what we both feared might be a boring evening, Sir Kenneth asked me to meet him for a drink beforehand. He had only recently received the KCB and when we met he was carrying his decoration in his hand. He asked me to fasten it round his neck as he said he had not yet got the hang of doing so. I found this little episode endearing and warmed to him from that moment.

Before we parted we made an appointment to meet early next morning. This would give us time, before catching our train, to go round the Cathedral together. But our rendezvous never took place. The National Gallery pictures were already packed, waiting to go to their hiding place beneath a slate quarry in Wales, and he had received an urgent message that they should leave immediately. Wishing to supervise their departure, he had caught the first train back to London.

Not long after the declaration of war, Dame Myra Hess instituted her concerts in a large room at the National Gallery. They proved a joy in those abnormal times and whenever my ambulance shifts would allow, and I was not too tired after a night on duty, I joined the packed audience at these

James McNeill Whistler, *Young Woman Seated, Back View*. Private collection

lunchtime performances. To reach the concert one had to walk through several of the bare rooms; without their pictures they were sad and reproachful and seemed to say, as the performers were heard tuning their instruments, 'This is all very well but we are being deprived of our rightful purpose.' The unspoken protest echoed my footfalls in the vast empty galleries, and I went away ruminating on the situation. As the art world in general had come to a halt and there were no pictures to be seen anywhere, I knew there must be others who felt the same sense of loss. What could I do? Why not use the gallery for loan exhibitions was the thought that came into my mind. The more I thought about it the better I liked the idea. Above all else it was thoroughly practicable, for owners would realize the risks involved and I felt certain that they would accept them.

Fortified by my recent encounter with Sir Kenneth Clark I went to see him in his impressive, sombre office at Trafalgar Square. Alas, this was a very different Sir Kenneth from the one I had met in Coventry. Without giving any reason, he summarily dismissed my proposal. But being a Taurean, a single refusal means little to me: I lower my head and renew the attack. I did so on no less than five occasions but each time with the same negative result. Despite all these setbacks I would not give up, but I was at a loss what to do. To have written a letter would have given him the opportunity to close the matter by a written refusal My only hope was that I might bump into Sir Kenneth at one of the concerts and broach the matter for one last time. I did bump into him and at long last was not turned away. Perhaps he was impressed by such tenacity or merely bored by this tiresome female who would not take no for an answer; at any rate he told me to put my ideas on paper so that he could show them to his trustees.

I rushed back to Kate to report the good news. Then came the question of getting to work; it was one thing to have a brainwave but another to put it into practice, for in the face of Sir Kenneth's opposition I had not even thought what the first exhibition should be about. Evidently it should be of British artists for not only would that boost their morale at a time when they needed an uplift, but in practice it was British work that would be most accessible in time of war. As Whistler (though American born) had exercised such a wide influence on his younger English contemporaries, he was a good starting point, from which would follow both established and emerging artists. I drew up a list of some 300 pictures which I believed to be among the most choice. All belonged to private owners, for the exhibition was to be strictly 'not for sale'. Sir Kenneth approved and so did his trustees. He had even become enthusiastic and went so far as to say that I would be heroic if I brought it off – which I thought was an exaggerated tribute. *British Painting since Whistler* was on its way.

That morning, when Sir Kenneth gave me the news I had so wanted to

hear, turned out to be another landmark in my life. I had gone straight from
night duty to the National Gallery still wearing my boiler-suit – the civilian
uniform – and carrying the obligatory steel helmet and gas-mask, and if I
was in a daze through lack of sleep my excitement very quickly jolted me
out of it as we got down to discussing the details. Sir Kenneth began by
telling me that he was far too busy to organize the exhibition and I would
have to help him. I was delighted by this unexpected suggestion, but something prompted me to ask him what time he got up in the morning. 'Eight
o'clock.' I suggested he rise an hour earlier. I doubt whether anyone had
ever asked him such an impertinent question, but it must have amused him
for when Queen Elizabeth – now the Queen Mother – came to visit our
exhibition, I heard him telling her what I had said.

I can truthfully say that up to that moment I had not considered I might
play any part; I was far too anxious for the project to materialize to think
what it might imply for myself. Disinterested actions do frequently bestow
rewards, I have discovered. Now I could leave the ambulance service to
return to my own field, but in a more exalted sphere. A request from the
National Gallery secured my release and I was allocated my very own office
in one of the world's greatest museums. The office was bare of all but a
desk, but a trustee and one friend came to my aid: Coutts Bank lent me
a typewriter through their managing director, the Hon. Jasper Ridley, and
Hugo Pitman produced two strong armchairs from his stockbroking firm of
Rowe & Pitman.

Almost at once Sir Kenneth was whisked off to work at the Ministry of
Information and I found I was left all by myself to put my scheme into
practice – a non-civil servant with all the resources of a great national institution behind me. About half the attendants were still at the gallery, the rest
having gone with the pictures to Wales; it was now William Gibson who
was in charge and to whom I could turn when consultation was necessary.
He was a stalwart Keeper of the Gallery and very supportive in all circumstances. Sir Kenneth naturally was kept well informed and approved all the
subsequent exhibitions.

There were no Treasury funds available for our enterprise but somehow
or other it was arranged for me to receive two pounds ten shillings a week,
this being the accepted 'separation allowance' given to women whose husbands had joined up, and because I was living with Kate at that time her
extreme generosity enabled me to manage. Believing that people would
be willing to pay and might appreciate the exhibitions more for having
done so, we decided on an entrance fee of sixpence, and the catalogue was
to cost fourpence. These sums seem paltry today but we managed to end
in credit to the extent of over £2,000. It would have been nice to have
been able to spend it on some modest work for the National Gallery, as a

commemoration of these exhibitions, but the surplus was duly swallowed up by the Treasury.

Whenever I want to get anything done I believe in starting right at the top, so I began by soliciting a loan from the Queen. With the advice of the two men already mentioned, who were her personal friends, she had acquired a few good modern paintings among which were canvases by Paul Nash, Matthew Smith, Augustus John and Sickert. I was notified immediately that she would grant my request, so I was able to begin all my begging letters with 'Her Majesty the Queen has graciously agreed to lend …', upon which everyone automatically followed. It was by no means easy to trace the whereabouts of all the pictures I had on my list and quite a lot of detective work was needed. There were no informative catalogues or any books to which it was possible to refer; not one single volume on a living British painter had been published since around 1923 when Benn had brought out their small series. But the dealers helped me to find what I wanted, primarily works they had handled themselves, while some of the artists filled in the gaps; the rest had to be found by following remote clues and, on the whole, I was quite successful. I must have written hundreds of letters in my own inexpert typing. I travelled all over England seeing collections and finding paintings I had not known. Once found, getting them to London was a formidable problem at a time when fuel was severely rationed. I fear that I often bullied our transport agent who, despite all restrictions, worked wonders; but he could not be expected to fetch one small canvas from some remote part of the country and on these occasions there was nothing to do but to find some kind person who would take me to get it. I had got into the habit of telephoning the Ministry to beg for more petrol for this special purpose and with the name of the National Gallery behind me I usually succeeded. Then came the day when Morton Sands, the owner of the largest collection of Sickerts, promised to take me to see Euphemia Lamb, from whose picture collection I wanted a couple by Innes. I had to arrange for the additional fuel vouchers and never thought to inquire about the make of the car, but as the official needed to know in order to assess the amount required, I was dismayed when Mr Sands told me with diffidence that, in fact, it was a Rolls.

Euphemia was Henry Lamb's first wife and was much loved by J. D. Innes, among several others; it was said that her photograph in his breast pocket saved his life when he was a soldier. She no longer lived in the world of painters but had retired to the country surrounded by animals. Into the kitchen where we were eating our lunch – she was renowned as an excellent cook – came turkeys, geese, ducks and chickens whose loud cackling made it difficult to talk. They too were given some of our food, just as Ethel

Walker's dogs had shared our tea. When the time came to leave we could not find Morton Sands until from a window on the first floor a call of distress was heard. This very correct former civil servant, in his Savile Row suit, had got himself locked in the lavatory and no pushing or pulling could release the door. Red with embarrassment he had to creep through the window and descend a ladder. We drove back to London in the comfort of his Rolls in which he was far more at home.

From all over England pictures arrived and finally came the great day for hanging, the most pleasurable of all possible rewards after the months of preparation. I find that the most exciting moment in the organization of any exhibition is when all the works are assembled around one and can be absorbed in their entirety. Not until then can one really assess how each may hang to its own greatest advantage and that of the show as a whole. This is when creative ability comes in, for good hanging is a minor art. In a general survey, strict chronological sequence is seldom possible, however desirable. The overall pattern and the look of each room are more important. Rhythm is the key to every good hang; rhythm of subject, size, scale and shape as well as of colour, tonality and mood – even in the application of *matière*, and as rhythm is fundamental to all areas of life, this is no dogmatic dictum. Quality also cannot be ignored; a wonderful painting may look less at ease if surrounded by unsuitable neighbours, while a really bad canvas is impossible to hang. To speak of 'hanging' may be confusing for the layman – I once dictated a telegram over the telephone which ran as follows: 'PLEASE SEND WILSON STOP WISH TO HANG IMMEDIATELY'! The operator could not believe her ears and I had to repeat myself several times and end up with a full explanation.

For the reasons above I do not believe in 'hanging on paper' before the exhibits arrive; this measured plan seldom works out for there are too many subtle elements that cannot be envisaged. I therefore had not the slightest idea as to how many of the National Gallery rooms we would fill, nor if the small canvases – well in the majority – would look lost on the vast walls. But it was a splendid change not to be restricted for space; as soon as one room was satisfactorily completed I could go on to the next, but when the next happened to be the long gallery, an eventuality I had not expected, I came face to face with a problem. There were plenty of paintings with which to fill it but they were all of too modest dimensions and the length of the gallery demanded a huge picture to act as a focus and hold all together. At such a late date I did not know how to find one but again Hugo Pitman came to my rescue, for being a friend and also a lender he by now felt himself involved in the show. When I confided my problem his eyes twinkled merrily and his nostrils quivered in a typical expression of mischief; he loved beyond anything to be 'in the know' and he had thought of a solution. In his country home he was temporarily housing an enormous mural by Augustus John; he was toying with the idea of buying it but had not yet made up his mind. My need for a large work became the catalyst, for although this mural, *Lyrical Fantasy*, was just the right size it could not be included while it still belonged to the artist. So Hugo consulted with his wife, John Sargent's niece, and they decided to buy it forthwith. It looked quite spectacular as it reigned over the room, and as very few critics had seen it before, it drew a wealth of publicity.

Among the exhibits for a later show I wanted to borrow another John, a drawing of Lawrence of Arabia belonging to Bernard Shaw. He had asked me to lunch to discuss the loan and as his apartment in Whitehall Court was so near to Trafalgar Square, I decided to walk the short distance. I was wandering in a leisurely way down Whitehall in plenty of time to keep my appointment, when the first meaningful siren of the war wailed out with startling and chilling surprise. Against the usual sounds of everyday life this abrupt shriek in the middle of the day blasted the ear and produced signs of panic, so that everyone ran in different directions without much idea where they were going. I ran with the rest, my heart beating fast, and plunged into the nearest doorway to find myself in a Ministry building where I had no right to be. In the urgency of the moment interlopers were not noticed and there I waited anxiously until the 'all clear' rang out, emerging from my shelter after a half-hour's delay. I was worried to have arrived so late for lunch but in those times social niceties were waived and Mrs Shaw warmly welcomed me at the door. I felt this homely, plump little person was accustomed to being the go-between; she did her best to put me at ease, sensitively aware how overawed I was at the prospect of meeting her formidably famous husband. She whispered that although he was a vegetarian, she and I would eat an ordinary meal – as if that could matter on such an occasion – which was touchingly thoughtful of her. There was no other guest so we were a trio but I did not feel shy as I had done at Winston's, and the reason for this was quite simple: I was not called upon to utter a word. Shaw talked ceaselessly and at such a pace that I wondered how he found time to breathe. When he was not expounding upon a whole range of subjects he would burst into singing to force home a point he was trying to make about music. The discourse was fascinating until he turned to art, and then I must say his comments were nonsense. But they were delivered with supreme confidence, as if every word were a pearl.

I had never paid much attention to them but had often had dreams which I could recount in every detail next morning. Shortly before my marriage broke up, I told Ivan of a fantastic one I had just had: I was hanging contemporary pictures on the walls of the National Gallery! We laughed about it as it was so impossible it should ever happen. Like other dreams it faded away and I never gave it another thought until the impossible became the reality.

Among the art critics and journalists invited to a press conference in advance of the opening of *British Painting since Whistler*, was Hugo Wortham, for long the *Daily Telegraph*'s distinguished 'Peterborough'. He had formed the habit of turning to me for advice whenever he had to write a 'par' on art, his own knowledge and love being directed towards music. He asked me for details about our exhibition and on account of our intimacy I told him of my extraordinary dream. Not realizing it was meant for his ears alone, and misinterpreting the dream as a wish, he wrote '... I have known Miss Lillian Browse for some years ... she always concealed from me her life's ambition. Now that she has realized it she confesses her days were filled with regrets that she could never hang picures in the National Gallery. Through the war her dream has come true ...'. This exaggerated, though apparently harmless 'par', was responsible for the furore that ensued. In public museums it was an unwritten law that everything be done in the director's name and that no individual be mentioned so, when at the press conference I faced a battery of journalists – I had been detailed by Sir Kenneth to do so – I had to endure their probings as well as I could as they tried to find out who was on the committee. I tried to focus attention on the pictures and owners but my name had already slipped into the news so that my evasive answers, to those experienced men, only served as a confirmation of what they had suspected – there was no committee at all. On the 23rd February 1940 the *Daily Mail* pieced together the story as if it had been given to them verbatim; to my great discomposure huge headlines apeared, the main piece of news on the front page: ONE WOMAN TO OPEN NATIONAL GALLERY – *Browse's Academy*. My principal worry was that Sir Kenneth might have thought I had betrayed his trust, but knowing how crafty journalists could be, he accepted my version of the affair.

In those anxious days there was little good news, indeed scant news of anything but war, and so in consequence papers throughout the country printed the *Daily Mail* story and the exhibition became the lead item. The *Mail* went so far as to repeat their big headlines when the exhibition opened in the following month. This time it was: WOMAN HANGS 360 PICTURES IN HER 'ACADEMY' – *The Queen lends work to the show*; then the storm broke. The *Daily Mail*, obviously pleased with its coup, followed it up with the announcement: R.A.s ATTACK BROWSE'S ACADEMY. Francis Howard, well known in the art world, wrote an ambiguous letter to *The Times* which was swiftly endorsed with far more annoyance by two Royal Academicians, Julius Olsson, President of the Royal Institute of Oil Painters, and A. J. Munnings. Their attack was chiefly against Sir Kenneth for having asserted that he had not chosen the pictures, but whereas he was well able to defend himself, I felt I needed some help. It was time for me personally to bring out my 'big guns' so I asked D. S. McColl, the influential critic and writer, and Sir Hugh Walpole to reply on my behalf, a task which they relished and splendidly performed. Mr McColl's letter hit the nail on the head by confirming that the National Gallery had become a Mecca during the war years: its concerts, its canteen and, not least, its exhibitions all proved themselves a triumphant success. He wrote: 'As one of those included by the Hidden Hand ... my judgement will be suspected of bias, but for what it is worth it agrees with the thousands who are daily refreshing their eyes at Trafalgar Square, as they have already refreshed their ears with music and other organs at one of the best sandwich-bars in London.'

In the same issue *The Times* published two more acrimonious letters from painters: one from J. B. Manson, former director of the Tate, and the other from Nevinson, who was complaining that his initials in the catalogue were the wrong way round! For feelings to run high among excluded artists is far from unusual when contemporary surveys are shown, and although at the start I had felt disconcerted, it was good publicity and sometimes comic. Among many others I received letters from a couple of eccentrics, one of whom threatened to take legal action against me for having ignored Cayley Robinson; the second sent a cutting from the *Daily Sketch* in which was printed a photograph of me examining Stanley Spencer's *Last Supper*, across which he had scrawled 'Sergeant Browse reviewing the 12 Apostles'! This sardonic caption contained a spark of truth for, as each day I entered those tall, black, closed doors reserved for National Gallery personnel, I had a sneaky sensation of being a 'somebody', reminiscent of the satisfaction I felt when, as a prefect, I could pass through the central doors of my school. But apart from all else it was thrilling to work in a place so bustling with life. Crowds from the services who were on leave, civilians tired and wan after long nights of the Blitz: they all flocked into the building which, I am sure, the majority had never visited before. Inside they found values true and enduring, a reaffirming assurance when it was most needed.

My office was situated in the publications corridor where I quickly made friends with the staff of young women who must have been rather surprised at my arrival. My special pal was the irrepressible Olive Cooke, the head of the department, who talked with the kind of breathless excitement with which children report a much enjoyed treat. Well versed in and enthusiastic about most of the arts, she would celebrate the birthday of a favourite Master by extracting from the library a photograph of one of his works which, together with flowers, she turned into a shrine and devoutly placed on her desk. As three of us were able to play the recorder – I very badly – we used to hold our own lunchtime concerts, which hardly rivalled those in progress overhead; we also set days when we decided to converse only in German or French. Although these were hilarious they were too great an effort and with relief we slipped back into English. But our funniest effort was our transformation of one of the photography dark-rooms. We had all bought some cloth, free of the ration, which Olive had triumphantly found; but it was so dreary in colour that before using it we tried to dye it. The sinks of the dark-room became a series of vats which were filled with an alarming purple liquid but the result was abysmal, the colour worse than before, and only Olive had the temerity to make up her material. All this we did with the utmost secrecy like schoolgirls up to a prank, and I never inquired whether the dye left any telltale traces.

On account of the camaraderie that existed between us it came as a shock when later I learned that one of our number, a twinset and pearls, golf-playing type, suspected I must have had lesbian tendencies. This was on the grounds that I had befriended a young woman whom I scarcely knew and did not particularly like. She came to assist me with a day's typing but as she appeared to be both homeless and ill, I gave her a bed for a couple of nights and succoured her as well as I could; one of those strangers who drift into one's life and after a moment's compassionate help, are never seen or heard of again. A similar one was a fellow ambulance driver, desperate when she found herself pregnant: she dared not confess her state to her parents so the only solution was a secret abortion for which she was quite unable to pay. I lent her the only money I had, laboriously saved up in a Post Office account, which she promised to refund as soon as she could. But despite professed gratitude and my repeated requests, all the letters I wrote were returned as 'unknown', for by this time I had left the station. The faithless experience taught me permanently, if expensively, a lesson. I was determined never to lend money again but if I could afford it and thought the cause worthy, then I would give it as a present.

During the run of *British Painting since Whistler* over 40,000 people came to see it; Queen Elizabeth was one of our most regular visitors for not only did she attend the original show but also all those that followed. Each time she came Sir Kenneth took a back seat, thoughtfully allowing me to con-duct Her Majesty; I was thrilled by the opportunity to be her guide and during these visits I almost forgot her royal rank: she was so natural and interested in everything that I might well have been guiding any other congenial visitor.

As the show was the chief topic of the day many other notables were among its visitors. I was particularly amused by Dame Edith Sitwell whom

I could not resist following through her tour. I watched fascinated as she passed at full sail through one complete gallery after another. She did not raise her eyes to the right or the left so that I wondered how she knew when to stop; but stop she did in the very room in which her well-known portrait by Wyndham Lewis was hanging. In front of it she paused for a while intently regarding herself then, mission accomplished, she walked out of the building with eyes similarly averted as when she had entered. So much for her proverbial interest in the arts!

A second version of our exhibition was planned for the autumn and I got as far as correcting the new galley proofs; but unfortunately the show never took place. The heavy raids on London had begun in full earnest; it was no longer safe to use the vulnerable main rooms, so I was allotted the smaller galleries on the lower floor, which meant that in future we would be restricted in scope. A collection of John drawings was already assembled, and though it was destined for a future date, the show could be brought forward to replace the one that we originally planned. 115 drawings, all of high quality, were stacked in one room awaiting the day of their hanging. One late afternoon I got a hunch, and providential it turned out to be. Should a bomb chance to fall on that room the cream of John's drawings would vanish. I summoned the head custodian and told him my fears, and though his assistants were just about to leave, they agreed to remain and remove everything to the comparative safety of the steel-lined corridor which was the National Gallery's shelter.

That very night the room was destroyed; the bomb that had fallen would have shattered the drawings: we had had an amazing escape. The owners never knew of their very near loss but for me the incident had an unexpected result. In view of the danger so narrowly averted, I thought it only sensible that a record be made for fear of a less lucky repetition, and so I had all the drawings photographed on the spot. When I saw the lovely prints set out before me, it seemed a pity not to assemble them in a permanent form. Happily Augustus John himself was keen on the project. Richard de la Mare was approached and despite the problem of shortage of paper, Fabers agreed to publish a book – the first of my small series of monographs. I wrote an awful, short, introductory essay which Augustus very rightly refused, a refusal for which I have ever since been grateful. He thanked me for the tributes that I had paid him but gently proposed that his friend, T. W. Earp, should do a small piece in its stead; gentleness was hardly one of Augustus's traits but as he had always treated me with kindly consideration, he let me down lightly this time as well. One of his excuses was that we did not want any personal details revealed in the text. I did not know many in any case and although he once asked me how many children he had and I was able to give an approximate answer, including his legitimate and illegitimate offspring, I had no more than a sketchy idea about his unorthodox marital life. He did not tell me he had it in mind to write himself about his life, which he did in *Chiaroscuro – Fragments of Autobiography*, published in 1952,* followed twelve years later by *Finishing Touches*.†

Exhibitions and monographs: Sickert and others

My slender volume was very successful and quickly went into a second edition, though one has to remember that during those years of great deprivation, nearly every new project was warmly acclaimed and a book on the arts was one of the rarest events.

The exhibition itself was so widely appreciated that various museums wanted to show it before its dispersal back to the owners. Some of the cities were considered too risky, but not Temple Newsam, the delightful country adjunct to the Leeds Art Gallery of which Philip Hendy was director. A dreamy-looking man with the air of a poet, his languid air belied the responsibility he was to assume when he became the director of the National Gallery in succession to Sir Kenneth Clark. After he had shown the Augustus John drawings, he took over other National Gallery exhibitions and so I was often in Leeds.

In the autumn of 1941 we launched a Sickert exhibition. Encouraged by the success of the Augustus John book and with the pictures again assembled, I thought it would be a splendid opportunity to produce another, this time on my favourite British artist. Being for the great part so low in tone, his paintings are difficult to reproduce; however, excellent photographers were close at hand and Fabers used printers of extremely high quality. On the practical level the project was simple but finding the pictures meant a great deal of spade-work. No one had yet produced a book on his art so that there was little to help me. Dr Emmons, Sickert's one-time pupil and friend, had recently published *The Life and Opinions of Walter Sickert*‡ but, as the title implies, it was no study of his work and besides it contained some misleading inaccuracies, for which Sickert's faltering memory must have been responsible. Although Emmons's book was in some respects useful, it lacked the information I sought. From the sales point of view, Fabers thought it would be wise to connect the name of some well-known author with that of the painter, and the obvious choice was R. H. Wilenski, for years their 'house-writer' on art; so while I was the

* Augustus John, *Chiaroscuro: Fragments of an Autobiography*, Jonathan Cape, 1952.
† Augustus John, *Finishing Touches*, Jonathan Cape, 1964.
‡ Richard Emmons, *The Life and Opinions of Walter Sickert*, Faber & Faber, 1942.

Augustus John, *Fishergirl of Equihen*. Fogg Museum of Art, Harvard University:
Paul J. Sachs Collection

editor and wrote on his life, Wilenski appraised Sickert's pictures. I learned a great deal from this experienced man and was grateful to him for his frankness; he did not spare his criticisms of the piece I had written but I realized their justice and respected him accordingly. Through them I gained a more professional approach.

I felt very sad that Sickert had died without ever seeing the book. I am not sure, as he was so ill at the time, that he even knew of the project, or that the National Gallery was to exhibit his work. Everything had been arranged with Thérèse Lessore, Sickert being incapable of it. During his long life he had missed due acclaim, and never enjoyed the sometimes phenomenal success that prominent artists are now apt to receive; an exhibition in one of the greatest museums – albeit as a wartime expedient – would have meant a great deal to him had it crowned his career in his lifetime.

Through the Sickert exhibition I was introduced to a less pleasant side of Sir Kenneth's complex character. Busy as he was, we saw him but seldom and I was anxiously waiting to obtain his agreement to the selection of pictures and the opening date – he was rather more careful than he had been at the start, owing, I suspect, to the critical letters. Willie Gibson and I telephoned him repeatedly but he was so involved with his particular problems – his work with the film industry was not going well – that we could never get a decision. Time was by now running desperately short, and so, with the approval of the Keeper, invitations were posted and the paintings all hung. The evening before the private view, Sir Kenneth arrived quite unexpectedly, accompanied by a few of his trustees who, I later discovered, formed the supposed committee. To my surprise, and in my presence, Sir Kenneth announced: '... if you, gentlemen, are not satisfied with the show then it shall be immediately cancelled.' The trustees were placed in an awkward position; they realized they were being asked to take sides and that there was something amiss. Apart from the fact that they knew me quite well, they could see for themselves that the exhibition was excellent. In order to offer some kind of suggestion which might perhaps justify their presence, one painting, and one painting alone, was moved to another part of the room even though it was not an improvement. Sir Kenneth then pronounced that they were content, while I stood by burning with indignation at such a petty show of injustice. But this was by no means the end of the matter, for next morning, when I picked up the telephone, I found myself on a crossed line. I was just in time to hear Sir Kenneth say 'she is quite intolerable'. Having no doubt he was referring to me I could not prevent myself from chiming in to tell him that I had heard his remark. I believed it quite possible that I had become a little too big for my boots on account of the small but fleeting fame the wealth of publicity had brought me, but on this occasion I knew I was innocent and did not hesitate to tell Sir Kenneth how very unfair I thought he had been. From then on our relationship was definitely chilly and he made one more effort to reduce me to scale.

The exhibition that followed was by William Nicholson and Jack Yeats, who at first glance may seem the most unlikely of partners, but each of whom, in their beginnings, was in 'publicity' – Nicholson through his posters and Yeats his broadsheets. Both of them worked with the strictest economy, thrusting out their message by means of bold black and white. Their individual temperaments and historical backgrounds being so far apart, their mature artistic expression loosened their early tenuous affinity and led them away from each other. We thought that the way in which each had diverged would make an interesting comparison.

As William Nicholson was a close friend of the Churchills, Sir Kenneth had organized a lunch in the gallery, prior to the opening, at which Lady Churchill was to be guest of honour. Neither Marguerite Steen, the writer with whom William Nicholson lived nor I had been invited and William was so incensed at this insult that he vowed he would not go himself. Ten minutes before the lunch was due to begin, he could nowhere be found; he was actually hiding in one of the galleries trying to improve upon one of his paintings. It was a conversation piece of the Churchills at tea, which several years previously he had painted at Chartwell. No amount of reworking could have made it better in essence, for it was too large and awkwardly composed, like others of this *genre* he had attempted. But William had found an excellent excuse and it was evident that no persuasion would induce him to budge. Sir Kenneth had tried but without effect so, in desperation, he had to swallow his pride and turn to me for help. I suggested to William that his absence would constitute an unforgivable insult to 'Clemmie' and that Marguerite and I were quite indifferent and would go for a 'binge' on our own. William very grudgingly succumbed to my argument and and to everyone's relief he went to the lunch. After the private view was over, a very different Sir Kenneth came and joined me on a seat in the gallery. Since Jack Yeats had not been able to travel to London, in his most winning manner Sir Kenneth proposed that we send him a joint telegram to tell him of its success, the wording of which he proceeded to discuss. I accepted the gesture for what it was worth, while Marguerite, who had no high opinion of Sir Kenneth, the man, dismissed the affair as being no more than might have been expected of him. I believe that their dislike was mutual.

Marguerite and I had formed a warm friendship which, on her side, had started unpropitiously. I had heard vaguely of William's liaison, which was confirmed on my visit to Bruton Street where I had gone to discuss his impending exhibition. My eye caught the name-plate on the door in the street which frankly described the *ménage* upstairs – 'William Nicholson and Marguerite Steen'. I was intrigued by its boldness and honesty, for an open announcement that they were 'living in sin' was simply not done in those non-permissive days. This was evidently an unusual and free-thinking couple.

William and I had been in deep conversation about the selection of paintings for his exhibition when a strikingly handsome middle-aged woman entered the room with enormous aplomb. Elegantly wrapped in a flowing black cape which she knew just how to wear, she had a presence that commanded attention. After a brief introduction she went out of the room leaving us to proceed with our talk, and it was not until later, after William had died, that she confessed her misgivings.

She and William had been fellow guests in Malaga in the spring of 1935, and though neither of them was any longer young, they had fallen in love at first sight. William had had a sequence of mistresses since parting from his second wife, Edith, but as he never had the heart to make a clean break, they vaguely remained in the picture. Marguerite was forthright, she would not tolerate this, and so adamantly she issued an ultimatum: for once and for all he was to make a firm choice, either they went or she would. William plucked up his courage and they were sent packing but Marguerite now felt herself threatened again. William had sometimes mentioned my name, but this was a professional matter so she paid little heed. When, however, she saw us together she got a big shock and told me the reason: 'When I saw another beautiful young woman having an intimate talk with my William, I thought despairingly "she is absolutely his type, here we go all over again". I metaphorically rolled up my sleeves preparing myself for another fight and I can't tell you my relief when I found I was wrong.' I was surprised and flattered at Marguerite's unsuspected interpretation, for I scarcely knew William at this early date.

Marguerite was so devoted to William that I felt that when he died, she died also. Her courage did not permit her to abandon her writing but the spark that had flourished, and perhaps reached its intensity, during their years together, was from then on extinguished. She never repeated the former success as a novelist that had brought her some fame, and as time passed she clung closely to me as one of the last links with her William.

The first French picture I ever bought for myself was during my days at Leger's: Dufy's *Regatta at Cowes*. It was very cheap and I liked its gaiety and 'Frenchness'. On the outbreak of war I, like others, was forced to sell some of my few possessions, so I offered the watercolour to Reid & Lefevre and was grateful for their thirty-five pounds. During my youth, with its seeming security, I was nevertheless niggled by another of my fears: I saw myself living alone and without any funds to support me. With the break-up of my marriage, the advent of war and an urgent desire not to seek help, this was the predicament with which I was faced and to which I responded out of character. Herbert Einstein, a private art dealer who, with his wife Angela, had also become personal friends, had been offered a small oil painting by Derain whose price was seventy pounds. He asked me whether I would buy a half-share and as the sale of the Dufy had yielded that sum I took my courage in both hands and was again bereft of my 'capital'. The Derain was finally sold at a profit and welcome though the money undoubtedly was, the transaction meant far more than that: it had broken the spell of my earlier qualms and although it took long for me to become financially stable, I never again fretted about money. Without underestimating its obvious necessity I had learned how to put it in its rightful place; this is just one of the reasons why I have grown to believe that we attract all our fears to ourselves, and that until they are faced and tackled with firmness, they will continue to plague us.

A little while after the Dufy affair, some time around 1941, I bought my most ambitious painting from an exhibition I had been asked to hang. The artists participating were only three: two emerging painters in their late thirties and a sculptor already making a name for himself. The show was to be presented at the Institute of Adult Education in the room where I had so often slept at lectures. During this exhibition of Piper, Sutherland and Moore, two diverse events stand out in my memory; I dropped a tiny Moore alabaster of the *Madonna and Child*, knocking off the Infant's head. Fortunately, Sir Michael Sadler, its owner, took it in good part and after it had been repaired only a fine telltale line was visible. Artistically the sculpture remained unimpaired, financially it mattered little, for its value was minimal and in any case it had not been bought for gain. The happier occurrence was that through this show I was able to buy arguably the finest of Sutherland's big paintings. Graham wanted to exhibit his important *Cliff Road*, so recently finished that it arrived with the paint still wet. As soon as I saw it, I fell in love with it and had the temerity to ask for its price, and as Graham and I were equally impecunious – he needing the sale and I longing for the picture – he said I could have it for fifty pounds, a sum I just managed to raise. But I was not the proud possessor for as long as I wished, for Graham's reputation was gaining momentum and I was continually being asked to lend *Cliff Road* to shows all over the country. I was borrowing so many pictures myself that I could hardly refuse, although lending presented a problem. The frame on the painting was solid and wide and a sheet of plate glass was fitted; being large it was so terribly heavy I could scarcely manage to lift it down, let alone to rehang it.

John McDonnell, the gifted buyer in Europe for Melbourne's Felton

Bequest, had often expressed his desire to acquire it, and so with great reluctance I sold it to him, and it hangs in the National Gallery of Victoria. My sense of loss can be understood for I only owned two other pictures, both by Sickert – a drawing called *Sally* and a tiny panel of beach huts at Dieppe. Moreover, I felt a sense of guilt towards Graham for having parted with his picture at five times its cost. But with the substantial sum of £250 I was able to buy something else that I coveted, and of a more manageable size.

On four subsequent occasions I made exchanges, each for a different reason. Lady Kendall Butler had loaned *Joachim and the Shepherds*, the most beautiful, I consider, of all Stanley Spencer's drawings, to the exhibition of *British Painting since Whistler*. While the show was still in progress she wrote to ask me if I could help her to sell it. The price she suggested was fifteen pounds and even in those days I thought it too low and, as I wanted to have it myself, I sent her a cheque plus another five pounds. This tiny affair pleased her so much that her son, R. A. Butler, came to the gallery especially to thank me for the 'generous gesture'. A year or so later the Chantrey Bequest begged me to sell them the drawing, which after much thought I consented to do; I had seen something else I could not afford and the Spencer sale helped me to buy it. I do not remember what I got in its stead but whenever I see the Spencer, again I feel sad that I parted with something so beautiful.

In the very early days of Roland, Browse & Delbanco, bronze casts of Henry Moore's little maquettes of *Family Groups* were being shown for the first time at the Berkeley Galleries in Davies Street. They were priced at a mere fifty pounds each, so I bought a cast to keep for myself, as did both my partners. Mine remained on my desk for some little while but finally I came to the conclusion that I was not really enjoying it, but was keeping it simply because it was a Moore. Despising myself for succumbing to snobbery, I sold the piece at a modest profit and bought a Rockingham writing set in its stead! I would still love to own one of Moore's large sculptures, having little or no feeling for the miniature in general, but apart from their size and the impossibility of placing one, their prices have grown far beyond me.

The last of my partings – I have already mentioned the Epstein drawing – was a painting by Innes, a jewel-like tiny panel, although bold in concept. At his best he is a painter of whom I am fond, but Hugo Pitman wanted to give it to his daughter, Jemima, and since I owed him a great debt of gratitude, and wished to have a larger example by Innes, I let him have it.

I think it is true of the majority of dealers that they will not consider selling their private possessions, however tempting the monetary gain; the *marchand* and owner are two different people and during my long career in the art world I have never found it difficult to separate them. On the rare occasions when an insensitive guest has tried to persuade me to part with a treasure, I have felt affronted, as I do not subscribe to the belief that 'everyone has his price'. I would not dream of asking any collector if he or she would be prepared to sell; this may appear to be lacking in enterprise but to me it is a question of good manners. I also dislike going into a home whose owners have died and the sale is *in situ*; it seems an intrusion into their private lives coldly to evaluate their personal possessions, those small, but often touching, everyday objects which still have the aura of their owners about them.

James Shand of the Shenval Press, which printed the National Gallery catalogues, invited me to meet Bill Williams at lunch during which Bill asked me to organize travelling exhibitions for CEMA. Sir William Emrys Williams, as he became, was the secretary general of CEMA – the Council for the Encouragement of Music and the Arts – the forerunner of the Arts Council of Great Britain. CEMA had arranged for a number of concerts to be held in industrial cities and towns, but they had not yet made any art exhibitions and Bill, quite rightly, thought that they should. Although some artists had found an outlet for their talents in the war artists' scheme, others were in dire straits so that everything possible had to be done to find them some work or otherwise encourage them to continue. I fully supported Bill Williams's plan, for apart from the lift it would give to the artists, it might be a stimulus for people in outlying areas deprived by the war of their normal recreations. No one came to London unless of necessity, since travelling was difficult and expensive, and the blitz was not exactly an attraction. So in an unpaid capacity I renewed my travels, hanging pictures in the most unlikely small towns and in the most makeshift of rooms.

One of the shows was to open at the National Museum of Wales in Cardiff and afterwards tour that country. I tried to make it essentially Welsh but other well-known painters were included. Knowing that an exhibit loaned by the Queen would be an added attraction, I once again wrote to Her Majesty and once again she consented. The exhibition was sent off well in advance but wishing to take extra care of the Queen's Matthew Smith, it was packed in a case all by itself and despatched just in time for the opening. I suddenly received an urgent call from Cardiff; my careful concern had backfired for when the Matthew Smith case was undone and the canvas examined, it was found to have damp patches on the reverse and the painting of fruit was smelling of fish. I rushed down to Cardiff to see what had happened and found the report had not been exaggerated: the canvas indeed was extremely wet and the odour it emitted could not be mistaken. The precious cargo had been unloaded and left on the platform and a porter, ignoring its 'fragile' label, had dumped a crate of fish on top

of it. The painting itself showed no sign of a stain but I immediately reported the mishap; the Queen simply thanked me for letting her know and
asked if the picture might deteriorate in the future. I replied that the pigment might possibly flake and that if this happened she should immediately
inform me when we could have it relined. I never again heard about the
affair and after the passage of so many years I think it safe to assume that
all is quite well.

This story reminds me of a little joke that William Nicholson played
while staying with the Churchills at Chartwell: throughout the night he had
worked on a *Still Life* in which was included a piece of fish that Clemmie
had given him from the larder. The following morning he was congratu-
lated on his truthful rendering of the subject; his hosts even said it was so
realistic that they imagined they could smell it. This was not surprising for
William was always good for a lark, and not giving a thought as to whether
it would remain edible, had hung the fish on the back of the painting.

These wartime journeys for CEMA were often attended by silly little
adventures; one particularly sticks in my mind because of the embarrassment it caused me. On returning from the West Country on one of those
night trains that stopped at every small town, I suddenly awoke to find we
had halted at what I assumed was a main station. I took it for granted that
it must be Paddington but as it was about five o'clock on a winter's morning and the black-out was really pitch black, I could not have deciphered
the name of the station even had the name-boards not been removed. I
hurriedly wakened the sole passenger in my compartment to warn him that
we had arrived back in London and we both pulled our knapsacks down
from the rack and scrambled out on to the platform. No sooner were we
clear of the train than it slowly pulled out of the station and to my horror
I realized we had got no further than Reading. Whatever my companion
might have thought about me, he was too disciplined to show any signs of
reproach, even though neither of us had any idea how long we had to wait
for another train. How idiotic I felt may well be imagined as we stood for
what seemed an interminable period alone on the dank and icy cold platform where it was too early, had there been a canteen, even to get a hot
comforting drink.

Apart from the exhibitions for CEMA another 'extra mural' job was
proposed. The Hon. Jasper Ridley, who was at the time chairman of the
trustees of the Tate Gallery and already a friend, had been asked to
organize a sale of pictures in aid of the Red Cross, which Christie's were to
auction free of commission. He agreed to do this on condition that I would
assist him, so once more I got down to my begging letters, this time in a
different cause. With the help of a committee and backed by the generosity
of a wide range of donors, we collected for sale over 300 pictures, almost

Thomas Gainsborough, *Portrait of the Artist's Brother*. Bode Museum, Berlin

Victor Hugo, *Jersey, 1855*. Private collection

Max Ernst, *Black Forest with Dove*. Private collection

Georges Michel, *The Black Cloud*. Private collection

Jules Pascin, *Seated Nude, Back View.* Southampton City Art Gallery

Joan Eardley, *Glasgow Slum Child*. Private collection

Odilon Redon, *Woman Riding Pegasus*. Henry Moore Trust

Roderic O'Conor, *La Ferme à Lezaven, Pont Aven*. National Gallery of Ireland, Dublin

Auguste Rodin, *Grande Danseuse, A.* Private collection

equally divided between old and contemporary. Christie's were functioning from Derby House – lent by the earl – as their 'great rooms' had suffered severely, and there, in October 1942, our two separate auctions were held. In the old master sale a large, genuine Murillo, the *Holy Family with Angels*, fetched 450 guineas, while a pair of typical, small oils by Guardi did not bring more than 700; a much exhibited G. F. Watts failed its reserve of a pathetic fourteen guineas and there was no bid at all for an Edward Lear, a good-sized watercolour of Albania. The modern sale that followed totalled £4,000 for 170 items; there was no reserve on them and they averaged a mere twenty-two guineas each. Among them were such well-known paintings by Sickert as *The Prevaricator*, a *Rue Aguado* and a portrait of Sir Winston smoking a cigar – now in the National Portrait Gallery – as well as canvases by Matthew Smith, William Nicholson, Innes, Conder and Nevinson; also two Steers, one of which was an early and therefore rare subject. It was a landscape by John that fetched the top price of 170 guineas. Any one of these paintings would now well exceed the total and some would sell for at least thirty times more; but we were able to hand to the Red Cross some £9,000 which, in the circumstances, was considered to be quite a moderate success.

The last show I organized at the National Gallery was in December 1942 – though I remained in my office until the end of the war – and was by far the most ambitious. The owners and public having responded so well to the exhibitions already presented, we thought we would try French art as a change from British as originally planned. There were not many French pictures in English private collections – the same may be said today – and even I shied away from asking the owners to expose their possessions of much greater value to the dangers in the centre of London. But everyone agreed that it would be a *coup* if such an exhibition were possible so I braced myself against expected refusals and sent out the selected petitions. Unfortunately, the Queen did not possess works by the Impressionists or the Post-Impressionists and I therefore had to find some other 'carrot'; my choice fell quite naturally on the museums whose directors all gave a heartening response. The Tate Gallery promised to lend a Cézanne; the National Gallery brought back from Wales a Manet and a Géricault, while the Courtauld Institute surpassed everyone else with a Van Gogh, a Degas and a Renoir. This was a splendid beginning; with such a fine nucleus of the big names the show augured well and indeed it more than fulfilled its promise; the thirty-three private owners lent all that was asked and the total reached eighty-one pictures. The complete exhibition, entitled *Nineteenth-Century French Painting*, was of such high quality that by any standards, even those of more propitious times, it was considered a 'knock-out' with the press reporting 'the most successful art exhibition ever held in

London ... drawing over 37,000 people in thirty days' – and this took place at the height of the war.

Only one painting suffered any damage at all – not caused by a bomb but through me: the window cleaner had come to do his job in my room and as the windows were a great height, he had placed his tall ladder upright on the floor which unfortunately was highly polished. I had only one painting in my room at the time whose details I was noting for the catalogue; it was a Matisse of a young woman seated against a clear *eau-de-nil* background. I had leaned it against the wall, opposite the windows, where it seemed to be perfectly safe, but no sooner had the cleaner reached the top rung than his ladder slid down with a crack to the floor, hurling the poor man some distance away. My heart took a leap but I have to confess it was not on account of his safety for, when I dared look towards the Matisse, my very worst fears were confirmed. The ladder had spanned the full width of the room; one of its feet had penetrated the canvas and a sharp cut was visible in the empty area in a spot most difficult to disguise. The one and only redeeming factor was that the cut was as clean as a knife's edge and subsequently none of the thin paint was missing. So after the restorer had repaired the damage, it could not be seen at all from the front and only the patch on the back of the canvas remained as a witness to the accident. The owners reacted with fine equanimity and were able to put a scar on one painting – however important – into perspective during this time of far more terrible happenings.

The same exhibition caused one other casualty and this time it was I who was injured. As I had never before possessed a bicycle and with transport being as scarce as it was, I thought it only sensible to get one quickly and teach myself how to ride. With a certain amount of trepidation, plus a great deal of foolhardiness, I rode daily from Notting Hill Gate, negotiating Marble Arch and Trafalgar Square rather through the courtesy of the drivers around me than through my own road-worthiness; in fact I was such an unsure beginner that I dared not relinquish my hold on the bars to signal the direction in which I hoped to go. In London I was lucky and had no mishap but ironically I met with my one and last accident while on a ride in the country.

I had an appointment to visit Audrey Pleydell-Bouverie from whom I hoped to borrow a lovely Degas. Her home was in Hertfordshire, not very far from where James (Hamish) Shand lived, so we planned to enjoy a day's cycling together and call on her at the same time. I put my bicycle on the train and met Hamish at the appropriate station, but by the time we arrived at our destination we were both rather tired and very thirsty for it was a particularly hot summer's day. Mrs Pleydell-Bouverie, known as eccentric, did not even offer us a cup of tea and she got another big black mark from me as her wonderful Degas of a *Repasseuse* hung totally hidden behind a huge and rather awful arrangement of flowers.

When the time came to leave I had been promised the Degas and we started on our way to Hamish's house where I was to spend the night; in the meantime there had been a small shower of rain, my bicycle skidded, and far too exhausted to try to correct it, I fell on the only hard curb we encountered during the whole of the day. The pain was so great I could not bear to be touched, and so an ambulance had to be summoned and I spent the night in the general ward of a hospital suffering from two broken ribs. After that episode I sold my machine and have never ridden another.

In 1943 my first book on Sickert was published by Fabers. Its text was but minimal and the notes on the pictures equally slight, but the black and white reproductions were excellently made on paper as good as could then be obtained. Moreover, it was the first volume to appear devoted to Sickert's actual work and, like the book on Augustus John drawings, it too was enthusiastically received and also ran into a second edition.

Hamish – whom I have mentioned as having introduced me to Fabers – had grown ever more interested in the pictorial arts and the lack of litera-ture on contemporary British painters fired him with the idea of a new project which he divulged to Fabers and me. The former had published a series on poetry small enough to be tempting in price, and Hamish sug-gested that they might be interested, in conjunction with his own Shenval Press, to embark upon a similar series but devoted to different aspects of the visual arts. They were to cost only half a crown each, which would make them available to students, and were to appear annually, five or six at a time. Fabers accepted the plan with myself as the editor, and the result was the Ariel Books on the Arts Series. They comprised fifty pages of black and white plates with an introduction to each artist by a specialist writer – and they were even hardbacked. Our first batch included J. D. Innes as painter, Barbara Hepworth as sculptor, Eric Ravilious as designer, Leslie Hurry for theatre and lastly the draughtsman, Constantin Guys, all but one of whom were as yet unrecorded in a book. The exception to our rule was the Frenchman, Guys; despite his nationality and the fact that a book on his life had been published, although long out of print, we thought it high time to bring him before a wider public in England. As general editor I proposed the artists, chose all the plates and found the appropriate person to write the short essays, a task that on the whole presented few problems. Only the Innes book involved me in an awkward situation which, however dis-comforting it was at the time, led to a friendship with another elderly man who, like Charles Marriott of *The Times*, was certainly old enough to have been my father.

It seemed quite clear that Augustus John was the best person to write about Innes since he and Derwent Lees, together with Innes, had in the early days of the century painted as a trio in Wales. The three produced some very personal landscapes which at times so markedly resembled each other that it is not always easy to tell them apart. I feel it was Innes who was the original, that he influenced John's way of seeing the country and not, as is said, the other way round. As Lees had died seventeen years after Innes, who was a mere twenty-seven, the only one left was Augustus. He said he would write a few hundred words but when he gave me his script I was dismayed and did not see how I could use it. However valid his comments might have been, they were expressed with such a near-brutal insensitivity that they would have been hurtful to Innes's family and I had no option but rejection – not for the same reason as he had rejected my text on him. Augustus had admired and been fond of Innes, but there was a quirk in his generous nature which occasionally induced him to make a cruel joke about his acquaintances or friends. This he did with a self-conscious chuckle as if he were trying, though sensing he had failed, to show that he was a wit. He took my refusal in very good part; it did not impair our relationship and whenever I needed I asked for his aid.

While I was still at Leger's it occurred to me that the penniless widow of T. Leman Hare, who had been the editor of *Apollo*, would be very much helped by a Civil List Pension. I scarcely knew what the pension entailed or how to set about getting it, but having been told that such a petition needed the endorsement of influential figures, the first I approached was Augustus. He backed me up without second thoughts and his signature was followed by the directors of the Tate, the National Gallery and others well known in the art world, and so with such a distinguished assembly of names my self-imposed mission was successful, although the payments awarded to Mrs Hare proved to be lamentably low.

There was also a moment when Patricia Preece, who married Stanley Spencer as his second wife, was in desperate straits; I instituted a fund for her immediate relief and again it was Augustus who was the most forth-coming. The only time I found him really tiresome was when we were preparing his book. I always went to see him in the early morning before he had started to drink; later in the day he was unable to concentrate and, besides, he was seldom alone. The vexed question between us was the selection of drawings as, understandably, he wished for the accent to fall upon his contemporary work, while I insisted, as far as I could, upon a larger proportion of the earlier. A compromise was reached but on account of the struggle I vowed I would never again attempt any book while the artist concerned was still living.

After the fiasco with Augustus's essay I had to think of an alternative author and my choice fell upon the notorious John Fothergill who had also been one of Innes's close friends. According to photographs and from reports, John Fothergill, when young, had been extraordinarily beautiful; he had known Robbie Ross and through him, Oscar Wilde, and with the former had opened the serious but short-lived Carfax Gallery. When first I saw him during my Cookham days before the war he was the proprietor of the famed inn, the Spread Eagle at Thame, a popular haunt of Oxford scholars as well as the minority who appreciated the food. His clientèle were attracted as much by the eccentricities of John Fothergill's dress and behaviour as by his unusual menus; they never knew if they would be received with studied rudeness or inherent charm, an uncertainty which appeared to act as a magnet for the Spread Eagle was always full to overflowing during summer weekends.

My aunt and uncle drove me over to lunch and I was eager, perhaps a little apprehensive, to meet such a character whose reputation had forcibly forestalled him. I was also curious to try his strange food and was not disappointed for on the menu were his famous black soup and blue potatoes, besides other delicacies from all over the world which at that time were novelties. Intrigued though I was by our original fare I was still more intrigued by the man: he knew he was the star and rejoiced in the role. A striking small figure with heavy-browed eyes that could either glare in scornful disgust or light up with a friendly twinkle, he sported a type of Puritan dress, severely black and with buckled shoes. A monocle hung from his neck like a jewel, relieving the sombre effect of the whole, and with this monocle he made plentiful play. His presence demanded correct behaviour and we saw what could happen in the case of a breach; one party of guests was requested to leave because their chauffeur committed the unforgivable sin of refusing his lunch, being accustomed to plainer food. Fothergill also turned away visitors whom he considered ill-mannered and vulgar.

This was the man to whom, some ten years later, I wrote about a fresh foreword for *Innes*. I received a reply which expressed his keen interest, including an invitation to visit him at Market Harborough and to spend the night at the Three Swans, the inn to which he had subsequently moved. As it was a wet, autumnal evening, I was wearing a raincoat and felt hat with a veil – veils then being in fashion – and I caught a train that got me there just as dinner was being served. I was received by a manservant who showed me my room and apologized that Mr Fothergill could not greet me himself as he was in the kitchen cooking the dinner, so would I go to his study as soon as it was over. I entered the dining-room somewhat tentatively but was immediately heartened by the sight of my table: it was thoughtfully prepared as for an honoured guest with a vase of fresh flowers, a bottle of wine and brightly polished silver on gleaming white linen; the service was also impeccable. After the meal I was shown to the sanctum and a few minutes later John Fothergill appeared. I do not know who was the more expectant. Upon my arrival my host, being curious, had asked his *maître*, 'What is she like?' The answer had been, 'A bit of an old frump' – the veiled hat and burberry had done the trick. Moreover, I had written on National Gallery paper and as my mission was concerned with a book on art, he was prepared to meet a blue-stocking. A look of surprised pleasure came over his face as he glanced to where I was sitting, while I was relieved by his friendly expression and the warmth of his greeting.

When he had written his essay on Innes, I spent many weekends at the Three Swans with John, his wife Kate, and always a number of his son's friends. I worked in the kitchen helping with the meals and to this day I use some of John's recipes as well as his many labour-saving devices – one of the most useful wrinkles being the easiest way to peel an onion – starting by cutting it diagonally across. John very rarely came to London but when he did visit the National Gallery to see me he was treated as 'special' by the young women in the Publications Department, for he often sent 'goodies' outside the ration which he was allowed because he was an *hôtelier*; his cakes and biscuits were eagerly devoured by all of us for elevenses. From the time that I met him I was never short of butter nor of that precious commodity, a lemon, and he spoiled me in various other ways. I suppose I represented a swan-song in his life because Kate was an invalid confined to her chair and therefore unable to share in his pleasures; neither was she interested in art.

After the first batch had been publicized, the Ariel series came to an end; costs had risen to such an extent that it was impossible to keep to the price and we were reluctant to increase it. This was a pity for the books were good value and not unimportant artistically. Moreover, I had started a further series and the artists concerned were disappointed that it did not materialize.

The Hugh Walpole estate

The death of Sir Hugh Walpole in 1941 had led to another very interesting assignment. Throughout the years the eminent novelist had been an avid collector of pictures: he was one of those men who deeply loved art in his own way, never allowed himself to be distracted by fashion, but followed his nose, buying here and there whatever happened to delight him. Among similar collectors whose names spring to mind were Sir Edward Marsh, Sir Michael Sadler and Sir Cyril Kendall Butler; 'Eddie' Marsh was one of the most obsessed and could not resist any painting or drawing that his slender means allowed him to buy. It did not deter him that he already owned far more pictures than he could ever hang, so that his apartment looked like a dealer's stock-room with piles of works stacked against all walls. I would say that Marsh, Sadler and Butler had a finer feeling for quality, but none was more thrilled by every new purchase than Hugh Walpole, whose taste was perhaps too eclectic. It ranged from old masters – most of them dubious, for he had been given some disgraceful advice – through the Impressionists and Post-Impressionists up to contemporary artists. Some of the names were completely unknown and I thought probably would never be otherwise.

The two executors of Sir Hugh's estate were Rupert Hart-Davis and Alan Bott of the Book Society. Both were appointed as literary men and neither being qualified to handle the pictures, they asked Sir Kenneth whom he would suggest to do this for them. It was kind of Sir Kenneth to refer them to me. Rupert Hart-Davis was serving with his battalion abroad and not available for our discussions, so that all my dealings were with Alan Bott. Upon my agreeing to undertake the dispersal of this large, haphazard collection, I was sent a draft contract offering me 'an over-riding commission of one per cent on the net total which the Walpole estate received … with the minimum fee of £100 plus reasonable expenses'. I appreciated the fact that the executors' duty was to keep overheads as low as possible, but the fee was really far too small for the work that would be entailed. There was said to be a total of 900 pictures but the figure proved to be understated. Mr Bott yielded to my ultimatum and so I went to Brackenburn, Sir Hugh's country home near Keswick where the collection was stored, to spend a weekend prior to making my report. Sir Hugh's secretary and devoted friend, Mr C., was in charge of the otherwise deserted house, over which hung a heavy pall of melancholy. For the two days I was there I worked without a break, carefully studying every single item until my eyes could scarcely distinguish which was a drawing and which a print. Mr C. extended whatever hospitality such a shell of a *ménage* could offer but at meals I was regaled with various lewd anecdotes which hardly relieved my depression.

The dispersal of an entire private collection always excites the art world. I knew that – unlike today – it would be more advantageous to effect such a sale through a series of exhibitions, and this was the course that I followed. Not a single item was to be sold in advance, a precaution which proved to be wise for, as expected, there were would-be acquisitors hoping to creep in through the back door and steal a march upon their rivals. Amusing ploys and claims of friendship were tried by collectors and dealers alike, and I must say I took a mischievous delight in thwarting these art predators.

It was not thought to be safe to bring the collection to London until
fourteen months after my Cumberland visit, as Alan Bott put it, 'after the
flying-bomb-cum-V2-rocket phase had passed'. Sir Kenneth had promised
that I could have storage in one of the National Gallery rooms, but their
own works were returning by the time we were ready and so I had to seek
other accommodation. Sir John Rothenstein offered a room at the Tate,
and there I spent night after night identifying, measuring and recording
the provenance of 945 items, excluding portfolios filled with drawings and
prints. Single-handed it was very slow work, as anyone who has made
a detailed catalogue will know. I thought I deserved my reward but it
was only a fleeting monetary fee and here I was surrounded by works of
art, some of them of enduring value. I was particularly entranced by a
Modigliani drawing – a pale tender watercolour of a head of a woman –
which in ordinary circumstances I could not have bought, so I resolved to
spend my commission on that. The drawing would also be a memento to
Sir Hugh for whom I had formed a retrospective affection, and as the value
put upon it was already known, I could not be accused of taking advantage
of the estate.

Agnew's were keen to hold the Walpole exhibitions but for various
reasons the Leicester Galleries were preferred, and in the early summer of
1945 three separate shows took place there. Buyers were so keen to secure
their first choice that they waited in queues for the doors to open: this was
a sight I had never seen and it augured well for the result. J. B. Priestley,
another art lover and the staunchest of friends, wrote in the catalogue such
a succinct introduction that I cannot resist quoting from it:

Hugh Walpole liked excitement and – apart from his work – he had three
unfailing sources of it: the first was in making new friends (and he had a gift
of friendship); the second was in discovering new books and writers; and the
third, which concerns us here, was in acquiring works of art. Nearly every
time one met him, flushed and triumphant, he had some new picture or
drawing to display. As this show and its successors will amply prove, his taste
was catholic, and it ranged easily from Constable to Klee. He loved the
Impressionists (notice the Renoirs); he was rich in Sickerts and Johns; and, as
the beautiful Claude Rogers examples testify, he bought wisely from such
contemporary schools as the Euston Road Group. He was, to my mind, the
best kind of collector, if only because he pleased himself and did not follow
fashion. Here as elsewhere he was a romantic, seeing each favourite picture
or drawing as an intensely personal communication. He did not merely buy
and own pictures, he lived intimately with them. And let us hope, in this grim
time, that a lot of other people, visiting this show, may he able to recapture
some of this happy excitement.

It has not been surprising, after this distance of time, to find from my files that the prices were even more laughable than I had supposed. Oliver Brown, one of the Leicester Galleries' two partners, had originally suggested that they should be even lower but finally gave in to the higher values which, because of the excitement, I felt were warranted. The top price of all was 1,800 guineas for *Garçons nus dans les Rochers à Guernsey*, a charming medium-sized oil by Renoir; two canvases by Braque, each a *Still Life*, fetched 550 and 150 guineas respectively (the latter being quite small); four watercolours by Klee each brought between seventy and ninety guineas, while a *Self Portrait* by Picasso reached the enormous sum of 450 guineas. By the time every work had been sold the Walpole Estate received just under £27,000. It is no wonder that I now find it difficult to think of a picture in terms of millions.

Few people today can know at first hand the significant role that the Leicester Galleries played during the period between the world wars, and I would like to digress to pay a small tribute to Oliver Brown and Cecil Phillips. They were the first London dealers to stage exhibitions by the great French masters of the nineteenth and twentieth centuries; they also introduced and continued to support many young painters – now contemporary old masters – besides taking chances on a handful of sculptors such as Moore, Epstein and Hepworth.

The best kind of dealers, in love with their *métier*, they were neither mad about money nor about power; they gave the wisest advice to the young who were interested and, because they were content with reasonable profits, they enabled the latter to start small collections. The gradual demise of this once notable gallery was one of the saddest events in London's art scene.

Linden Gardens

By the time I went to live there with Kate, Linden Gardens had come down in the world, yet it remained one of those unexpected byways that make London so endearing. As private property it boasted tall cast-iron gates to keep it aloof from the busy main street; there was also a commissionaire who guarded its privacy and was responsible for its tidiness. The whole had an air of faded Edwardian grandeur as did many houses at Notting Hill Gate. Like the park railings, the gates were later removed and melted down for munitions, while the commissionaire, like his job, also disappeared.

Kate had a flat in a country-like house, one of a small group right down in the corner; each was set in its own spacious garden, in one of which grew a rare mulberry tree. No. 42 had originally been bought by a family who had come to this country as refugees from Alsace. In order to accommodate further relations, it had been extended into the garden until it became a large rambling building in a winningly higgledy-piggledy fashion. In the course of time, as the family contracted, it was divided and leased out as flats, and whether by accident or design, the lessees were always connected with art, either 'fine' or 'applied'. It is said that Sir Henry Irving lived there for a while and built a miniature theatre on its premises. When I first came to know it, the tenants included Kate, who was teaching voice production at RADA, and Audrey de Vos, one of the most eminent ballet teachers in London, whose best-known pupil was Beryl Grey. To her studio dancers from various countries repaired whenever their engagements brought them to London; they came to polish their roles or simply to keep in practice. Two commercial artists occupied other flats, one being shared by Bryan Rawlinson, actor/producer and playwright. With my involvement in art, I added one more to the list.

But none was more active than Louie Boutroy, the granddaughter of the original owners, who inherited the house on the death of her aged mother. An uncle who had lived with the family had started to collect photographs of events that particularly interested him, and Louie and her sister Alice had become involved in his hobby, which they gradually turned into a profession. They called their reference library of photographs after the family name of Richgitz. By the time Alice died, during the war, the material had accumulated to such a degree that it was too unwieldy for Louie to manage, even with the help of the young George Anderson, who had come as an evacuee from Wales. Louie was reluctantly persuaded to sell the library to *Picture Post*, and accompanied it for a while as supervisor, but the role did not suit her inherent independence and she quickly regretted the sale. As soon as another established collection (the Mansell) came on the market she decided to buy it and start again. The Mansell Collection which remained intact for some years after Louie Boutroy's death has now been sold to Times-Life and Katz Pictures Ltd. Today it comprises thousands of prints, photographs and slides on every subject up to the 1930s and, like the original Richgitz Library, is invaluable to writers, publishers, television researchers and editors – a fascinating example of a mere hobby developing into an asset of near-national importance.

Because No. 42 continued its tradition of having its occupants even loosely allied, it formed a little oasis and I think we all felt that it had a special aura about it and that we were lucky to live there.

Kate's studio flat was on a top floor and the living room had an expanse of top-light which though fine for a painter in time of peace, was highly dangerous in a war. During those fifty-seven nights of continuous bombardment, we tried to reach home before it was dark so as not to be caught in the street, but as the flat offered little protection we started taking shelter in the Underground. After a couple of nights, both Kate and I felt we would rather risk being killed in the comfort of our beds than dossing down on a platform where hordes gathered nightly. In his *Shelter* drawings Henry Moore has imbued these sleepers with an air of nobility which I must say was not as I saw them. Their spirit of acceptance did have a grandeur, but the actual sight of them rolled in their rugs and heaped on the ground like so many sacks, their mouths dropped open in a chorus of snoring, I found repulsively sordid: a sad state of indignity to which man was reduced by the instinct for self-preservation. It is easy to talk glibly of the 'comfort of our beds' but those nights were so frightening that only dozing was possible between the precious time when the 'all-clear' sounded and the next wail of 'enemy aircraft approaching'. I made a resolution that when all was over and I could be certain of a night's uninterrupted sleep, I would never again grumble about anything, but like most other vows this one has not been kept.

Degas Dancers

Towards the end of 1943 I was twice more connected with Faber & Faber; they had commissioned R. H. Wilenski to write a new *Dictionary of Art* and asked me to be his assistant at a fee of three shillings an hour. I reckoned I could help him in my spare time but the project was early abandoned, for Wilenski fell ill; moreover his increasing age had slowed him considerably. The second idea was suggested by me and as it was something very near to my heart, I was delighted to see how eagerly Richard de la Mare responded. I wanted to do a book on Degas's ballet dancers. With my ever-growing passion for this supreme artist, reinforced by the experience of my first profession, it seemed to me an obvious way to combine two of the arts about which I knew something. And how very enjoyable such a task would be. Many fine books had been published on Degas but none had focused its entire attention upon any one of his various themes; little did I think that mine would become the acknowledged definitive work on the subject.

I was fully aware of the difficulties I would encounter because of the war. I had it in mind to trace the history of the Opéra, but this could only be accomplished in Paris and I had no idea when I could get there. Photographic material was also a problem because it was not obtainable from Europe; but perhaps beyond all was the question of copyright that had to be negotiated through SPADEM, the notoriously difficult copyright agency who collected all fees on behalf of the heirs and who were also situated in

Paris. I did not, however, worry too much; the important thing was to start right away. Somehow the obstacles would be surmounted and hopefully the war would not last that long.

Again London dealers gave the fullest support and American museums, so rich in material, were, as always, unfailingly helpful although correspondence was inevitably slow. Fabers, knowing that I was unable to make any arrangements regarding the copyright, accepted the responsibility themselves. I fear this involved them in no little trouble before the matter was finally settled, which was not until communications could be opened again.

The book was to contain 120 black and white reproductions, with just enough in colour to indicate the range while keeping the cost at a moderate figure. I was also allowed several *vignettes* for which I have a great liking. These little sketches being so intimate bring one very close to the master and give a clearer insight into his private thoughts than many a completed picture. As the book gained momentum with more and more material coming to hand, Fabers were marvellous and each time agreed to an extension, so that by the time we went to press, *Degas Dancers* had become nearly twice the size originally envisaged. No author could have wished for a more harmonious arrangement with a publisher and I look back on our collaboration with gratitude and pleasure.

I had at first thought it was my bad luck that M. Lemoisne's great *Degas: Catalogue Raisonné* was being printed while I was working and was therefore not available for me to consult and so reduce much of my spade-work. But I realized in time that I must have been influenced by his extensive knowledge and might perhaps have repeated the few errors he made. As it was, I did my research independently and have disagreed with his dating on several occasions.

Quite unexpectedly, I had only one year in which to work at leisure. The advent of Roland, Browse & Delbanco interrupted the flow so that most of my time and my thoughts were filled with this exciting venture, which I shall shortly arrive at. But as soon as possible after the end of the war in Europe, I rushed over to Paris where, among other museums and libraries, I spent much time in the Musée de l'Opéra, whose records I found in such a confused state that I was able to identify some material they did not even know they possessed. I also had the unique experience of going all over Garnier's huge Opera House, a complete world of its own in the heart of Paris. My mission was to find out whether Degas had painted any of his various *Classes de Danse* series in that particular building, which might be recognizable from architectural similarities. Only one picture could be placed there with certainty, the rest of the *Classe* paintings having been set – some retrospectively – against the background of la Salle de la rue Le Peletier.

Before the advent of electricity, fire was the theatre's greatest enemy. The Opéra, which performed opera and ballet, had already known many different homes when in 1763, while in the Palais Royal, this theatre was burned down. Eighteen years later it was established in the second Salle du Palais Royal when that building too was destroyed in the same way. The fire, which took place on a June night, was the subject of Hubert Robert's painting now in the Musée de l'Opéra. For the next forty years and for different reasons the Opéra was moved from one place to another until 1821 saw the inauguration of the Salle de la rue Le Peletier, the theatre which was to witness the rise and fall of the Romantic ballet, the revolution in stage mechanism and the replacement of candles and Argand lamps by gas lighting. This theatre with its famed *foyer*, built in the gardens of the former Hôtel de Choiseul, was meant only as a temporary home for the Opéra but actually served the purpose for over half a century, until it too was burned to the ground. The Salle Ventadour served briefly as a substitute until Garnier's Nouvel Opéra was completed and opened its doors on 5th January 1875 to an important and brilliant audience.

In the Cabinet des Estampes I had enthusiastic help from Mlle Nicole Villa – a professional encounter which led to a friendship that has endured until today. I was also lucky enough to trace and to meet a very old lady who had posed for Degas as a child. This one living link with the great man brought him into focus as a human being, whereas before he had been a fabled, distant figure. Suzanne Mante, with her mother and sister, appears in two pastels done in the 1880s, yet despite the passage of more than sixty years, Suzanne remembered Degas quite well. He was, she told me, a kindly old man who wore blue spectacles – this to protect his ever-failing eyesight – and who used to stand at the foot of one of the staircases in the Opéra as the *rats* were running up. He would ask them to pause while he made some quick sketches, and in the book I reproduced a few of these as well as two finished pastels. I was less fortunate with a second dancer – as far as I could discover there were only two alive – for her vanity would not allow her to admit to her age and she refused my requests for an appointment.

On account of the various delays I have mentioned, *Degas Dancers* was not published until 1949. But soon after its appearance it led unexpectedly to my re-entry into the ballet scene, this time as a critic and not an exponent.

Part Four

Settling Down
After the War

Forming a partnership

The last two wartime shows at the National Gallery were organized by the Tate. Its director, Sir John Rothenstein, had returned from the States to find that the acclaimed exhibitions, and in his own territory, were being held at Trafalgar Square. He probably felt that it was high time for the Tate to assert itself as the custodian and promoter of contemporary art. Without knowing anything about the politics that went on between the various museums, I sensed that all was not well, that there was discord behind the scenes. This may have explained Sir Kenneth's last-minute intervention in the Sickert exhibition.

The war in Europe over, it was time to consider my future in the new post-war art world which was beginning to emerge. In it, Sir Kenneth Clark was an immensely influential figure, and I found he was disposed to find a place for me in the new structure. I was enormously grateful to Sir Kenneth for having given me the privilege of working at the National Gallery and allowing me to retain my office until the end of the war; also for having recommended me to the Walpole executors. Now he suggested that I might take the position of art director to the newly formed Arts Council. Philip James was then its acting director, 'acting' because he was really a book-man with a less specialized knowledge of pictures, and it was intended to elect somebody permanent with a wider experience of visual art. With Sir Kenneth Clark's name behind me I felt quite sure that I would have been offered the post, but I let the matter drop and Sir Kenneth rightly interpreted my silence as the refusal which I should certainly have conveyed to him directly.

As it turned out Philip James grew into his job and successfully continued his directorship for many years, and although I did not know what the future might hold, I never for one instant regretted my decision. It was essential that I should earn my own living and the Arts Council position would have made me secure; apart from the salary and a pension, it would also have carried a certain *réclame*. But I knew in my bones this was not what I wanted, that I could never work with a committee; I am too impatient to tolerate long pros and cons; or perhaps too certain of my personal judgement. I am always willing to work from behind and my tendencies make me a faithful Taurean; it is said that one born under this sign is equally happy at the front or the rear but never in the middle.

Sir Kenneth interested himself one more time in my future, as I learned many years later in a letter from 'Mr Harold' Leger: 'I feel it would be of interest to you to know that Sir Kenneth Clark came to see me at the gallery informing me that your intention was not to return to the Leger gallery in the future, which may explain why I did not press you to return to me.' I was surprised to say the least for I did not remember telling Sir Kenneth any such thing. I did discuss matters with Willy Gibson who proffered the following advice: 'If you love pictures do not join a museum, you will be swamped by administrative duties and never handle a painting.' His advice, though appreciated, was unnecessary for I had neither the necessary academic qualifications nor the slightest desire to work within museum confines.

Having taken it for granted that, like Mr Oldham, old master dealers avoided contemporary art, I noticed with pleasure and surprise that my former German teacher and his partner came to the National Gallery exhibitions. Since the days of my tuition under Dr Roland, I had only met them casually when viewing future sales, or in the streets of that compact West End region, the hub of London's art trade. On these occasions only polite exchanges passed between us – on the current state of the art market or perhaps my progress in German. Then one day in the summer of 1944, Dr Roland telephoned to say he would like to see me and we arranged to meet in my office. The purpose of his visit was to tell me that he and Mr Delbanco wanted to start a gallery in the West End, and to change from old masters to modern art in which both had always taken a keen interest. Their training had well equipped them to handle old masters for each had taken a degree in the subject and Mr Delbanco was considered to be a leading authority on drawings, but now they both felt that they would prefer to deal in the works of the nineteenth and twentieth centuries. Being shut in an office can be very dull, for clients only come by appointment, and the idea of an open gallery with its more lively atmosphere of changing exhibitions, and resultant steady flow of visitors, seemed to be much more attractive. Also Dr Roland laid stress on a point which he knew would appeal to me, that they wished to encourage young painters, unknown but gifted, who could not find a gallery to accept them.

I came into the picture because it appeared that the whole plan depended on me: if I would collaborate they would go ahead, if not, they would continue as before and renounce the whole proposition. The terms they offered were a full partnership – the third of my divided career – and if I agreed we would look for some premises so as to open as soon as peace was declared. I could not give an immediate answer, nor did Dr Roland expect one, but being a man who customarily takes every step possible to insure against contingencies, he asked if, at least, they could have first refusal of me. This quaint expression made me feel as if I were a painting for sale and upon which a half red spot had been placed as reserve until the client reached a decision. But in this case it was the 'painting' and not the client who had the ultimate say!

The proposal was flattering and totally unexpected for these two men were comparative strangers; with one my relationship had been no more than master and pupil, the other I knew even less. Moreover, I had never thought of running my own gallery, though once propounded the idea was attractive, and I was puzzled as to the reason for this generous offer. I had not a penny to put into a business while they, admittedly with little fluid capital, had a small stock which included some very good paintings. I felt that there must be a snag and that I needed advice; the best person to give it was Hugo Pitman who was not only experienced and successful in business but also keen on the arts. He once told me that nothing delighted him more than to shut the office door behind him and to take himself off into this different world. He did so most weeks by spending an evening in Augustus John's studio, where he was usually among a group of young artists sitting at 'the feet of the master'. Occasionally I went with him, but I did not care for the atmosphere of hero-worship at these gatherings.

So I telephoned Hugo and explained my dilemma; his advice was to accept if the idea appealed to me and if I thought the people concerned were reliable and honest. Just before we parted he nonchalantly said, 'By the way I have a couple of thousand pounds doing nothing in particular; take it as your share in the business; you'll feel better if you're able to contribute something. If in due course you're unable to repay me I will take pictures in lieu of the money.' Such a thoughtful gesture augured well for the future and from the moment Roland, Browse & Delbanco came into being, Hugo was always known as its 'god-father'. I was able to repay his loan while he, already overcrowded with pictures, supported us by occasionally buying something from the gallery.

With my own instincts backed by Hugo's approval, I had practically decided to join the two men but as yet had given no affirmative reply. Warily, I was still weighing the pros and cons when Dr Roland called again to see me. This time he asked for a positive decision as the matter had become urgent: he had learned that the lease of No. 19 Cork Street was for sale and the price was temptingly low. This was understandable because the 'doodlebug' era had not yet come to an end and few dared invest in any new property. The charming small house, which I had known in the days when it was Freddie Mayor's gallery, had been empty and neglected throughout the war, but for how much longer would it be available? I went to look at it once again and realizing, as had the others, its full potential, I was completely won over and then and there gave my agreement. The opportunity was too good to miss despite the grave risks that the purchase entailed, and we could only hope that the house would be standing when hostilities finally ended. We arranged to meet to plan the organization of our new gallery.

Because my two partners lived near Swiss Cottage, it was there that our rendezvous took place, not in any smart West End restaurant but in a tatty small café near the Underground. In this modest environment Roland, Browse & Delbanco was born. The simplicity of the venue was more than fortuitous: it was to indicate the unostentatious tone of the gallery, reflecting the temperament of each of the partners.

It may seem surprising that at this first discussion we talked more about our general attitude to art than we did about business. We accepted that with our small capital and the necessity to accumulate an entirely new stock, our overheads must be strictly controlled, each partner taking the minimum salary according to individual needs. We decided against a partnership contract on the basis that a piece of paper would be no deterrent if, in the future, one of us wanted to withdraw; nor did we think that it would be necessary to have two endorsements on our cheques. Right from the start we trusted each other and during the thirty-two years of the gallery's existence we never had occasion to regret it.

I must have been exercising the legendary feminine intuition, for I was casting in my lot with two comparative strangers who already knew each other intimately. But I had a strong feeling that we could make a team, as the longer we talked the more apparent it became that an important denominator existed between us and this was a deep love of painting. We were also in harmony with the ethical approach that should pertain to art dealing, and though we naturally hoped to earn a comfortable living, it would have to be governed by respect for our *métier*. We were determined always to put quality before profit, not to buy or exhibit simply for gain. This may sound smug, but it is just how it was. Without any ambition to become internationally powerful, we would not sacrifice our private lives on the altar of 'big business', so that however ready we were to work hard during the day, we were not prepared to allow commerce to impinge on our private lives. This meant no entertaining of clients at night unless, of course, they had become friends.

From the start we resolved to remain independent by operating within the limits of our own resources and neither seeking nor accepting outside finance – a self-imposed restriction which often proved to be thwarting if a beautiful painting at a moderate price had to be renounced because our capital was exhausted. Today it would be quite out of the question to run a gallery like Roland, Browse & Delbanco on similar lines without considerable backing. The art trade in those days was small and exclusive; it had not yet become a fashionable profession or a field for the private speculator; nor had the auction houses altered their function by assuming the role they have subsequently played as the dealers' most powerful competitors. Good pictures were plentiful in galleries and sales, while prices were reasonable and frequently low, so that alert eyes reinforced by knowledge could often make a very nice 'find'. As the trade mainly focused on the big names while ignoring a large number of interesting artists, we took the opportunity of exploring that field and were able to introduce various unknowns as well as recalling those of past standing who through the years had slipped into the shadows.

The name of the gallery gave us some food for thought and we ran through the usual gamut. Although the sum of our names was a rather big mouthful – one well-known critic, reviewing our first show, spent several lines complaining about the length of our title and the space it took up in his columns – we came to the conclusion that it would be more explicit to use all the three and in euphonic order. I was particularly in favour of this arrangement which would avoid my repeating that I was not the secretary.

Whilst I am on the subject of names I would like to explain why, until now, I have made a distinction between the designations of my partners. As I had said, each of the two had taken similar degrees in Germany, the country which gave birth to the art historian, but while Dr Roland is proud of his title and prefers it to be used, Mr Delbanco is apt to treat it with disdain and will teasingly say that 'every other German is either a doctor or a baron'. Upon the advent of the gallery we formed the habit of calling the former by his surname and the latter, because he disliked the name Gustave, became simply 'G'. From now on this is how I shall refer to them both.

Roland, Browse & Delbanco in Cork Street

Immediately peace had been declared and my partners released from their war duties, we were able to take physical possession of our building. Our gamble had paid off for it was still standing, and we were faced with the thrilling prospect of putting it in order, as having been empty for such a long time it was badly in need of refurbishing. Because of the atmosphere of the house, which had once been the mews cottage to Lord Sandwich's mansion, we wished to retain its intimate character and furnish it, as nearly as possible, as a private home. We felt that clients seeing pictures in such a setting could more easily envisage how they might look hanging on their own walls; we also wanted the gallery to be friendly and inviting so that all would feel quite free to come in.

As the building had already been used as a gallery, no structural alterations were necessary; in any case they would have been out of the question for, apart from the cost, neither builders nor materials were possible to find so soon after the years of disruption. From the mass of demolition we were able to obtain enough battered wood for our storage racks but new carpets were non-existent, and although G. thought that linoleum would do – an idea firmly rejected by Roland and myself – we managed to lay hands on a curious medley of second-hand Wilton pieces which, though on close scrutiny they resembled a patchwork, served our purpose at the time. Regency furniture seemed a good compromise as a setting for pictures of all periods and as it had not yet come into fashion, we succeeded in buying in a Christie's auction eight cane-seated ballroom chairs for the sum of fifty shillings a piece. The chairs were unusual in that on their backs brass handles were fitted to lift them more easily, and many years later, with the luck of the sale room, the rest of the twelve came on the market. Although we did not need to have any more, we thought it a pity not to reunite them and so we added the four to the rest. These little chairs meant so much to me as a symbol of an environment I had cherished that when the gallery once and for all closed its doors, their appearance at Christie's, forlornly lined up and awaiting a new owner, was one of the most poignant moments. Perhaps this small incident, more than any other, brought home to me the finality of a chapter that had been so fulfilling and happy.

I think that the gallery hinted to visitors that a woman was behind the scene; men on the whole did not bother with detail. But to me they were very important. For the chairs I ordered three sets of squab-covers, each in a different colour, and from this selection we were able to choose whichever best suited the current exhibition. The flower arrangements also became one of our features and were likewise selected according to what was on show. That all this care did not go unnoticed was confirmed by a woman visitor's remark: 'I have come to see the chairs', while her companion responded 'and I to see the flowers'!

As the woman in our trio I was given my own office – one in the basement which had been Freddie Mayor's retreat – while my partners shared

Ludwig Meidner, *Portrait of Felix Müller*. Private collection

Adolph Menzel, *Mr Atkinson*. Private collection

another upstairs. We gradually got used to each other's habits and foibles and despite the small squabbles inevitable among people of such different temperaments, who were in close contact each day of the week, the partnership thrived without any near breaks and the gallery continued to flourish. That we were an odd number was a definite advantage for it meant a majority ruling was possible, but even this course was not rigorously followed if it was clear that any one opinion was by far the best informed of the three. When it came to buying there was never a problem if what we called an 'RBD picture' was the one we were considering; we would just look at each other in implicit assent and except in borderline cases discussion was unnecessary unless it were about price.

Hardly a day passed without at least one artist, often still a student, bringing in work to show us; it was part of the normal routine, and however busy we happened to be we always made time to look and tried to be helpful. Knowing our reactions were important to them and that they found these visits embarrassing – they could also be embarrassing for us – we did our best to make positive criticisms. The actual percentage that, rightly or wrongly, we found really interesting, was abysmally low; but contrary to what most young painters think, we did always hope to find someone. I believe it was Roland who had the best flair for recognizing potential among them, and if G. and I did not happen to share his good opinion, he would on occasion buy the work for himself.

Among the secretaries who worked for us, Mariegold Proctor (now Mrs John Heron) was with us the longest; she remained in our employ for some fifteen years and only left to get married. She was passionate about literature, poetry and prose, and had a talent for writing which she has never seriously developed, so just out of interest she wrote impressions of us with humorous, if favourably biased, insight. We thought these so charmingly and amusingly expressed that I have been tempted to quote them; they sketch random observations of three disparate people, the duration of whose partnership, I have been told, caused some surprise in the trade:

ROLAND, BROWSE AND DELBANCO – *An Appreciation*

by Mariegold Proctor, 1960

I have studied this partnership for several years. At first 'the trinity' as they sometimes facetiously call themselves, seemed marked by their profound disrespect for each other's judgment. Later this proved superficial, and I saw they had in common a deep appreciation of the best in human quality, so that they would more often say about a client, 'What a nice man' than 'He really has a good eye'. On their comments on artists, this consciousness of human values has a bearing. About a generally esteemed painter of the stark Realist school one said, 'It looks as though he has looked through humanity and found nothing there'; and about a painter inspired by Turner, 'Yes, his colour is beautiful and he paints with great taste, but I can't believe in him – that woman he goes about with!' This human appreciation is by no means irrelevant. It may explain why they do not entirely support completely abstract painting, considering it in the last resort a barren intellectual pursuit, lacking passion; it is perhaps one reason why they so greatly admire Josef Herman who reaffirms Munch's reverence for 'human beings who breathe, suffer and love'. They will say 'finally the artist makes the best apology for his works. He believes in them so utterly; otherwise he would commit suicide.'

But there is nothing sentimental about their attitude. They themselves would emphatically state that quality is the final arbiter. Their aesthetic integrity is absolute. This respect for human values is only a symptom of a broad and civilized outlook reflected also in the catholicity of their taste. They have no prejudices in favour of any particular dogma or school. The joys they provide are manifold; the grace of a Courbet *Flower Girl*, or of a Rodin or Emilio Greco sculpture, the elegance of Modigliani, the tenderness of Pascin, the purity of Ingres, the rich sensuous colour of a Ruszkowski, the elemental excitement of a Vlaminck, the charm of Constantin Guys …

Each partner has a strong personality which never results in impossible conflicts for humour is the saving grace. Each contributes to the character of the gallery. Mr Roland, always immaculate, is friendly, affable, courteous, quick in his response. He is full of impatient enthusiasm, unsmilingly expresses dogmatic opinions, but often retracts with humour and meekness. He has a strong will, not immediately apparent. His business-like method and competence are plentifully tempered by an occasional whimsy and a tendency to sign himself 'Monticelli' or 'Henry Moore', so closely does he identify with the figures he admires. And this devotion to those artists in whom he ardently believes is one of his outstanding characteristics. He will undertake the most monotonous tasks in order to spread a knowledge of their work. Many students also will remember with gratitude his careful analyses of their paintings.

Miss Browse, elegant, original, but never *outré* in her Edwardian dress, is full of proverbial subtlety and intuition. She has a delicacy and perfect sense of fitness invaluable in any difficult human relations. Though dignified and extremely fastidious in her taste, she is never precious, and before you know her well the timbre of her deep unrestrained laughter is reassuring and so is the colloquial style of her letters. Her extravagance is only equalled by her generosity.

Her housewifely qualities, as her partners would call them, though the word in our English sense is very far from what they mean, are of the utmost importance. She not only arranges the flowers, chooses cushion covers in harmony with whatever is being shown on the walls, but also washes marks off the paintwork and suggests structural alterations. Even the tray on which the tea-cups rest was chosen with a thought to the colour of the Lucienne Day curtains in the office with their Klee-like design. The most perfect of hostesses, she makes casual visits pleasant social occasions. It is she who, so to speak, makes a home for the exhibits, is responsible for the trailing plants, for giving a sculpture a natural setting and the whole gallery a cherished feeling. Her love of order seems, rarely enough, to bear a relation to a sense of beauty. To make order under her direction seems only like the preparation of a garden for planting. Yet with all her feminine attributes, she is thoroughly shrewd and logical.

Mr Delbanco modestly affirms that he is nothing without his jokes. I would add that the deeply ingrained solecisms of his speech also seem an indispensable part of his personality. He too shows the utmost kindness and patience in dealing with young aspirants and when forced to give the unwelcome answer will do so without wounding their self-esteem. His jokes are never at their expense. He is no respecter of persons and you may even hear a young client, a man of indecision, saying plaintively 'You mustn't tease me, Mr Delbanco'. He has the reputation with his partners of talking a great deal but, I imagine, it is not noticeable to most people as he also listens with sympathetic attention. He is not only concerned with the personal problems of artists. I have known a distressed middle-aged lady, initially seeking a valuation, pronounce him 'a real philosopher' after twenty minutes' acquaintance. He is always benevolent but not always polite, will answer gruffly when preoccupied, interrupt conversations and seldom thank you if you pass him a cup of tea. He will excuse himself from one conversation and being engaged in another, will forget the first. He is a great advocate of the spirit of compromise, is incapable of offending or being offended. He is interested in everything from politics to kitchen gadgets.

I shall have given a wrong and sentimental impression if I have presented Roland, Browse & Delbanco merely as charming dilettanti rather than as people able to calculate readily, with an immense background of knowledge and experience paying minute attention to what goes on in the art world. Otherwise they would not and could not be art dealers.

I have never delved into the history of Cork Street but have been told that, in Edwardian days, it was noted for its disreputable small hotels to which prostitutes would take their clients. No 'lady' would walk down the street unaccompanied by a male, if at all, a situation which applied also to the charming Burlington Arcade, now so popular with tourists that within its precincts one may meet acquaintances from all over the world.

When we opened the gallery, and for some long while after, Cork Street was still mainly orientated towards male needs and desires. Although the hotels were no longer there, many of their premises had been taken over by some of the finest tailors in London. So much so that we teased a few clients by saying that they only visited the gallery when they were on their way to a fitting. But carnal appetites were by no means neglected, for Cork Street remained one of the West End's most notorious locations, a beat jealously guarded by 'regulars'. The *filles de joie* sauntered up and down the street or stood chatting in groups as long as they dared, with one eye carefully looking out for the police and the other expertly scrutinizing each male passer-by. In order to rest their weary feet they frequently took recourse to our railings, upon which they would sit like so many birds on a telephone wire. Sometimes we had to ask them to move for it became evident that they were embarrassing those who would pause to look in our window. The whole scene was a novelty and I was in the front row. Intrigued to discover how such transactions were made I would hurry down to my office below in the basement, where voices were magnified, hoping to eavesdrop on this form of bargaining, but I always arrived a little too late and my curiosity was never satisfied.

To the immense amusement of my partners and myself I was twice taken for a prostitute. We had found as a carpenter an elderly refugee who scarcely spoke one word of English and early one morning I arrived at the gallery to find him waiting at the locked door. As I fumbled in my handbag to retrieve the key, I was mystified by his extraordinary behaviour: he stood looking terrified, wildly gesticulating and shaking his head in a gesture of negation all the while repeating 'No, no, no' as if I were about to murder him. He only relaxed when I unlocked the door and he realized I was not propositioning him.

We got to know all the girls on our beat and exchanged daily greetings with them; the eldest was a motherly figure who had a young daughter studying ballet, so she and I, with an interest in common, would discuss Covent Garden performances. One afternoon, on my way to Soho, she stopped me to admire the outfit I was wearing; she said, 'I could knock you down for that dress' and as it was made of black and white plaid I told her I thought it would get dirty too quickly (standing about in the streets was in my mind). With a smile still lingering about my face I went on my way, when all of a sudden I had the impression that a young officer in uniform was following me. He had seen me talking to my obvious prostitute friend and had taken my smile as an inviting factor. As he drew level he realized his mistake but it was too late to withdraw; very red in the face he stutter-ingly asked whether he might invite me to tea. I thanked him politely but excused myself as I was in a hurry to get to the butcher – the basket on my arm endorsing the reason. I had tried to let him down as lightly as possible by pretending not to notice that anything was amiss.

Early exhibitions and gallery artists

Today there are hundreds of galleries in London, many of whose names I do not even know – I once counted over twenty in Cork Street alone – but when ours opened in 1945 we had but a handful of competitors. A new gallery was a rare event and anticipated with eager curiosity, so that our first exhibition was of the utmost importance and demanded the most careful thought. It was not only designed to arouse interest by the wide range of commitment we hoped to maintain, but above all to indicate that quality, irrespective of fashion, would in the future be our keystone. As a London gallery we decided to begin by paying homage to British art, with the result that the choice for our first show was a loan exhibition of the best English drawings we could possibly accumulate, starting backwards in time and coming right up to date. This is where my connections became particularly valuable for I already knew the majority of collectors and established artists, who greeted our project in the most helpful way by lending whatever was asked for. We gathered together eighty fine drawings, a handful of which we had acquired, beginning in the late seventeenth century with Kneller and Marcellus Laroon and ending with John Minton and Leslie Hurry. It was not our intention to limit ourselves strictly to period or country, for such confines would have been economically inadvisable and a waste of experience. On the other hand we had neither the space nor the means seriously to deal in old masters, and so we would only buy when the opportunity occurred and concentrate on the present and last centuries, mainly in Britain and France.

Our second exhibition was prompted by what we had in stock and comprised English and French eighteenth-century paintings; not very originally we entitled it *The Age of Grace*. It was dominated by *The Four Seasons* by Boucher, an important set already owned by my partners, and included, among others we had been able to buy, works by Hubert Robert, Moreau le Jeune, Reynolds and Romney as well as a superb portrait of his wife by Gainsborough and a sketchily evanescent small Watteau. This truly delicious, poetic little canvas was once offered to Georges Wildenstein, and I have never forgotten his cynical reaction. Pretending to be uninterested but nevertheless asking its price, he was quoted 4,000 and asked 'Four thousand what?' I have always regretted I was not quick enough to answer that it was guineas not pounds, the proper retort to a disparaging question.

Professional fees were formerly quoted in guineas and as those in the art trade justifiably regarded themselves as professionals – as did estate agents or dealers in bloodstock – they always worked in this currency. Georges Wildenstein was notorious for his ungenerous attitude towards his fellow dealers in general and although the majority could not compete with his own rich and powerful firm, he habitually denigrated any fine picture that was not in his possession.

That we were able to buy, when we opened the gallery, without any real capital, a group of paintings by such artists as I have mentioned, gives some idea of the state of the market. It makes the mouth water to think back to those times, but all was not so easy as it may be thought. It was far from unusual for an excellent picture to remain in stock over years; there were very few English clients for expensive paintings; the museums were stagnant or penniless; and the international market had hardly come into being. It was really a case of many good pictures seeking very few buyers – the cry is just the opposite today and I am still not sure which situation is preferable.

William Nicholson was one of the first English painters to join the new gallery on a regular basis and, from the time when he started showing with us, his name became indelibly linked with that of Roland, Browse & Delbanco. He had previously been attached to the Leicester Galleries but he now put himself under our care; it was more likely Marguerite who had prompted the change for William was blissfully unaware of business matters and was like a trusting child in the hands of his agent. The Leicester Galleries, always modest, were selling his paintings at ridiculously low sums, far less than was asked for those approaching his stature, but William never weighed his artistic worth and accepted their values without question. We doubled his prices to their warranted value to Marguerite's satisfaction and William's surprise.

One of William's quirks was to collect truant hairpins which he picked up off the pavements and stuffed into his pockets. In his hands these harmless objects became dangerous weapons for whenever he thought that one of his paintings needed adjustment – and he usually did – his hand automatically went to his pocket, out came a hairpin, and using it as one of the tools of his trade, he would scratch on the surface of the canvas quite sure he was making an improvement. When I realized the danger that threatened his pictures, I made a point of never letting him see them alone; I always went with him as he walked around the gallery trying to stop him but often without success. So these fine scratches on many paintings may even be regarded as a mark of authenticity. I hope that no unscrupulous person will, in the future, be tempted to add them.

As William worked slowly his production was small and his first exhibition covered only one floor; on the other we hung a group of French drawings which ranged through the period from Corot to Picasso. This show and others ended our first year of trading and we felt that the gallery had been satisfactorily established. It had been greeted with appreciation by public and press; it had earned the respect of dealers, scholars and painters, and its atmosphere had proved so inviting that everyone knew they would always be welcome to come in for no more than a chat.

Soon after we opened I had to go into hospital for a cartilage operation on my knee. I sustained an injury while playing hockey at Cookham, a sport in which I would not have dared to participate while I was a dancer. Hoping the trouble would heal with time I endured the pain until it was evident that I had to do something about it, especially as I was unable to climb the rather steep stairs at Cork Street. Since my surgeon worked at the London clinic, it was there that I went for my operation, and as two weeks in hospital would have been a great waste of time, I took with me my *Degas* manuscript, photographs and typewriter and managed to get on with my work. I could not understand why so many nurses filed in to see me when I was recovering and one day I asked for the reason. I was told that the visits were instigated by the matron who thought that her staff might usefully learn something about form from the photographs of drawings by the master. She was an unusually enlightened matron!

Another small happening on this occasion makes me chuckle inwardly whenever I think of it. I was very much alone at this particular time and did not relish the thought of seeing myself into hospital without anyone to accompany me. Neither friends nor relations were presently available and fearing lest I might indulge in self-pity settling down in an empty hospital room, I sent myself flowers well in advance so that they, at least, might greet me. The sight of them on my bedside table cheered me considerably and I thought of them many years later when I chanced upon the tenet: 'It is better to light a candle than to grumble about the dark.'

Our second year's shows began with a theme especially dear to my heart. *The Lyrical Trend in English Painting* was another part-loan exhibition and in the foreword we explained that we had 'tried to bring together such diverse artists as Turner, Whistler and Hitchens – to name but a few – assembling pictures by English painters of the last 200 years whose bond was their lyrical quality'. As the title suggests it comprised mainly landscapes and apart from the old masters mentioned above, it included Alexander Cozens, Richard Wilson, Gainsborough and Bonington. We showed three pictures by Samuel Palmer – then treasured only by the *cognoscenti* – and a *Moonlight Landscape* by Joseph Wright of Derby. It may justifiably be claimed that Wright was one of the artists we brought back into the limelight after a long period of obscurity: we bought all his good paintings that came up for auction, gradually dispersing them among museums and dealers. One American dealer became as enthusiastic as we were and on each visit to London he would come to the gallery to see if we had purchased any more in his absence. Similar opportunities occurred among other such painters, unrecognized or forgotten but of artistic value. This hitherto untapped vein was moderately rich and because, as I have said, it was largely ignored, the pictures in question could be bought very cheaply, usually for no more than a few hundred pounds. That they took time to sell was nothing unusual and we were all quite accustomed to the discipline of patience.

Other British artists of the past for whom we acted as 'midwives' – as G. liked to put it – were Fuseli, James Ward, Roderic O'Conor and Walter Greaves as well as the French painters le Sidaner and Marcoussis, and Hayden (French by adoption); but way above all was the role that we played in re-establishing the reputation of Rodin.

During the run of the *Lyrical Trend*, Douglas Cooper, man of wealth, scholar and collector, notorious for his rudeness and withering judgements, came into the gallery to see the show. We had just concluded the sale of the Bonington which was one of the paintings owned by ourselves, and as the new owners were admiring their purchase, Douglas Cooper boomed out, his voice penetrating against the room's quietness: 'That picture is not by Bonington.' With this helpful remark to the friend he was with, he marched out of the gallery in his forceful way. It was a moment of dismay for the sale was significant and the clients were new; seeds of doubt might easily have been sown in their mind but fortunately they took no notice. The painting was well documented and extremely attractive and they evidently had faith in our judgement for the sale went ahead just the same. It was a great pity that so gifted a man should apparently have had such a large chip on his shoulder: Douglas Cooper had a rare feeling for painting which, strengthened by imagination and much erudition, made him an outstanding figure in modern art. Had it not been for his general unpopularity he might well have become an inspired director, at one time, perhaps, of the Tate.

Theme exhibitions needed help from outside and we could not borrow too frequently, so, as we had intended, they were interspersed by our shows of contemporary artists of whom we were gradually gathering a circle. Two Polish-born artists, settled in England, were among the earliest of these; Henryk Gotlib came after *The Age of Grace* and Josef Herman, sharing the galleries with William Ratcliffe – one of the least known members of the Camden Town Group – followed *Currents of Post-Impressionism in France and England*.

So our first exhibition of a contemporary artist was one of Henryk Gotlib who, like Marcoussis (originally Markus) was born in Poland where he became one of the leaders of the Formist movement. At the age of thirty, in 1922, he left Cracow for Paris but at the end of the 1930s the approaching war caused him to uproot himself once again and move to London, and subsequently to make England his home. Whatever his Fauvist background, when we first saw his paintings his palette was of soft, mellow colours. His figures melted harmoniously into their backgrounds as did the solid forms in his landscapes. He became attached to the country around Rye, defining its features in a personal way; although at a point he seemed influenced by Bonnard, the affinity was based on little more than colour and not at all on his vision, which was entirely his own. His forms seem achieved entirely through paint but underneath he is an excellent draughtsman. I am struck by the tenderness which pervades his work, in his case a reflection of the man himself.

At Gotlib's first exhibition I fell in love with one painting and was toying with the idea of buying it, but in my terms it represented quite a big sum and I was not at all sure I could afford it. While I was dithering the picture was threatened: a man we knew slightly came into the gallery and said he might like to buy it. I suddenly felt quite panicky for fear I might lose it, and so while he was upstairs viewing the rest I quickly stuck a red star on its frame. When our visitor descended he was very annoyed to find it was no longer available and not having the courage to tell him the truth, I invented a story about a client who had telephoned, but felt sure he did not believe me. I was not very proud of the trick I had played but was not too worried because the man concerned, David Edge, had the reputation of buying a picture on the spur of the moment and, on second thoughts, cancelling the deal. He was even more furious when he learned the true story and shunned the gallery for years. When finally he decided to resume his visits, he asked me to dinner and to this day I do not know why.

David Edge was conspicuous throughout the art world as a mysterious, magnetic and unpredictable figure who did not fit easily into any category; and because the world is mistrustful of those human beings whom they fail to understand, his doings were frequently regarded as suspect. Exotic in his taste, deliberately outrageous in speech, he could not resist buying antiquities and works of art that attracted his amazingly quick eye. Many he claimed as 'extra-ordinary' masterpieces, and although he was inclined to see the objects he bought through rose-coloured spectacles, I know that on occasion his assessments were justified. On one side of the coin was a gentleman of means, but the other side did not quite tally for on it was etched a person of shadowy substance, a *quasi*-adventurer who deceived even himself. He rather enjoyed the enigma he set and was always able to laugh at himself; it pleased him to say that when he was staying in his villa in Venice, his London friends claimed that he was imprisoned there; and that when he was living in his London flat, his Italian friends said the reverse.

When I was admitted to his chosen circle, David was assuming the lifestyle of a Doge and his London apartment was furnished accordingly.
Period paintings hung over tapestries and gilded candelabra, as well as the
dinner-service, glittered on top of a malachite table. Later he transferred his
allegiance to the near East, whereupon his London *décor* was changed, and
he, of an evening, dressed as a sheikh. He bought and restored to an unbelievable grandeur an obsolete palace in the kasbah at Tangier, transform-
ing it into a fantastic abode. The palace was one of the sights of Tangier,
to which visitors were allowed entry on payment of a fee in aid of a Society
for the Prevention of Cruelty to the Animals of Morocco.

On my visits to him in Tangier, I was allotted the entire quarters of the
former harem which looked down on the little walled garden; outside my
bedroom a small fountain played and tuberoses filled the air with their
heady fragrance. David could identify with the Arab mind, although by
birth and culture he was a European. He enjoyed his daily visits to the
colourful market where he would offer such outrageously low prices for
fruit and flowers that he knew they must provoke the good-natured hag-
gling without which mutual pleasure could not be aroused. At the other end
of his spectrum was the Moroccan royal family whose members, *incognito*,
would attend some of his parties. It pleased him to introduce me as a rich
English woman, quietly indicating that I wore a diamond necklace. It was
in reality paste but it looked rather splendid on account of its age and I
never gave David away.

When it reached his ears I was to remarry, our curious friendship came to
an end as abruptly as it had started for, although our relationship had been
entirely platonic, he had reckoned on our spending our old age together –
so at least he confided to one of my friends.

Apart from an exhibition held six years before, Josef Herman had
developed his own style and theme in isolation and we presented the first
show of his drawings fifteen months after our opening. Josef became an
integral part of the gallery, remaining among our artists until the very end
when, envisaging its closure, he had already resolved not to tie himself
down to anyone else. He had long been accepted as a leading British painter
and had made his name through our firm, and so after such a long and
fruitful partnership, he did not relish the idea of a new attachment. Josef's
loyalty to us was only one key to the constancy of his resolute character;
firm as a rock – which even his appearance suggests – he stands by his
beliefs as a man and an artist and from them he cannot be shaken. When
he no longer lived and painted in Wales among the miners who were his
chosen subject, he did not abandon the theme of the labourer. They are to
him the salt of the earth, he salutes their application and dignity: all are
artisans as he is himself, each simply fulfilling his destiny. I have a deep

fondness for this stalwart being whose understanding is profound and whose advice is detached. He is always the same 'come fair wind or foul' – a trait both unusual and precious.

Perhaps one of our most surprising exhibitions – at least to Josef Herman's admirers – was a collection of his portraits we had gathered together and presented in 1973. We had long been aware that he was an excellent and perceptive portraitist who, not being a professional in this branch of art, was free of the concessions to convention and the restrictions that normally beset this category of painter. Concentrating on the physiognomy of his sitters, who were nearly always among his own circle of friends, he devoted himself to painting the face, believing it to be the essence. The portraits mainly represented those involved in the arts, including my partners and myself: quite a bold move when we were present for comparison. Josef ignored the much quoted dictum that 'the eyes are the mirrors of the soul'; he either painted them as dark blobs in the face or drew, as in my portrait, no more than their outline. Although the tenor of this portrait is severe, which I never feel, even if I may give that impression, I thought that the painting was so very fine that I decided to buy it. It now hangs upstairs outside my study where my husband, Sidney, does not often see it; like the average husband he cannot be unbiased and his reaction to Josef's canvas is to say: 'But I thought you had rather nice eyes!' The show included a few rare commissions among which was a portrait of a wealthy industrialist whose wife was indignant when she saw his red nose. Although she admitted that he was a drinker, he never touched anything but a glass of champagne and that did not turn the nose red!

The second artist who made his début with us and also remained until our closure was the exuberant Philip Sutton. He had been a pupil at the Slade School of Art, then under the directorship of William Coldstream who, knowing our interest in up-and-coming young artists, used to call our attention to his most promising pupils in the hope that we might share his opinion. As soon as we saw some of Philip's work, we were sufficiently impressed to include him in a show, and ultimately to give him his first one-man exhibition, which took place in 1956. Philip is what one calls a 'real painter', his one and only language being that of paint. Like Matthew Smith he is a hit-or-miss artist and by this I mean no disparagement; he works directly on his canvas without preliminary drawings, intuitively and very quickly, so that among all the paintings that pour out from his studio there must inevitably be a high percentage of failures. The use of pure colour was rare among modern English artists – thanks perhaps to the influence of Whistler – but Philip on the contrary always adored Matisse and also revels in the most vivid of palettes. His canvases are suffused with a

Renoir-like joy that is alien to contemporary art. In modern parlance it is known as escapist, but I prefer to call it refreshing.

It is not surprising that, among contemporary old masters, Sickert was always 'in residence' at Roland, Browse & Delbanco. Although he was far from easy to sell on account of the low tones that he preferred and in which most of his finest pictures were painted, we nevertheless always kept a number in stock awaiting the more enlightened eye. Sickert's recognition, reflected as always in the prices obtained, has been slower than those of his circle, and he is still enormously undervalued. There is more fluctuation in his sale-room prices than in any other artist of the Camden Town Group and this is because we live in an age when decorative values are prized above all else – hence the phenomenal success of the Abstract Expressionists.

Admittedly Sickert's paintings are difficult to hang and only reveal their subtleties when placed in full daylight, but it is wrong to accuse him of not being a colourist, for in his tones can be discovered a whole lovely range of delicate transitions. On the rare occasions when he used a much lighter palette – always excluding the trivial *Echoes* – his prices have risen accordingly, the most striking example being the charming *Brighton Pierrots*. Although there are two almost identical versions, one came up for sale (it had already been offered in 1983) in 1996 and, for Sickert, fetched the unheard of sum of £200,000 'under the hammer'.*

Before the close of 1946, we took the bold step of making an exhibition of sculpture – bold because there was little market in the United Kingdom for sculpture, generally considered an art for museums. The revolutionary change in this country's status in the areas of music, ballet and sculpture was then in its infancy; Henry Moore had not yet become a 'must' and the rest, as I have said, were practically unsaleable. With our pioneering spirit we decided to show a group of young and little-known artists, and in order to give them an interesting foil, their sculpture was placed against a background of old master drawings. I think that this show intrigued the three of us more than it did our visitors; neither did it meet with financial success – but this we had anticipated. As a dedicated publisher will sometimes print a prestigious book which he knows will have a limited sale, so we occasionally indulged in what we considered a fascinating but unsaleable exhibition.

A much later example of these disinterested exhibitions consisted of a collection of Fuseli drawings from a folio discovered most unexpectedly in New Zealand by Peter Tomory, then director of the Auckland Art Gallery. We knew that none of these outstanding drawings would be for sale but as Peter was anxious that they should be seen by a wider public than was possible in New Zealand, he suggested that we should show them in

---

* The picture is now in the Tate Gallery.

Henri Matisse, *Lying Nude*. Private collection

London. We jumped at a prospect so full of interest and one that added further valuable insight into Fuseli's oeuvre.

Other exhibitions during our first five years ranged through seventeenth-century Dutch paintings; *British Romanticism*; Henry Moore – maquettes and drawings; a fine part-loan show of Degas with thirty-six works in his various media and, in contrast with today's magnificent tomes which sometimes surpass the exhibits themselves, there was not one reproduction in the modest catalogue!

It was Sir Kenneth Clark who told us about Margaret Kaye and how much he admired her fabric collages, which he thought we should inspect. When we evidently showed our distaste at the notion of exhibiting the applied art of needlework, he told us quite firmly not to be 'snooty' but to reserve our judgement until we had seen it. G. and I were immediately won over and although Roland, always a stickler for keeping to 'pure art', was never behind our few deviations, we nevertheless decided upon making a show. Kaye did not employ the minute, regular stitching usually associated with needlework pictures, but with remarkable boldness she constructed compositions of animals and birds by sticking a medley of materials on a board. She united the whole through a variety of crude threads, much as a painter might use a glaze. The best of the collages had the kind of vitality that Lurçat retained in his tapestries; while the incongruous materials were used with the certainty of a Schwitters. Despite several shows we never succeeded in establishing Margaret Kaye to the extent her originality deserved, for buyers were suspicious of pictures in fabric which they did not believe could associate with oils. Today all is changed and all is accepted to an alarming degree, but Kaye has changed too in the meantime. She now produces quiet, subtle, small collages and paper has replaced textiles.

Together with Kaye's show we presented a second with no other connection than that it was equally bold in conception. We had bought a large sketchbook of dashing, late eighteenth-century drawings but there was no indication as to who was the author and so we decided to christen him 'The Master of the Giants'. Stylistically near Fuseli, of the circle of Romney, Blake and Mortimer, his pseudonym was prompted by the theme of the drawings, the giant-statured heroes of Greek and Roman mythology. Considerable speculation and interest were aroused among those who had specialized in English drawings; some did not realize that we had invented the 'Master' and fruitlessly searched for him in the dictionaries, while others put forward different suggestions as to the artist's identity. One scholarly collector, having browsed through the material in the Victoria & Albert Print Room, proudly informed us he had solved the mystery and that the unknown artist was actually Prince Hoare. Most of the drawings had by then been dispersed and for a while the attribution was generally accepted; later they were 'given' – in art world parlance – to an obscure artist, James Jefferys. In Bénézit's dictionary he is described as a marine painter who spent a few months in Rome; this sounds so unlikely that without infallible proof I cannot imagine how this name was arrived at.

The few exhibitions I have highlighted, which greatly contributed to the gallery's good name, give some indication of the fun that we had and the richness of subjects available. Theme exhibitions were then a rarity, for old master dealers hardly ever made shows, while the small number who worked in contemporary art mainly confined themselves to one-man exhibitions. A kind. of exception was the Leicester Galleries whose annual small survey, *Artists of Fame and Promise*, was equally valuable to painters and buyers. But because of our experience in the past and the present we were able to wander over the centuries and I, quite naturally, was O.C. exhibitions. I have often been asked how we divided our duties. In fact the tasks seemed to separate themselves. Roland, very orderly, looked after our finances and, by and large, kept the gallery books; G., very disorderly, viewed all the sales and attended to matters which allowed him to wander, for he hated being confined to the gallery. I used to tell him he was like a bird whose tail had to be salted to stop it flying away. We had made a rule that one of the partners had always to be in the gallery, and if Roland and I were absent together, one could never be sure whether G. would remain. Apart from these broad, general distinctions, each was involved in every procedure and we did nothing without consultation, and because we were three it was never too difficult to reach a compromise when we differed.

Exhibitions, however, acted as show-pieces. The serious business was buying and selling. It has never been possible to run a West End gallery on contemporary exhibitions alone, so to some extent they are an altruistic endeavour and we accepted the fact that many ran at a loss. No painter can work in a vacuum for ever, with an increasing number of pictures around him and without any outside reaction. His work must have an airing in some show or other, and even though sales may be disappointingly low – even non-existent – at least there is a satisfaction in seeing them hung in surroundings away from the studio.

Dealers are accused of taking too high a commission and from the artists' standpoint the accusation is understandable, since after paying commission and the rising cost of materials, so little is left to live on that most have to fall back on teaching. But galleries' overheads have likewise increased so that the smaller ones have no option but to charge more and more – the usual old vicious circle. We, however, reckoned that a firm of real substance should be able to carry such extra burdens without passing them on to the artists, and we continued to charge one third – as did the

Fine Art Society and perhaps others – while the rest have risen to 40 or even 50 per cent.

But no business can afford to be entirely magnanimous and, as I have said, all exhibitions carry certain advantages; they attract visitors who may become clients and they also used to have publicity value. Nowadays a review has become an unexpected bonus, for, as I have said, critics are given too little space – even had they the time – for the endless number of shows they are invited to cover.

During the first five years of the gallery's life we had sold forty pictures to public bodies and museums, about one third of which comprised works by old masters from varying countries and of different periods. Such disparate painters as Piero di Cosimo, Murillo, Boucher, van Goyen, Wright of Derby and Zoffany, were among those we dispersed and at prices then normal but now hard to believe, for they ranged from as little as 150 guineas up to 2,500. But by far the most incomprehensible situation of all was the extraordinarily delayed appreciation of Turner, whose genius was not acclaimed, at least price-wise, until the years that followed the war. A splendid large oil that our gallery handled went to a museum in the United States for the sum of £5,000; now several more digits would be attached.

Outstanding among our museum sales of the twentieth century were those that closely reflected my personal taste: the Tate bought Gwen John's important *Self Portrait* as well as two Degas bronzes; the Aberdeen Art Gallery had William Nicholson's *Studio in Snow*, one of my favourites among all his landscapes, and a good early Vlaminck, also a landscape. The Victoria & Albert and the Leicester museums had canvases by Paul Nash and Innes respectively, and a fine Sickert, *Dieppe*, went to the Sydney Art Gallery. Moore's sculpture and drawings went all over the place as did drawings by Herman and Minton, Augustus John, Sickert and Hurry, to name but a few. When Sir Trenchard Cox was its director, the Birmingham Art Gallery bought so much from us, by old masters and new, that he used to call us his London office.

The mention of John reminds me afresh of an amusing and somewhat eccentric happening which, considering his early attachment to gypsies, was not altogether surprising. We had bought a pair of good early panels, neither of which bore a signature, and as this was unusual I wrote to 'Dodo' (his wife, Dorelia) to ask whether I might bring them for him to sign. She responded at once with an invitation to lunch and I took the two pictures to Fordingbridge. Their *ménage* was such that she had forgotten all about me and so my arrival was unexpected. But as various people popped in and out of this open, Bohemian household, one more or less was of little consequence. Dodo looked at the panels and gave her approval, whereupon we all sat down to lunch; the paintings had been placed on a chair facing me and as Augustus was opposite, his back was towards them. He had already grunted that they were not by him but Dodo took no notice of that; then during the meal he suddenly rose from his chair, stood in front of the panels as if in rapt concentration, after which he returned and whispered to her. It appeared that he had been consulting his pendulum and as it had given the affirmative swing, he was ready to concede that the paintings were genuine. The meal over, I followed him up to the studio where he signed both the panels in a shaky hand. I have known other instances of artists not recognizing works that they painted in earlier years, but never before and never since have I come across one who professed to solve the problem by divination.

Rupert Hart-Davis, that dear and distinguished man-of-letters, whose family had long been among William Nicholson's friends, decided it was time that a full-length monograph be published on the paintings of this sensitive artist. The matter was discussed with Marguerite Steen and together they agreed that I should write it, a proposition to which I consented with pleasure, not only because of my affection for William and my admiration for his work, but also because no amateur writer would lightly refuse a commission from the firm of Hart-Davis. I had been sorry to miss working with Rupert over the Walpole affair, and this was a second opportunity to do so. I thoroughly enjoyed my sessions with him, and felt like a pupil under his stylish guidance; he used to tease me whenever I wrote 'naturally' or 'of course', saying that these expressions were meaningless.

On considering the project it seemed to me that, as William's *oeuvre* was relatively small, it would be a good idea to publish a *catalogue raisonné* instead of a simple monograph. I very soon discovered what a boring task the compilation of a complete catalogue could be and vowed never to undertake another. Up to this time I had intended, at some future date, to make the definitive catalogue of the paintings of Sickert and had already been granted the rights by Thérèse Lessore, his widow. For years I kept my records up to date but as pictures began to rise in price and hence change ownership with quite alarming frequency, I gave up the chore of trying to keep track of them, and, bearing the Nicholson experience in mind, I left the task to a future historian, namely the dedicated Wendy Baron.

For a full thirteen years after his death in 1949 the body of Sir William Nicholson K B E – for he had been knighted, much to his surprise – lay like a pauper in an unmarked grave next to his family in the churchyard at Newark. This disturbing revelation came out of the blue in a plea from Marguerite to do something about it. She had found herself in so ignominious a position that she had not dared even to attend William's funeral. She was an outcast in his family's eyes for his second wife had refused to divorce him – Marguerite longed for their marriage – and although she had not been the cause of the break-up they held bitter feelings against her. William's daughter, Liza, had not joined in the feud but her mother and Ben continued their enmity. As the funeral arrangements had been made by the family, Marguerite justifiably thought they would attend to a headstone, but as the years passed and nothing was done she decided to take matters into her own hands. But Marguerite could not afford the modest cost of a stone, a revelation which shocked me deeply. In her cottage at Blewbury, where William had died, she lived on little more than her pension; the royalties on her books had gradually diminished as had her impetus to continue her writing. Like William, she too had been careless of money. When they had it they 'blew it' with no thought for the future and both had been cheated out of thousands of pounds by an accountant in whom they had had complete trust.

At her request I wrote to old friends and buyers with an appeal for subscriptions. In answer to my letters the money was collected and in the summer of 1962 a simple headstone with beautiful lettering was at long last erected. I never forgave Ben for refusing to contribute the moderate sum of ten pounds. In a long rambling letter which covered in circles every scrap of its pages, he said that he thought a stone was unnecessary for his father's work would suffice as a memorial – in essence this, of course, was quite true. But his attitude was haughty, with no thought for others, and was not mitigated by his promise to present one of his own paintings to the Tate Gallery as a commemoration of his father. Despite Ben's professed admiration for him, the promise was never fulfilled. I could not help feeling that Ben's letter to me was meant to be kept for posterity but such was my resentment that I tore it in pieces, making quite certain that it should not be preserved.

Ballet again, from the front of the house

In 1949 *Degas Dancers* had at long last been published and I was thrilled by the huge, flattering press it received. As far as I know there was only one dissenting voice – a teasing review from Sir John Squire in the *Illustrated London News*. He wrote that the book 'is of necessity, owing to the art paper, very heavy in hand. But still books are not published for the convenience of reviewers who like to be able to hold them up in armchairs, or even in bed, and reluctantly go to an upright seat and a flat desk to pass their jaundiced opinions on them.' Lawrence Gowing's review in the *Spectator* was the one I prized most of all, not only because I, like so many in the art world, regarded this distinguished man's opinion with respect but also because, among the general literature on Degas, he felt able to write: 'In this important and delightful inquiry only one piece of equipment is now necessary, Miss Browse's book. Even the great *Catalogue Raisonné* recently published by M. Lemoisne at twelve times the price is hardly more indispensable.' I did not expect any extraneous results from this review but, although I cannot remember the exact order of events, I know that it led in a roundabout way to my subsequent appointment as a *Spectator* critic – not on art but on ballet.

Having definitely decided to give up ballet upon our return from the Holland engagement, the practice of dance no longer played any part in my waking hours, but in my sleep it remained surprisingly persistent. I have already told how I was able vividly to recount my dreams many days after they had come to me (e.g. the hanging of contemporary paintings upon the walls of the National Gallery), but now I was having the most persistent dream which recurred spasmodically over several years. It still makes me chuckle to recall it! Having lived in Cookham my daily journeys to London on the Great Western line made me very familiar with Paddington station, so it was there, on one of the platforms, I was standing in a neat fifth position and about to perform a *changement de pieds*. In this step the dancer springs from the ground as high as possible and lands, again in the fifth position, but with the alternate foot in front. I must explain that, by nature, women do not have the same ability to spring from the ground as do men, but there I was performing this simple *pas*, only jumping so high that my head struck the iron girders which held up the glass roof. Since I have always had a lot of thick hair I was protected from damaging my skull. Whilst poised at this lofty height I looked down on those ordinary mortals below to see if they were admiring my extraordinary feat (they were not!), then slowly I descended to the ground finding it more difficult than to leave it.

I had already written a few ballet reviews for the *Sunday Times* on the occasion when its regular contributor, A. V. Coton, had gone to New York to research a book. He had asked me to take over during his absence, telling me, in so many words, that he knew I would not try to 'pinch his job', as he feared some other colleagues might do. As I had enjoyed this temporary role, I was excited by the prospect of returning to ballet on a permanent basis, and from the other side of the 'footlights', and so with alacrity I accepted the *Spectator*'s offer.

The scene I re-entered was very different from the one I had known years before: British ballet was now at the peak of its triumph with its senior company established at Covent Garden, having proudly attained Royal status. It boasted no less than five ballerinas among whom Margot Fonteyn was the *assoluta*; Robert Helpmann was dancing and Ashton composing his inimitable ballets for the senior, as well as for the junior companies, to which latter John Cranko, the brilliant young South African, had been appointed as resident choreographer. The richness of London's ballet was further enhanced by the advent of smaller young British companies and the visits of foreign ones, as well as by some famous choreographers. The Ballet Rambert was celebrating its twenty-fifth birthday; the Ballet Workshop, its tenth programme; while Markova and Dolin had but recently formed their Festival Ballet company. Balanchine came to stage his *Ballet Imperial* followed by his *Trumpet Concerto*, and Massine created a Scottish ballet, *Donald of the Burthens*, with the two Scottish artists, MacBryde and Colquhoun, as his chosen designers.

London had indeed become a centre of ballet for, during my first two years as a critic, no less than eight overseas companies came to perform in the capital. They came from Sweden, from Spain and from India; the New York City Ballet made its European *début*, and seasons were given by the Marques de Cuevas Company and the Original Ballets Russes, both of whom were the inheritors of the de Basil repertoire. Roland Petit and his company came on a second visit from Paris but missing were some of the sparkling young dancers who had created such a sensation in 1946. The saddest absence of all was Jean Babilé, one of the most compelling male dancers I have ever seen, who, for reasons that were not disclosed, never again appeared in London. There was also a performer of a quiet pattern, of whom few will have heard but whom I have never forgotten. Paul Draper,* the nephew of the famous Ruth, was a tap dancer to classical music. I cannot praise his artistry more than by placing him, in his own way, in a class with Fred Astaire. But his dancing to Bach – one of his favourites – was necessarily remote and deliberately impersonal, far too esoteric for popular appeal, and to our great loss he also faded away. He gave a short one-man season at the Mercury Theatre to which I was drawn over and over again.

The first half of the fifties was a busy and exhilarating period for critics and one during which the English public surprised itself by taking ballet seriously. They had even become *balletomanes* so that audiences were vast and hugely enthusiastic though not, at this stage, well informed. I was delighted to have two reserved seats for each and every *première*; also flattered, but at the same time quietly amused, by the near-deferential treatment with which critics are courted. I realized how little this really meant but it was novel to be thought to have power, for though the *Spectator* had only a small circulation, its long honoured history commanded respect and some of this brushed off on me. I was always convinced that nobody read my reviews and that, if they did, they took little or no notice. This belief

---

* His appreciative obituary has recently appeared in *The Times*.

gave me an extra feeling of freedom to write what I thought without mincing words, especially as I was independent of my very small fee.

On re-reading my reviews at this distance of time, I find them rather cheeky but honest. In my efforts to be strictly unbiased I was no respecter of persons and freely criticized star dancers and choreographers when it seemed to me warranted. One such review led to one of my not infrequent fracas with Uncle Hubert whom I one day happened to meet outside Fortnum's. From the look on his face it was obvious to me that an explosion was imminent, and although I could not guess how I was at fault, I was to be quickly enlightened. He was incensed at the 'disgraceful' review I had written in the current number of the *Spectator*. I had complained that a famous ballerina's performance showed that she had been neglecting the class-room – a comment quite normal to those who appreciate the rigid régime of a dancer, and which simply meant that she had become careless. Dancers on all levels attend daily classes to keep well in practice and correct any faults that inevitably creep in, but my uncle could not know this and gave me no time to explain. He ended his onslaught with 'and anyhow who cares what *you* think?' and just for once my reply came off pat: 'I suppose that the *Spectator* does, otherwise it would not pay me'; and on that note we parted. Although I appeared to be so sure of myself, such small seeds of censure find vulnerable pockets in which they may lie fallow for a very long time and unexpectedly germinate when they are least welcome, and that is what happened in this case.

During one of Balanchine's visits to London, A. V. Coton had invited the famous man to dinner and had asked me to make up a trio. The occasion should have been marvellously interesting; instead, for me, it was full of embarrassment. Balanchine and 'A.V.', as he liked to be known, chatted quite easily together, but when they turned to me to contribute I was too shy to utter a word. It was a repetition of the day when I took tea with Churchill but this time there was no excuse; I was no longer a novice but a fully fledged critic, and in contrast to those who had done little more than attend a few classes in order to learn something about the language of ballet, I had received a full professional training. This being so, there was no need for my *gaucherie*: I had failed my host and felt very ashamed for I knew that the evening meant much to him. When I searched my mind for some explanation I could not arrive at a logical answer – could it have lain within those deflating words: 'Anyhow, who cares what *you* think?'

Ballet, like the other interpretative arts, may be savoured on differing levels, and while I was witness to much beautiful dancing, transporting performances were few. Technical perfection is a joy to behold and one marvels when aware of its stupendous difficulties (today it has become even more remarkable), but the rare, supreme moments are something apart.

They are not born only of years of hard work combined with all natural physical qualities, there must be another, an ungraspable element, which can only be couched as pure magic. Such bewitching experiences send flashes of ecstasy shuddering throughout the whole of one's being so that one hardly dare breathe for fear of breaking the spell, and these are not transient, fleeting sensations, but may be recaptured at will. I had been transfixed, those long years ago, by Pavlova's presence on stage – a magnetism felt by all those who saw her – and have never forgotten that last poignant moment, the final quiver of wing like the swan's farewell sigh before the silence of death overcomes it. Pavlova created a role out of nothing: the *Dying Swan*, composed by Fokine for her, is technically so simple that any dancer could perform it with ease, but she transformed it into the theatrical miracle that evaded even her greatest successors.

In my adulthood I felt Ulanova's ecstasy as, possessed by the intoxication of a young girl's first love, she, as Juliet, leapt into her old nurse's lap with all the bewildered agility of a sprightly impala – yet the ballerina was already in her forties. Many times have I seen Markova's Giselle and been entranced by her ethereal Willi, but Olga Spessivtseva, in the same role, I found to be even more wondrous. Very tall, slim and wispy, she was simply perfection in Giselle's mortal and immortal states. Her mad scene, so haunting, became a tragic reality when she suffered a breakdown and was confined in a home, but unlike Nijinsky who never recovered, Spessivtseva emerged having regained her sanity, though never again did she dance.

Those who love ballet feel sadly deprived because they never saw Nijinsky perform; there is not even an old film, such as was made of Pavlova, to give some tiny glimpse of this fabled dancer. One can therefore do nothing but accept the reports which unanimously proclaim him a genius – as one writer put it 'he was a superb and instinctive artist to whom technique was only a servant'. So all those *fouettés*, flying *swallow* leaps and *entrechats dix*, which never fail to bring down the house, are spectacular and brilliant technical feats but they are, after all, 'only servants'.

In the spring of 1954, Martha Graham came to London with her company. It is known that she was anxious about this enterprise, having heard how disinclined the English are to accept the unknown in art. I had waited so long for this first appearance, had built up in imagination some intense, hyper-Expressionist exponent of modern dance, that it was a relief to find her so different, yet creative beyond anything I could have imagined. During long years of continuous experiment she had developed her own dance language and themes: no fairy-tale scripts for this pioneer, but serious searching into the problems of man and his relationship with the fundamental forces of life. Her original apprehension was proved to be justified for her art form of deep and unusual beauty, opening vistas quite new to ballet, met with a hesitant response from her audiences, while most of the critics were equally reserved. Strange though it seems, it was not immediately apparent that here was a kind of modern Diaghilev. Martha Graham had chosen her composers and designers with much the same flair as that world-famous impresario; in their quality they matched her beautifully trained dancers and, as all were at one with her particular aesthetic, the whole was perfectly harmonious. Richard Buckle and I could not keep away and were in the theatre night after night so that in a subsequent review I was able to report 'each successive visit confirms the certainty of her genius as well as the beauty of her mind'. Such rare experiences glitter like stars in a sky too frequently overcast, and it is these which help to sustain ballet critics through the many arduous evenings that are implicit in such a profession.

The repertoire of the classical ballet is far more circumscribed than that of music, even of opera, and very much more so than of the 'straight' theatre, so unless there is some outstanding feature to lift them out of the norm, *Swan Lake*, the *Sleeping Beauty* and even *Giselle* – not to mention my particular *bête noire*, the *Nutcracker Suite* – also become tedious through endless repetition. As the Royal Ballet had four outstanding ballerinas who starred successively in each new production, the press were invited to the *première* of each change of cast. The production and designs had been reviewed the first time, so little was left but to stress the contrast between the individual rendering of the leading roles, but repeated comparisons make for dull reading and might even be odious. I also came to dislike the inevitable *divertissements* which usually have nothing to do with the story: designed as they are to give many dancers a chance, which is a valid reason, they often seem to belittle a ballet by imparting to it the timbre of a dancing display.

I had foolishly thought that writing for a weekly would give me plenty of time to prepare my critique, but I had reckoned without those not infrequent *premières* that took place the evening before we went to press. On these occasions I would sit up for hours until there was little time left for sleep, for I found that reviewing was unexpectedly difficult and that my experience as a dancer was not an asset but rather a stumbling block. I came to the conclusion that I was probably a better judge of painting than I was of ballet; I was all too aware of the dancer's problems while of the painter's I knew next to nothing. But as struggles should not be of concern to the critic, the final result being what really matters, I think that an observer with flair and experience may better assess the artistry of the whole than a practitioner too deeply involved.

During the year 1954 I was already working on a new book; together with the *Spectator* and my days at the gallery, these three involvements tired me out. Fatigue was probably a contributing factor towards my developing the dreaded complaint from which I still suffer today.

Trigeminal neuralgia, about which doctors know little – neither the causes nor any cure – was to give me extended periods of agony with occasional intermittent weeks of respite. When it got to the stage that I could not clap a dancer because the repercussions through the body set off an attack, I knew it was time to stop being a critic and spend the evenings at home on my book. The decision in any case had been taken for me as, with excellent timing, the *Spectator* had just appointed a new editor and he, in his turn, wanted to appoint new writers. I was one of those who had to go to make room for them. It was with some relief that I came to the end of my four years on the paper.

'In sickness and in health'

Apart from a few traditional observances, religion had played no part in our family life. My mother, continuing the way in which she had been brought up, had observed the two most important dates in the Jewish calendar by going to synagogue at the New Year and on the Day of Atonement. Although my father had never gone with her, she had felt it her duty to take her two children, and when we were old enough we had also fasted for the required twenty-four hours. We had had little idea as to what it was all about but liked behaving as adults; however, the rule which forbade us to clean our teeth lest one drop of water should escape down our throats, had seemed to be going a little too far. Unbroken by meals the day seemed interminable and in our longing for food I fear that we had our eyes on the clock rather than on the powers above. As a family we had kept only partially to the dietary laws, for while no pork was served at our table, illogically shell-fish was allowed, my mother being very fond of oysters. These my father would bring home as her treat, and because Jack and I were never left out of anything, we were always allowed to taste some. As a result of this early education, oysters have remained one of my favourite delicacies.

The New Testament did not exist for us: it was not only forbidden but never mentioned and, until I was grown up and free to choose for myself, I was not really aware of its contents. Curiously enough when the time came for Jack to read his barmitzvah, it had not been a rabbi but a Protestant parson who had given him lessons in Hebrew. But although we were liberal in many respects, it was no less unthinkable that either Jack or I should marry outside the Faith. My father sincerely believed – perhaps my mother also but she was less inclined to voice her opinions on the subject – that those who were Jewish were God's chosen people, and when later I learned that the English think the same of themselves, I reckoned, with amusement, how lucky we were to have the ultimate of birthrights.

As most children did at that period, we had said our prayers every night before settling down to sleep, but as we grew older this good habit lapsed, at least as far as I was concerned. It took many years and painful experiences before I learned the true meaning of prayer, and that there is a spiritual side to all life which finally triumphs over everything. During this time there had been a flicker of faith but I had not been driven to explore it and it was not until later that I was taught that when the moment is ripe, then and only then comes the awakening; that no striving can help, no bouts of impatience, for 'it is no good blaming a rosebud for not being a rose, nor an acorn for not being an oak tree'.

On one occasion during the war I had been involved in a séance, unsolicited and very unwelcome because I believe any tampering in the occult to be undesirable and at the worst, highly dangerous. I must begin by explaining that my father hated the more flamboyant Semitic characteristics – in fact ostentation in whatever form. He was so much against the wearing of jewellery that my mother had only the minimum – rings and earrings were especially taboo. Apart from her wedding ring and a discreet diamond-bar brooch, she only owned one of the gold 'slave-bangles' that were much in fashion but very 'quiet'. I think she regarded it in the nature of a talisman for she never removed it from the upper part of her arm, and as the gold was extremely thin, it became more and more dented with the passage of the years. During the war I was to be reminded of this bangle in a most uncanny way.

The head of our ambulance station was a striking looking, elderly woman, Mrs X, who puzzled me by a certain air of strangeness. One evening she had invited me to dine at her home together with a daughter and a friend. As I only knew her in her official capacity I wondered why I had been singled out.

The meal had passed off without incident but afterwards, while we were drinking coffee, my hostess put her cup on the arm of her chair, closed her eyes as if in sleep, and started muttering in a language which I took to be Spanish. Bewildered, I looked towards her daughter who seemed quite undisturbed by this bizarre occurrence, and who assured me in the casual manner of one accustomed to such an everyday event, that her mother had gone off into one of her trances and was talking through her normal Spanish medium. The latter appeared to be entirely bilingual for the advice that followed was in impeccable English. Mrs X first addressed her daughter, and after her in order of proximity, her friend. By this time I was becoming agitated because my turn was next, but encouraged by the others' matter-of-fact acceptance, I stayed where I was to face the ordeal. Fortunately I was not called on to make any response but was told that 'on the other side' there was a large, middle-aged woman with the brightest of blue eyes and wearing a gold bangle on her arm, who was distressed by my unhappiness and was longing to help me. She had not previously 'spoken' to me and on this account needed more time in which to explore the details of my trouble. I was to promise to be in touch again. At that time I had not lost anyone excepting my own darling mother, and the description, although vague, fitted her well enough. Of the bangle I remembered nothing at all.

I never again went to Mrs X's home as I had no intention of becoming involved in Spiritualism; I firmly believe we must make our own decisions, including our mistakes, which can only be salutary if through them we learn, and should not be by-passed through the guidance of spirits, even supposing that to be possible. All the same I had found myself disturbed by the evening, particularly when, later, I recalled my mother's bangle. When Jack returned from Burma at the end of the war, I asked him if he knew what had happened to it. He told me it had been impossible to remove it from her arm so, as she would have wished, she was buried wearing it. I subsequently found out that Mrs X thought I shared her extra-sensory perception and that this had been the reason for the invitation to her house.

The war years with their conflicting emotions had dragged on, an over-long drama which mostly comprised players uprooted from the normal course of their lives to play many parts, however bizarre, that happened to fall to their lot. It had been my good fortune to have been moved from my ill-fitting role as an ambulance driver to return to my accustomed world of the arts, but as my working life grew towards its modest success, my private life had continued lonely and desolate, heightened by an ever-gnawing feeling of guilt. Had I been able to attach a modicum of blame to the husband I had abandoned, my conscience might have been assuaged a little, but there had been no flaw upon which I could seize and therefore no comforting shred of mitigation. The wheels of fate, however, had turned not slowly but inevitably and I had attracted the very predicament I feared and was brought face to face with living alone.

As I endeavoured to get accustomed to my new plight, I looked on those friends who had made lasting marriages with a glance that was wistful, perhaps tinged with envy, and in this state I paid a visit to Kate. Her husband John being stationed at Gullane, they had invited me to Scotland for a few days' respite. Through no fault of theirs I felt like an intruder, a third player breaking in on a duet. One late afternoon, cloaked in misery, I wandered listlessly down to the beach. The sun was just setting and as it intermittently shone through the fast-moving clouds, it flooded the grey sea and the vast stretch of sand in a light that was radiantly golden. Not one living creature offended the stillness, and as I stood there alone against this endless expanse, the soft breeze and moving sunbeams enfolded my being and I felt myself weightless, lifted up to the heavens. My body was left with its feet in the sands while the 'I' floated into the glorious Unknown. Transfixed and joyous, without the will to move, least of all to return to my material self, the magical moment, a lifetime in seconds, passed like a whisper and half-dazed I strolled back to the house. I had no wish to seek for a rationale but was content to allow what I vaguely believed was a mystical happening to remain within the depth of my being.

After the war, with Kate and her husband settled once more in Linden Gardens, our little coterie had been joined by Joan Dashwood (then Joan Cherry), who had leased a flat that was part of my premises. Joan, at the time, ran her own bookshop in Queensway where she specialized in literature for children. Kate and I had already grown close having shared good and bad fortunes, and now with Joan's coming we formed a trio of friendship which, despite separations, endured over years. Both Kate and Joan were earnestly searching for their individual paths towards faith: the former was studying under a Christian teacher, the latter inclined toward Buddhism. The three of us would often talk of belief though as yet I had not found a way to it, but I had glanced with much interest at one of Kate's books, the *Autobiography of a Yogi* by Paramhansa Yogananda, which I promised myself I would read one day. Little did I guess in what desperation I would be driven to its study.

Some ten years later, when still living alone, my worst attack of trigeminal neuralgia rendered me prostrate and speechless for weeks, unable to swallow a morsel of food. Kate succoured me in every possible way; my eldest god-daughter, Jill Balcon (Day-Lewis), read poetry to me as only she can, but most of my friends did not come as they knew that I could not and should not try to talk. It was a period of utter despair: I knew I would not die from such a complaint but how could I continue to live with it? Reading was all that I could do in order to pass each interminable day and I knew without doubt that this was the time to turn to the *Autobiography of a Yogi*. I found in its pages my first glimmer of hope. Like the rays of spring sunshine, its message of faith started to melt my frost of despair; I read it over and over again as some read their Bible, determined, upon emergence, to find my own guru. But 'it is not for the pupil to seek his own Master', the Yogi had said, and although I made several abortive attempts to seek one I eventually realized that it was true.

The solution to my quest, as is usual, came when it would and quite unexpectedly. When I was well enough to return to the gallery, one of G.'s friends, Henry Joachim, a musician, called in one day to have a chat with my partner, but G. was engaged and asked him to wait. After a time Henry departed without ever having seen G. but whilst he was there we started to talk and Henry, who knew about my ordeal, tentatively asked if I would try faith healing. I replied that I was willing to try any cure for both orthodox and unorthodox methods had failed, but he was really leading to something besides and, apart from giving me the name of a healer, he suggested I read the short editorials in the *Science of Thought Review*. This small periodical, published privately, and now the longest running magazine of its kind in the world, was edited by its founder, Henry Thomas Hamblin, of whom Henry Joachim had become a devotee.

Mr Hamblin was the son of a Baptist deacon and of humble education. The family being poor, this son, as a youth, had resented the poverty under which they all lived and was determined to make himself rich. He brilliantly achieved his worldly ambition by founding a firm of opticians that for years after his departure still bore his name, and which in his time took the lead in that field in its fine spacious premises in Wigmore Street. But, contrary to expectations, he was far from happy: in fact he was in a state of total despair, which seemed to be centred in his own soul. After horrible experiences which made him psychologically ill and which he tried to shake off by immersing himself more and more in his business, he realized he was not following the divine pattern of his life and that therefore he had lost all sense of God's presence. He was pursuing, albeit successfully, the kind of career that was not intended for him. He abandoned his business and with few worldly possessions retired to the country to pursue what he now knew to be his proper calling, to impart through his writing how, over the years and despite many struggles, he had succeeded in living a life of faith. All this is told simply in his book *My Search for Truth*, which touched a deep chord in me, as had the *Autobiography of a Yogi*. Yogananda had opened the most esoteric of doors; Thomas Hamblin had spelled out, with all the simplicity of a child's ABC, how he had been able to step through it. His teaching was suited to the Western novitiate and particularly harmonized with my temperament. Henry Joachim had been sent as a messenger; through him my Master had found me.

Faith healing did not help my neuralgia at all but Mr Hamblin's message began a change in my life, slow and imperceptible as it had to be. Each subsequent attack again made me lose hope, but at last I accepted my affliction as chronic and was only too grateful that a drug had been found which could alleviate the pain. I even came to regard it in the light of a blessing without which I might have still remained in the dark.

Positive thinking gradually informed my life and I decided to take a few

Edgar Degas, *Danseuses*. Private collection

Amedeo Modigliani, *Caryatide*. Private collection

Henri Hayden, *Still Life with Bass and Glass*. Private collection

Auguste Rodin, *Balzac*. Formerly Kodak, present owner unknown

Charles Despiau, *Serene Head*. Johannesburg Art Gallery

Josef Herman, *A Short Respite*. Private collection

Jean Baptiste Carpeaux, *Wild Horses*. Private collection

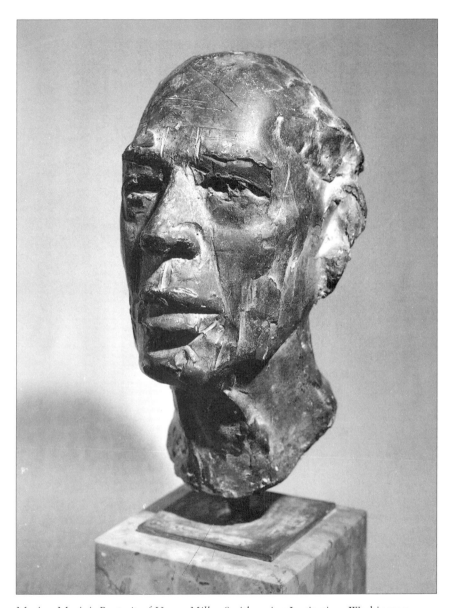

Marino Marini, *Portrait of Henry Miller.* Smithsonian Institution, Washington

Walter Sickert, *Portrait of Israel Zangwill*. Scottish National Gallery of
Modern Art, Edinburgh

practical steps to bring some companionship and more material comfort into the emptiness which pervaded my home. My first aim was a house-keeper and Willy appeared, loyally to remain for some twenty-four years; then, with someone to look after it while I was at work, I would set about getting a dog. Since leaving South Africa I had not had a pet, and as animals had played such a large part in my life, I missed them tremendously and felt incomplete.

Jokingly, I would prophesy, but to myself, that when I had got thus far with my plan, then a husband might appear to complete the *ménage*, and this was exactly what happened. I was no longer striving or feeling sorry for myself since I had counted my blessings and knew I was lucky. I had many dear friends; work that I loved, which fully absorbed me and was fruitful enough to let me live as I pleased; I also enjoyed a very strong constitution. No one has everything, I told myelf, and if the right partner should never appear, I would still be content. Deep down inside me I felt truly joyous. I had had a glimpse of inner serenity.

In this happy state of trustfully floating downstream, I met and one year later married Sidney Lines.

It was indeed strange we had not met before as we had mutual friends and might easily have gathered in one of their homes. From them I had learned of his wife's recent death – tragically sudden after a dinner party – and how wonderfully bravely Sidney had borne it.

Robin Fox had asked me to organize a Sickert exhibition as one of the events of the Sussex Festival season of which he was honorary secretary for 1962. I had never met this eminent theatrical agent but was rather curious to do so as my mother had been intimate with Robin's family in London and often used to talk about them. Moreover, his aunt, the actress Lily Hanbury, who was famed for her beauty and adored by my mother, had been one of my godmothers. Just at this time, Robin's wife Angela and I were both invited by Nora Littler to stay at her villa in Cannes. During the visit Angela and I became friends, and so when the festival opened in Brighton with a gala dinner in the Pavilion, the Foxes asked me to spend the weekend with them when we would go to the dinner together. There I was introduced to an extremely tall and good-looking man whose face, aglow with the broadest of smiles, effectively belied the grievous loss he had sustained only two months before. I was deeply impressed by Sidney's courage, but I cannot pretend this was some *coup de foudre*, for marriage was far from our thoughts. I had made peace with living alone while he, having treasured twenty-four years of happiness, reckoned that no man could expect any more.

There were still many years of physical suffering before me but now I had Sidney as a great comfort. The day after our wedding I was struck down again and he tells wryly how his honeymoon present to me was a mincer because I was unable to chew any food.

The turning point came when we were in Hong Kong where I travelled with him on one of his long business trips. On the advice of his staff I tried acupuncture again – I had already had abortive treatments in London – this time with the most eminent Chinese professor. This elderly man with the quiet smile of the Buddha changed the whole course of my trouble by eliminating the alarming fear which brought on and worsened every attack. Back in London I was lucky enough to find two excellent women practitioners and they, with my occasional use of the only effective drug, made it possible to live with this agonizing affliction. Today, after more than forty years, I can, with inexpressible gratitude, say that the worst of this disorder is behind me.

I may have dwelt upon this subject too long. On one level my illness was a curse, but it turned out to be an inestimable blessing, and I could not try to paint my own portrait without bringing it in and out of my story.

Part Five

Roland, Browse & Delbanco

The rise and fall of London as art centre

I believe it is true to say that Roland, Browse & Delbanco's most fertile years were those up to the early sixties. By that time the seeds of revolution had germinated and were lustily growing in the aesthetic as well as the commercial soil of the art world. Around the year 1955, mainly because Sotheby's had become so lively under the brilliant guidance of Peter Wilson, the centre of the art market moved from Paris to London, as I have said. The days gradually passed when it was necessary to go to Paris three or four times during the year in order to buy French pictures for stock. Normally two partners went on these trips, the third being left to look after the gallery, and we took them when possible in careful rotation, for apart from the 'finds' we were able to make, the visits were fun on a personal level. It was such a pleasure to zigzag one's way up and down the narrow streets of the Left Bank; to see what was on offer in the numerous small galleries; to pop into favourite dealers for a chat and an *apéritif* – sometimes to lunch in their pet *bistros* – and always to discuss or buy a painting, a drawing or a piece of sculpture with someone whose knowledge commanded respect.

The detonator of the huge price explosion was the sale of Impressionists from the Goldschmidt collection that Sotheby's held in 1958. From that moment, the art market changed and ethically not for the better. Against the new range of prices connoisseurs and art lovers stood little chance of buying, for investors had sensed the spectacular scope of gambling in an entirely new area. Sotheby's continued to rule over this market with its centre remaining in London, but when the firm bought Parke-Bernet of New York, in spite of Peter Wilson's protestations, the centre of the Impressionist and Post-Impressionist market inevitably moved to New York. The best of these pictures had come from the States to be put up to auction in tax-free London but as the majority of buyers were the rich from

America – dealers, private people and well-endowed museums – it was indeed senseless to import these works only to send them back after the sale. The Japanese too had entered the field and whether they journeyed to New York or London was a matter of indifference to them; therefore London was fobbed off with trivial French sales, although there are occasional exceptions.

By 1950 the United States had assumed a new role through the onslaught of Abstract Expressionism. For the very first time America took the lead in the development of Western pictorial art whose non-objective form had, many years earlier, already been pioneered by Kandinsky. This esoteric movement, which swept all before it in the country that was the first to accept it widely, shattered the concept of traditional standards, thus opening the flood gates to the stream of indulgence that has informed the succeeding 'isms'. English taste on the whole is far from receptive to pictorial aspects which seem to deny as their basis a recognizable human experience. Nor for that matter does it take very kindly to overtly theoretical manifestations. The Cubists, for instance, with their stress upon form at the expense of both light and colour, have never met with general approval in the United Kingdom. But whereas these artists evolved their expression with carefully considered control, the Abstract Expressionists threw their caps to the winds, obeying none of the canons to which art, through the ages, has in varying ways paid its homage. Once the barriers were down all hell was let loose and we now have the situation that 'anything goes'. Still much in favour are ludicrous objects which may claim to be neither painting nor sculpture, as well as transient, private happenings, the conceit of whose perpetrators renders one speechless.

There had to come a swing in the opposite direction despite the forebodings of a few pessimists that 'easel painting' was a thing of the past, and there is evidence that this is so. The dissenters, as is normal, have gone to the other extreme with often tame, hyper-realistic canvases. But this is a beginning, a small sign of hope that sanity may be returning. It would seem that all avenues have been explored and that Picasso had the last word. But art, like life, is full of surprises and a Phoenix, one day, may arise out of the ashes. Meanwhile a number of really good painters, though of their time, have kept to the mainstream; they have been neglected and are still largely ignored by the 'élite' but fortunately not by a new generation of art lovers.

The excitement aroused by the Abstract Expressionists admittedly made much else appear dull. The painters being the rage in the States commanded prices as enormous as their canvases, and Sotheby's, alive to every fresh chance, cashed-in in New York once again.

Before the spectacular rise of the Impressionists, Christie's had held all the main picture auctions which, as I have said, had comprised exclusively old masters, but with the popularity of the later French schools they could not afford to neglect such a market and so they were forced to try to compete. A huge effort was needed as much ground had been lost to Sotheby's but, contrary to general expectation, their challenge succeeded and they are now running neck and neck with their rivals. The last to awaken out of its torpor was Phillips (formerly Phillips, Son & Neale) whose import, still minor but gradually growing, may yet constitute a break in the monopoly.

The two powerful firms who seize every occasion of spreading their tentacles have played Tweedledum and Tweedledee with each other, much to the diversion of those in the trade. When one makes a move the other responds, although Sotheby's has usually been the innovator. Each has a grand emporium in New York and now in many other parts of the world; and has instituted the holding of important sales in the evening at which the auctioneers sport evening dress as do some of the 'audience'. Such sessions are worked up to present an 'event' approaching the exclusivity of a charity *première*: the preview is by invitation, champagne is served in the flower-bedecked galleries and frequently television cameras are present. When both auction houses, just 'by chance', simultaneously introduced a buyers' commission against strong opposition from the trade, Christie's tried to steal a march over Sotheby's by reducing the ten per cent charge to eight; today they are equal at a higher level.

One of the most amusing changes in sale-room fashion is the advent of the Victorians, caused no doubt by the ever-growing dearth of fine French paintings of the nineteenth and early twentieth century. Christie's would formerly have offered such 'minor' works in their Monday sales – they would never have been allowed to enter the hallowed doors of King Street on a Friday – while Sotheby's, with their accent on books, did not touch them at all. I have not made any definite calculation but I would say that a large proportion of picture sales now held by the two firms in New York as well as in London, comprise Pre-Raphaelites and other artists of the same period. They are no longer untouchables but highly prized. When this flow has been exhausted one wonders what next – real estate, antique motor-cars, garden furniture, even personal belongings of the rich and notorious have all now become grist to their mill.

Having usurped the art dealers' function by wooing and capturing private buyers and sellers, these famed auctioneers found themselves placed in an unaccustomed and awkward position. In the days when they catered exclusively for the trade, no guarantees had been necessary. Their clients, being dealers, were fully responsible; they took their own risks, backed their own judgement with their own money and were fully accountable to their own clients. But a private person buying at auction could not be expected to spend thousands of pounds without some assurance of authenticity, so in came the system of 'expert' advice, without which no work by any known name would be accepted for sale. This system has led to uncomfortable situations which have been settled as quietly as possible, for the 'expert', being human, can sometimes be wrong!

The power given to 'experts' is too often unwarranted, for although there are naturally fine serious scholars among them who also have a feeling for quality, there are equally those who frankly rely upon nothing but provenance, as well as others who, upon the strength of one monograph, however superficial, have become classed as 'specialists'. In my experience, among the least reliable are frequently members of the artist's own family. Because they still bear the enchanted name, it is taken for granted that their word is law even though their knowledge is minimal.

I have no feud against the two major sale rooms with whom I have always been on excellent terms, but there is some resentment against them both among scholars and in the trade. I do not pretend that every art dealer is without reproach: that would be nonsense and would never be credited, for the art trade is tricky and by its nature lends itself readily to shady, if not downright dishonest, practices. Clients, except the few who are knowledgeable enough to judge for themselves, are entirely in the hands of their dealers; the relationship is one based on trust. Probity, therefore, is the first essential, not only in commercial ethics but also in scholarship. It is easier for individual galleries to ensure this level of conduct than for the big corporate firms.

I am occasionally consulted by Christie's and Sotheby's when the work of an artist, upon whom I have concentrated, poses a problem to them. Sometimes it is clear-cut and there is no need for hesitation; but when I am doubtful I can only advise that I myself would not touch the picture. It is then up to them what they choose to do. There are always enigmas such as works that are painted in the manner of somebody else, experimental essays that may be just as atypical as the works of an artist's youth often are: all are equally difficult to attribute with certainty. I once turned down three early panels by Sickert which Roland had bought in Paris. Apart from their obvious derivation from Whistler, they were otherwise anonymous and might have been painted by Roussel or Maitland. But as their provenance turned out to be flawless, I had made a mistake and I had to eat my words.

On one occasion I personally suffered from the same kind of unfortunate mistake having been made in the past. Roland, Browse & Delbanco had sold a most beautiful Whistler, *Symphony in Red*, to a friend and well-known small collector. I had fallen in love with this bewitching painting and had asked John Bryson, the purchaser, to let me have first refusal if he ever needed to sell it. Some years had passed when he honoured his word and his price was 2,000 guineas. As this sum represented a great deal to me, I consulted Colnaghi's, who had handled much of Whistler's work and were better acquainted with its current value. A former director, who was then long since dead, had kept careful and detailed records on Whistler. To my dismay his notes revealed that he had had doubts about this very picture. Neither I nor my partners had had any qualms and had sold it without hesitation, but Colnaghi's were famed for their knowledge and honour and so I could not lightly dismiss what they had told me. Despite my own certainty I dared not take the risk for if, in my turn, I was forced to a sale, I would have had to disclose this dubious assessment with a result that was not hard to guess. Sadly, I felt obliged to renounce my claim on the painting. Today it hangs in the Boston Museum of Fine Art and its authenticity has never again been questioned. I quote this small story simply to illustrate how mistakes may be made by the most upright, informed and well-intentioned advisers.

It must be said that the auction rooms, Christie's and Sotheby's in particular, have contributed greatly to the wide if indiscriminate interest that art now enjoys, and whose growth did not begin until after the Second World War. It is only a pity that the role they have played should all too often have had the effect of reducing art works to the level of share certificates. Quite understandably, buyers are attracted to their cleverly publicized auctions, for they not only offer an enormous variety, far in excess of that of a dealer, but an element of glamour is, for some reason, attached – a kind of kudos that is linked with their sales. Uncertain buyers feel reassured that around them are others who covet the same item. But I wonder if they realize that the spirit of competition may induce them to pay a much higher figure than they would ever contemplate in a gallery. It is amusing to observe that the proverbial ditherers, who at a dealer's can never make up their minds, must, in an auction, decide on the spot. The hammer waits for no one.

The majority of pictures sold at top prices – millions of pounds are now commonplace – go to a handful of billionaire buyers, the Getty Museum, an occasional public gallery who may, with difficulty, scrape the money together, or the odd dealer acting on behalf of a client. Smaller firms find it impossible to compete at prices that have soared so high, so that without some fairly strong financial backing they have to be content with a much reduced stock.

Because it is such big business, art has attained an unprecedented media value: the most notorious sales are shown on television and record prices are headlined in the press. A typical caption that years ago started the ball rolling concerned a painter of little artistic value. It announced '£66,000 record for a Laura Knight' (when she was alive the painting would hardly have fetched £6,000). Journalists, always alive to sensation, are equally pleased when they sense a fall. Today there are even publications, akin to those recording the value of secondhand cars, which print the current prices that individual 'big names' should fetch according to their size, subject and date – quality does not seem to matter. (I regard these publications as thoroughly offensive.) Fortunately, however, there is some coverage, un-related to price, in the more serious journals. Important public exhibitions are usually reviewed and given generous space, but sadly – and probably because there is a plethora of them – dealers' shows by living artists are practically ignored.

I was once asked by the *Economist* to write on the subject of investment in paintings. When the article was written I found that the words allowed to me were mostly taken up in condemnation of the current situation, an attitude eminently unsuited to this journal. I realized that it was not at all what they wanted but there it was and honestly written, so I duly sent it off to the editor. Needless to say, I never heard any more: the article must have landed in the dustbin.

As Roland, Browse & Delbanco was independent, and therefore modest, we happily had few downright investors as clients but many smaller buyers instead who really loved painting, and whose every purchase constituted a thrill. Their interest and knowledge had been encouraged and advanced by the growing number of art exhibitions of all kinds and periods, of which the superb Royal Academy winter exhibitions used to be unique – since the war there are also those of the National Gallery, the Arts Council, the Tate and other national museums. The latest of these exhibition galleries is the Barbican and though it may be churlish to have reservations, we are in danger of seeing too great a plethora of shows whose artistic worth is not inexhaustible. In my opinion the Barbican is *de trop* – the Hayward would have been more than sufficient – while the museums themselves are com-pelled to launch shows in the hope that they might augment their impover-ished exchequers and keep their institutions lively. I well remember being asked by a taxi driver where the National Gallery was – today such a query could not arise.

Roland, Browse & Delbanco and the avant-garde

As time progressed we sold less and less to museums. The rising price of old masters caused us to give up buying them and limit ourselves, as we had originally intended, to the more recent schools, while the twentieth-century artists whom we favoured had, by this time, become well represented in most of the public galleries. Abstract Expressionism and all that followed having swept into fashion, museum directors, with justification, wished to bring their modern collections up to date. In my view, they reacted too strongly for, in paying tribute to present history, they surrendered their judgement and became addicted to changes of style. They have fallen for objects that are often intriguing and quite entertaining, but ridiculous when taken too seriously. At the end of a tour of some splendid art gallery in which high quality is the rule, such objects come as a shock, a mocking conceit, and further acquaintance does not make them acceptable.

Our trio of dealers could not support them and accordingly we suffered, since the market was buoyant and some dealers seized the opportunity of doing good business through work that we shunned. Rightly or wrongly we stuck to our guns, an old-fashioned gallery by contemporary standards. But I suppose that it was some kind of integrity which would not let us profit by what we did not believe in. It was not comfortable to be out of step with trends that were so widely accepted. However, as from the start we had vowed to be 'our own men' , there was no other course we could follow. One should never suspect the motives of others because of one's own in-ability to conform, but I cannot help feeling that there are far too many art historians, critics and also buyers who will support any movement or indi-vidual artist because they are fearful of not being 'with it', as well as some dealers, without personal aesthetic standards, who follow wherever com-mercial advantage may lead them.

Discoveries and revivals: O'Conor, Rodin etc.

During the years 1950 to 1960, Roland, Browse & Delbanco presented some interesting, even notable, first one-man exhibitions in England. Constant Permeke, whose show was organized in collaboration with the Belgian Ministry of Education, was, next to James Ensor, the most im-pressive figure in contemporary Belgian art. This exhibition was mainly disinterested as nearly all the exhibits were lent and not for sale. Two other artists whose reputations we hoped to establish in England were Hayden and Marcoussis, both of whom were born in Warsaw and left it to work in Paris in the first decade of this century. Marcoussis was an early adherent of the Cubist Movement, while both he and Hayden were among the group of young foreigners who formed, with their French contemporaries, the phalanx of what was later to be termed l'Ecole de Paris.

Roderic O'Conor, the Irish painter who worked in France, was an ex-citing discovery and quite the most important we made. Until we launched his first English exhibition, his paintings remained virtually unknown, and we were able to buy many of them at the sale of his studio in France. Financially independent, he had neither the need nor the desire to exhibit his work, for he was said to have disliked art dealers; he did, however, show occasional canvases in various group shows, being one of the early members of the Salon d'Automne and of Les Indépendents. He broke his rule with regard to dealers when in 1937 he exhibited fifteen pictures at the Galerie Bonaparte in Paris. Having been no more than a name to a few, on account of a mention in Clive Bell's memoirs, he now takes his place among the most noteworthy artists in the circle of Gauguin at Pont Aven.

It was still worth subscribing to sale catalogues from Paris when, in 1956, one from the Hôtel Drouot caught our eye. The catalogue stated that upon the recent death of Mme O'Conor – O'Conor himself had died sixteen years earlier – the contents of his studio were to come up for sale, an announcement which intrigued us considerably. One never knows what treasures might be found in an artist's *atelier*, especially one with O'Conor's background and as withdrawn and mysterious as he; and so Roland went to Paris with *carte blanche* to buy all the paintings he thought had quality, regardless of how many there might be. We did not fear that he would be over-committed for such an unknown would not fetch high prices.

Roland bought something like fifty oil paintings whose arrival we awaited with tremendous expectancy. Great was the excitement when they finally arrived and as the cases were opened we inspected the haul. It was clear that, artistically, we had made a *coup*. How financially successful it would be we could only guess, but as the inaugural show would be in the nature of a 'feeler' we decided to link it with Matthew Smith as a draw. We put Matthew's exhibition on the upstairs floor so that everyone would have to pass through the O'Conors before they could see the Matthew Smiths. Combining the two made some sense for Matthew was one of the few in the United Kingdom who had known and admired O'Conor; there was also a painterly affinity between them, so much so that Matthew swore it was he who had painted one of O'Conor's *Nudes*, although in style and in subject he did not relate to him until some twenty years afterwards.

The exhibition roused considerable interest, not least among members of O'Conor's family, several of whom came over from Ireland especially to see the show. They had each inherited a small sum of money from the uncle whom none of them had ever seen and whose work was equally unfamiliar. From this exhibition and those that followed, the Tate and the Museum of Modern Art in New York acquired their first examples, as did the Scottish National Gallery of Modern Art and some of our provincial museums, also those in Australia and New Zealand. Private buyers gradually became interested and one New York dealer, as enthusiastic as ourselves, bought some of the finest examples for dispersal among his clients in the States.

Jean François Millet, *Peasant Girl Resting*. Private collection

The first really large comprehensive exhibition of O'Conor's work was held at the Barbican Art Gallery in London in 1985. Paintings came from as far as New Zealand as well as a few from the States and what made the show especially interesting was the inclusion of a number of his lively drawings. By 1971 Roland, Browse & Delbanco had already made five one-man exhibitions, so we were the acknowledged dealers in O'Conor. It was therefore not surprising that among the ninety paintings on show at the Barbican no less than forty had passed through our hands.

When the partners gathered over coffee or afternoon tea we used to compare notes on the shows we had seen, or hold long discussions on painting which at times could be surprisingly argumentative. During our conversations we found ourselves returning to the neglect from which Rodin had suffered since his death in 1917 at the height of his fame, and all of us wanted to rectify it. If we were to stage a show by the great sculptor we would have to seek the collaboration of the Musée Rodin in Paris, the only source of Rodin bronzes. The sculptor's huge private collection of works of art as well as the vast number of his bronzes, plaster casts, terra-cottas, drawings etc. was given by him to the French State on the understanding that all would be housed in Rodin's home at Meudon and the Hôtel Biron in Paris, the latter being loaned to him for the rest of his life. It was officially decided that the Musée Rodin could make twelve bronzes from every cast they thought desirable, a rule that is strictly adhered to. The trouble was that we had never met Mme Goldscheider, the director, who had the reputation of being unapproachable. Then came the news that the Tate were raising funds to buy Rodin's large marble, *Le Baiser*, which they had had on loan for the past fourteen years. Through this situation we saw a chance to set up a rapport with Mme Goldscheider. We knew that Sir John Rothenstein was on good terms with her and so we evolved a disingenuous scheme: if the Musée would let us have a Rodin exhibition, we would devote the proceeds of the sale of our catalogues towards the Tate's purchase while giving publicity to their appeal. Our plan was disingenuous because we did not think the Tate should buy this dull piece of sculpture. The big marble version, enlarged by Turcan, Rodin's *practicien*, is lacking in tension and vitality, an assessment endorsed by Rodin himself who considered the marble to be 'soft'. Feeling slightly hypocritical, although our goal was deserving, we sought Sir John as an ally; through his good offices a show was arranged with Mme Goldscheider's enthusiastic help. It is difficult to believe now that we were taking a chance but this was indeed the fact: sculpture in general was still looked at askance and Rodin, through contemporary eyes, was seen as *démodé*.

In 1953 we held our Rodin exhibition, the first for twenty-two years; nobody knew just what to expect but all were surprised to find it so beautiful. As our gallery did not have room to show any large bronzes, we kept to the medium-sized and tiny pieces – the latter were hardly known to exist. There were figures and studies brimming with freshness whose vitality served to give a glimpse of the master and compensated for the absence of monumental groups. Among the small bronzes initially shown were the first five of the series of *Danseuses*; some little heads from the *Burghers of Calais* and various sculptures of hands both healthy and deformed, the study of which had so interested Rodin.

Artistically the show was an enormous success but the sales at the time were modest: visitors, though attracted, were still hesitant and even the *Danseuses*, today the most coveted of all the small pieces, were not snapped up, although they were priced at £350 – even then a modest amount. Now some of the *Danseuses* fetch a hundred times that sum but they are rarely available; those who missed buying are kicking themselves. But this is the usual story.

Quite soon after our initial show, Kurt Valentin, the perspicacious American dealer, presented a similar one in New York; the ice had been broken, Rodin began to re-emerge at last and to be valued as one of the world's greatest sculptors. As a result of our efforts during the ensuing years, enhanced by those of Kurt Valentin, the Musée Rodin refurbished itself, a 'face-lift' that was badly needed. Cécile Goldscheider was so grati-fied by the turn of events that, unofficially, we were appointed the agents for Rodin in the United Kingdom, and until the museum had exhausted its total of castings of the smaller pieces we wanted to show, we continued to make these important exhibitions.

One morning when I went to the Musée Rodin where I had an appoint-ment with Cécile, I found this highly intelligent, very reserved woman in a state of unusual excitement. She mysteriously produced for my inspection a tiny, explosive figure in plaster and carefully passing it into my hands asked me if I knew what it was. Hardly giving me time to reply and know-ing how thrilled I would be, she divulged the secret I had half guessed – it was *Nijinsky* by Rodin. For years the moulds for it had lain in a drawer alongside other numerous fragments, but anyone who has followed the complications of casting knows how difficult it is to envisage the positive (the cast) from seeing no more than the shells of the negative (the mould). These two were diminutive and very intricate so no one had paid them any attention, but when our demand for small pieces increased and everything was examined more closely, *Nijinsky* was discovered and then cast in bronze.

It is well known that Rodin had championed Nijinsky when, in 1912, the dancer's final curtain in *L'Après-Midi d'un Faune* had scandalized Paris audiences and enraged squeamish critics on account of its 'bestial eroticism', and that the eulogy, which Rodin wrote for *Le Matin*, was said to have prompted Diaghilev and Nijinsky to go to the studio to thank him. The great dancer then went on subsequent visits and Rodin did drawings of him in the nude, but as no mention was made of any sculpture, its existence remained completely unknown until shortly before I called on Cécile. *Nijinsky* was shown in our next exhibition and we felt privileged to be the first to introduce this little treasure to the public.

The bronze has come to be known as *Nijinsky in L'Après-Midi d'un Faune* though I have never been happy about the identification. This beautiful ballet, choreographed by Nijinsky, was conceived in a two-dimensional form, echoing that of a frieze. The arms of the dancers take angular positions and like the heads and also the feet they are placed in profile as on Greek vases and frescoes, while movements are made with jerky abruptness. All is quiet and contained, full of subtle nuances, as the performers dance in a leisurely way to Debussy's haunting score, whereas Rodin's *Nijinsky* is overflowing with vigour. I felt as I handled this magnetic atom, this tiny embodiment of pent-up energy, that at any given moment it might dart from my grasp like a tightly curled spring just released. The mood of the bronze with its imprisoned power is far more suggestive of the fierce Polovtsian warriors from the *Prince Igor* suite, although as Nijinsky never performed in this 'ballet' I do not suggest it as a title. I think it is most likely that Rodin just seized a moment, and made mental notes, while the dancer darted freely about in his studio. This was his practice with his female models. As far as I know there is no drawing for the bronze and only one for any of the *Danseuses*, namely the first, *Danseuse A*. Rodin must have had an acutely retentive eye.

In a Rodin exhibition in the summer of 1956 we were showing the big cast of the *Danseuse A*, the single one of the series that was enlarged. I desperately wanted this piece for myself, not only because I thought it so fine but because the subject was nostalgic for me. It would also provide a fascinating foil to the *Danseuse* by Degas I already had – the latter in a classical, static position, the other one in a free movement – a pose quite impossible to hold without aid. The price of the bronze was £2,000 but as I could not spare such a sum, it seemed I would have to renounce it.

During the time when I was a critic I had noticed a tall, handsome young man who attended all the Opera House ballet *premières*, gallantly manoeuvring the stairs to the stalls despite his two artificial legs. He managed this feat with the aid of two sticks which frequently pinned my long dress to the ground whenever I was in his near vicinity – evening dress and black ties being the norm at Covent Garden *premières* especially for those who sat in the stalls. I had not seen him for two or three years, being no longer a regular attender at Covent Garden, when suddenly one morning he appeared at the gallery during the run of a Rodin show. He spent such a long time examining the sculptures, ascending and descending our difficult stairs and obviously making comparisons, that I became fascinated by his obvious enthusiasm and could not resist approaching him. We quickly got into a long conversation during which he decided upon the bronzes to buy; I told him, on my side, of the piece that I coveted and how I had made an unusual but abortive attempt to secure it. Although never a gambler, especially not on horses of which I had seen enough in my childhood, I had made an exception in this single instance and had staked a small sum on a Derby outsider, which, as far as I knew, was still running.

Just two weeks later a letter arrived for me marked 'Strictly Personal'; it was from Robin Howard, for such was his name, a name now honoured all over the dance world for the magnificent service that he rendered to the development of British Contemporary Dance, and to which he devoted his life and his fortune. While I do not have Robin's letter before me, its contents will ever remain in my mind; it ran '... I do not know if you were serious about wanting *Danseuse A*, neither do I know if you were just giving me sales talk. What I do know is that no one should have this bronze rather than you, and while I will not offer to give it to you, I will, if you allow me, pay for it now and you shall refund me whenever you can.' And this marvellous suggestion was from a complete stranger! It was just as unexpected as Hugo's had been when he put up a 'little capital' to help me finance the gallery – small wonder that I believe in the essential kindness of man.

I accepted Robin's offer in the spirit it was made, for who could have refused such a generous offer. But I doubt whether I would have been able to accept had I not known that I could repay him. Soon after this episode I lost touch with him, but many years later when we met again and I reminded him of his charming gesture, a look of surprise came over his face – he had forgotten all about it.

Since the growing demand for Rodin bronzes has caused their prices to rise – and in comparison with other sculptures they are still far too low – many false pieces may be seen in the sale rooms mainly stamped 'Alexis Rudier, fondeur'. These are the casts that have become the most favoured because it is erroneously thought that, as they bear the name of Alexis, who was Rodin's near contemporary, they must have been cast during the sculptor's lifetime and therefore under his supervision. This is a fallacy for the foundry continued under that name for thirty-five years after Rodin had died, when it was changed to 'Georges Rudier'. While I was writing the first draft of this book in 1987, for the first time, two wrong casts of the *Nijinsky* were offered for sale, and in the hope of protecting this unique piece, I wrote a short article highlighting the danger, which was published in the *Burlington Magazine*. Probably with justification, we felt that we knew more about Rodin bronzes than anyone else in the country; we had handled a very great number of them and consequently had got their 'feel'. False bronzes are those cast from other bronzes instead of from the original plaster, and although there are various tests to be made, none is really conclusive. The thickness of cast is rather vague, variations of size are difficult to measure, especially on a very small scale, while the seam which Rodin liked to be evident can, without doubt, also be left.

When Peter Wilson was still its Chairman, Sotheby's announced in one of their catalogues that a group of small Rodins were to come up for sale. As we were suspicious, we decided that we would examine them separately for fear that otherwise we might influence each other. When back at the gallery we compared notes and we found that we were in exact agreement as to which pieces were false – less than half of the bronzes had passed our scrutiny – and as we felt a certain responsibility *vis-à-vis* the Rodin market, we decided we ought to let Sotheby's know our opinion. Peter Wilson immediately called a meeting and, in view of our serious apprehension, it was decided to invite Georges Rudier, the current owner of the famous foundry, to come over from Paris to give his own judgement. He was therefore present at our second meeting when he also condemned four of the bronzes, but that still left a couple in abeyance. Peter then asked if we were satisfied but I had to reply that, personally, I was not. With his genius for diplomacy he found a solution: he would announce before selling that this and this piece had been doubted and if any would-be purchaser would feel more secure, he would send the bronzes in question to the Rodin museum for their unbiased adjudication. I had never before heard any auctioneer make such an announcement from the rostrum, but Peter was as good as his word and his behaviour, in the circumstances, could not have been more correct. That was the last time our gallery made any protest although there were, and still are, occasions to do so.

Balzac at Hemel Hempstead

One Rodin affair, which at first seemed a triumph, has since caused me nothing but frustration. Sidney, who, at the time, was a senior director of Wiggins Teape, the company specializing in the production of fine paper, had introduced me to one of his business associates, himself the head of Kodak in England. Norman Brick, a high-spirited and impish man, had started his career on the shop-floor of his firm and had risen to his high position entirely through hard work and flair. No respecter of hierarchy, forthright in speech, he is wonderfully refreshing in his enjoyment of life, and above all in his lack of pretentiousness. We both liked him enormously and when he came to our home he found our pictures so much to his taste that he asked me to help him form his own small collection.

When Kodak were moving to new premises at Hemel Hempstead, Norman persuaded his board that they should have some good paintings with which to embellish their more important rooms and, as he usually got his own way, I was entrusted to buy these and, backed by a not inconsiderable sum, was given *carte blanche* to select as I pleased. Having accumulated a nice group of contemporary paintings I still had an appreciable amount in hand when the idea suddenly entered my head that this might be an opportunity to redress an omission that for long I had felt was lamentable. Although Rodin was well represented in our museums, there was no *Balzac* in England; I knew that two casts of this famous masterpiece could still be made out of the limited twelve, and although my assignment did not include sculpture, I suggested to Norman how grand *Balzac* would look in Kodak's gardens which were then being planned. Neither of us could think of any connection between the great writer and photography which might be used as a reason, but Norman agreed that it should be purchased and, through his insistence, his colleagues consented, though I very much doubt if they knew Rodin's name. Cast No. 11 was then put in hand – No. 12 soon after went to Japan – and I felt I had achieved something of value in that the great piece would come to this country, and only just in time. I held detailed discussions with the architect gardener as to how and where it was to be placed, for it needed a screen of trees and thick shrubs to mask the hideous background.

The great day came when it was due to arrive – I had asked Henry Moore if he could be on the spot when the case was unpacked, and before the crane lifted its noble content on to its permanent site. He would advise in which direction to place it for the sun to strike it most advantageously. Henry was horrified when he saw the, as yet, unplanted area, barren and grim against the window-pitted architecture. The other views from the site were equally ugly – a filling-station and a roundabout along which incessant traffic was circulating. 'I would never allow one of my sculptures to stand in so awful a place,' he declared discouragingly, but I was still confident that, after a few years of growth, the greenery would hide all the unsightliness and form a bower which would embrace *Balzac* and set him off very well. How wrong I was!

Norman, by this time, had been promoted to the chairmanship of Europe and had no further say in the matter; he could not be present at the unveiling and no other director thought it worthwhile to attend, nor any of the press whom I had alerted. It is not every day that the world's greatest sculptor takes the trouble to drive for an hour or so to site a masterpiece of the past. The occasion, which should have been an important ceremony, passed by as a non-event. Henry went back on his cross-country home journey without an official to thank him; he had given so much of his precious time and nobody had had sufficient courtesy even to offer him a cup of tea. I felt quite ashamed that I had troubled him.

With Norman away, none of our carefully laid plans for the planting were ever fulfilled; on the contrary, the site was even worse than before with transport being considered more important than art. Most of the area which was meant to be landscaped had been turned over to parking, and *Balzac* stood lonesome, diminished in scale, an incongruous afterthought in a factory setting. I doubt if he received one passing glance from his owners or anybody who passed by daily.

The monument was starred in the Rodin exhibition at the Hayward Gallery in 1986, a fact that should have made even Kodak's directors aware of the importance of the sculpture they owned and that it should be treated accordingly. During the exhibition Sidney and I overheard a woman visitor say that she wondered how a firm like Kodak had come to acquire such a piece. Her remark implied as much surprise as if she had known that the Board comprised only philistines; I longed to tell her how right she was and how very much I regretted the sale. My hope was that one day *Balzac* would be rescued and placed in appreciative, fitting surroundings, for I could not help feeling it could be bought at a price – a price well in excess of its cost – for its owners, even though they thought nothing of it aesthetically, would make quite sure of its current price. Now my fond hopes had been dashed to the ground for after its *réclame* at the Hayward exhibition Kodak had obviously received a fine offer – probably from America or perhaps Japan – and the famous piece was to leave England for good. This was the only bitter happening in the whole of my career in the art world. I had thought that I had done something of real worth for my country by bringing to it a world-famed piece of sculpture: now it was to depart for ever and there was no redress. I contacted Nick Serota at the Tate in the hope of stopping its export since we had reason to believe it had not already left (I even offered to head the list of potential buyers myself), but he reminded me that there was nothing to be done for the sculpture had not been in the country for the necessary period of fifty years.

Although good sales were obviously welcome there have been other occasions when, in retrospect, I have equally regretted a particular transaction. At the time the buyer professed great excitement and apparently loved the work in question just as much as I did myself, but several years later when its price had risen, and although they were rich enough not to need the money, the profit proved far too tempting and the great treasure was surrendered. Greed once again won the day. We often used to say we were bad art dealers because we were too fond of painting; but we would act in the same way again because dealing in art is something special and totally unlike any other form of commerce.

Sickert again

In 1953 I organized a Sickert exhibition for the Scottish Arts Council in Edinburgh; and as 1961 was his centenary year, the Arts Council in London celebrated the occasion with a large show at the Tate Gallery, which again I was asked to organize. Agnew's and ourselves, among the art dealers, also presented good centenary shows. These three events, taking place simultaneously and each comprising fine pictures, were evidence of the richness of Sickert's large output, and of his unceasing application. Preceding that time, I was more than usually immersed in the study of my favourite English artist, for with his centenary looming ahead, I was preparing my second book on his work – far better I hope and certainly more informative than my first somewhat amateurish effort. The volume on this occasion was published by Rupert Hart-Davis, beautifully produced as always, and if the excellent colour-blocks had not been mislaid when, sadly, the firm changed hands, I believe that a reprint would go very well, as its second-hand price is sufficiently high to suggest it is still in demand.

A quite different volume that has since superseded it is Wendy Baron's big reference book* (not a *catalogue raisonné*); its patient erudition far surpasses mine but we two have never been in conflict. Wendy's interest in Sickert had originally been fired by one of the shows in our gallery, and for her doctorate she wrote her thesis on him, which she developed into her book. We refer to ourselves as 'Sickert's two ladies', a designation, considering his *penchant* for women, I think he might well have approved; while G., with the teasing he could seldom resist, said that Sickert was awaiting my arrival in heaven to thank me for my hard work on his account.

There is a third woman who should not be forgotten and who was every bit as devoted; she had the advantage of knowing Sickert intimately – an adverb I use without the slightest undertone. Having met him on the top of a bus when she was still an art student, she took, in 1917, a small studio in Fitzroy Street which happened to be in the same building as his and thereafter she encountered him frequently. I am referring to Miss Marjorie Lilly, a quietly enthusiastic and modest woman, whose delightful *Sickert:*

* Wendy Baron, *Sickert*, Phaidon, 1973.

the Painter and his Circle* gives a first-hand description of his working methods as well as his approach to teaching: the kind of insight that only a fellow artist may impart. She lived just long enough to see her book published for she had fought against ill-health for many years and died within weeks of its appearance.

Scottish artists at the gallery

In the sixties the gallery was still full of vigour: we launched exhibitions by various sculptors including a few from abroad. Among the latter was Emilio Greco who had never exhibited outside Italy, where, with Marini and Manzù, he was the most prized. The Japanese, too, thought highly of him and devoted an area in a public garden exclusively to his bronzes; but in London he met with only slender approval, the main condemnation being his elegance at a time when such a quality was 'old hat'. A few years ago I suddenly came upon a quite large, beautiful bronze of a *Bather* by Greco that had been erected in Carlos Place, the gift of an Italian firm of bankers. This was a delightful surprise.

Apart from those already mentioned as being attached to the gallery, there were also such painters as Norman Adams, Bernard Dunstan, Leonard Rosoman and Anthony Whishaw, all of whom have now established reputations in England. We exhibited Zladislaw Ruszkowski, another Polish artist, whose last exhibitions showed that he possessed the rare faculty of continuing to develop into his late seventies and beyond. We gave an unknown artist, Arnold van Praagh, his first exhibition which was based entirely on the theme of Toulouse-Lautrec. Despite the fact that it was completely sold out – mainly to a South African collector – he never repeated this initial commercial success. Another of our artists was Robin Philipson who though born in Lancashire became an eminent Scottish painter. In Scotland his wide reputation rested not only on his quality as an artist but on his position at one period as head of painting at Edinburgh College of Art, and later as President of the Royal Scottish Academy, a role he fulfilled for years with *réclame*. We gave him his first exhibition in London and he continued to show at 19 Cork Street for the rest of his life.

Since the early days of the gallery we had been interested in the work of Joan Eardley, another Scottish artist. Although we had seen only a handful of pictures when she participated in a small show in Cork Street, we immediately felt that she was a painter whom we would like to include in our circle. But as she was a rather solitary being, carefully guarding her privacy,

---

* Marjorie Lilly, *Sickert: The Painter and His Circle*, Noyes Press, New Jersey, 1973.

we were unable to make contact until 1961 when I was invited to her private view at Aitken Dott's in Edinburgh, and afterwards to meet her at lunch. I went to Scotland half expecting to be greeted by some resistance, but as it happened we set up a *rapport* and an exhibition was agreed for the future.

At this time Joan was spending much of her time at Catterline, a tiny fishing hamlet on the north-east coast of Scotland, although she retained a studio in a tenement in Glasgow, now long demolished, where she made her touching pastels of children. The kids of the family who lived in the building awaited her arrivals with expectancy; Pied-Piper-like they would follow her upstairs, tempted by the biscuits and sweets she had ready, which they munched while she made her studies.

The year after our meeting I went to Catterline in order to choose the work for her show, and I found with pleasure that our first affinity had not been merely transient but that even our evalutaion of individual pictures tallied exactly, so that some were discarded after a quick glance while the majority I eagerly accepted.

Completely oblivious to personal comfort, she lived in one of the fisher-men's tiny cottages that fringed the cliffs and overlooked the wild north-eastern seas. Her studio was in a similar cottage, but without any heating, and so very derelict that its front door had almost come away from its hinges and was kept closed with the aid of some string. In the formidable winters she would stand on the shore with her canvas or panel lashed to the easel, and her hands muffled up in her gloves. But she was not unaware of the comfort of others and had made thoughtful preparations for my short stay.

Joan was persuaded to come down for her opening and wore freshly washed trousers for the occasion, though she was uncomfortable among our visitors and spent most of her time in the National Gallery studying her favourite masters. Her reputation had preceded her first serious exhibition in London, as this was, and it was not only eagerly awaited but scored a great success. Her only reaction was one of contentment because as she told me: 'Now I shall be able to buy an estate car in which to carry my pictures.' In fact she was already quite well off and could have bought one if she pleased, but material matters concerned her so little that she was oblivious to this fact.

Despite her sturdy appearance Joan was not well. However, she chose to ignore her ill health. When she left London she went straight to Glasgow to consult with her doctor, a visit I feel sure she had deliberately postponed until after her exhibition had been launched. By this time the breast cancer had gone too far to be contained and she died shortly afterwards, in 1963; her singleness of purpose had signed her death warrant, the art world had lost an outstanding painter and her friends a fine human being. She was then only forty-two. Although our acquaintance had been very short, her death affected me deeply and I count it a privilege to have known this woman who seemed to combine the best in both sexes and who, among the dedicated artists I have met, has not been surpassed by any.

Joan's pastels of Glasgow children have sometimes been considered sentimental but a remark she once made to me is evidence of her practical realism. The Samson family of Glasgow, her favourite models, comprised six little boys and the same number of girls, all of whom had become adults long before their time, as happens in the poorest of families. Each of the girls had a very marked squint which was faithfully recorded by Joan, while all the boys' eyes were perfectly normal. Knowing it was possible to correct this fault I asked her one day why it had not been done, and she answered that the girls' eyes had now been made straight, ruefully adding, 'so they are no longer of use to me'.

After Joan's death, Aitken Dott and we ourselves divided the best pictures left in her studio which her family were ready to sell, and so we were able to make a few more exhibitions. With Eardley and Philipson in the gallery group, we reckoned we had the two leading painters among the vibrant contemporary Scottish schools of their day.

I long had a grudge against public bodies, a grievance I have aired in the press for what on the face of it seemed a general policy of deliberately ignoring contemporary Scottish artists – I mean those who still live and work in Scotland. The Tate Gallery, for instance, in 1960, did not buy but were given a painting by Anne Redpath, while in the following decade the only Scottish purchases were two oils and two prints by John Bellany who had, in fact moved to London. Despite several attempts by succeeding directors, three important Joan Eardleys were at different times refused, until at long last, after years of effort, one of her oils was belatedly bought. Robin Philipson still awaits entry.

As far as the Tate Gallery is concerned – other museums may have different procedures – it is the trustees who make the final decisions about new acquisitions, as the staff do not have votes. All the director and his keepers can do is to select in advance, put works which they think are desirable before the board, and presumably argue each individual case. But if the board in the end makes a bad decision it is not they, but the director, who bears the brunt.

The appointment of trustees is of the utmost importance, for much hangs on their ultimate decisions. But it is extremely difficult, if not well nigh impossible, to find an adequate group who are willing to serve, and while it is obviously prudent for a director to be able to call upon informed advice, how among laymen, who come and go at regular intervals, is it possible to find such a body, not only far-seeing but with knowledge and taste? The Tate tries the method of including some artists which on the surface appears a very good plan, but artists without blinkers are almost a phenomenon, the majority being prejudiced towards their own formal aims, and so one questions the wisdom of their admittance at a time when the visual arts are more polarized than ever.

Perhaps a solution to this knotty problem would be that the director, in consultation with his keepers, should decide upon works they wish to acquire and their order of importance; while the trustees, though with an interest in art, would be confined to advice on the museum's running, especially on finance and the raising of money, this being the area in which most are at home.

A variety of exhibitions

We only ever handled two Surrealist painters and in 1962 we made a joint show of them in which the exhibits were mainly of the second half of the 1920s. Max Ernst and Etienne Cournault were born in the same year and we followed the same pattern as with Matthew Smith and O'Conor, combining one painter, already famous, with another who was almost unknown. Cournault, the relatively unknown, had won a reputation as an engraver, the field in which he had begun his career; but his two early shows, which were of paintings, had passed by unnoticed, just as had happened to Max Ernst. A third was arranged but he forgot all about it and his pictures never got as far as the gallery – an unusual oversight for any artist to whom the date of a show is usually as threatening as the sword of Damocles. Some official recognition came in 1961, thirteen years after his death, when he was included in *A Hundred Years of French Painting*, an exhibition which the French Government sent on a tour of Japan. G. wrote in our catalogue 'Cournault's works, as those of Max Ernst, reveal another Sur-Realist whose dream world is no less valid, no less rich in invention,' and as Cournault was fascinated by the human head his rendering of it 'delved far below the ordinary appearance and sought the synthesis of expressive power and crystallized form.' He was essentially a draughtsman whose flat surface paint, with which he sometimes mixed sand – as did Picasso – served as a toned background for his probing line while he threaded his way over the canvas as finely and surely as the spider weaves its web. This analogy is strengthened by his attraction to small creatures for he owned a large collection of butterflies; in his last years he turned them to account by making a series of beautiful monotypes of which they were the theme. Cournault felt he was most nearly related to Klee; Jacques Villon was one of his closest friends. But unlike these two he has not yet made a name. I think we were bad impresarios.

The gallery having become known for its attractive exhibitions, we tried to maintain a lively variety as well as a rhythm in our annual programmes; we ran through some of the historical trends with *Fauvism, Cubism* and *Expressionism,* and as the Romantics appealed to us warmly, we bought good examples whenever we could, and in 1965 made one especially fine small show, *From Géricault to Courbet.* Keith Grant was welcomed as a contemporary Romantic whose spiritual home was the far north (and now he actually lives in Norway); an erupting volcano, the Aurora Borealis, the twenty-four hours of the ne'er-setting sun, all set alight the embers within him, contrasting sharply with his earlier, cold and stylized forms of the fjords.

Still indulging our taste for provocative titles, we continued with themes, sometimes suggested by pictures in stock which struck us as having a common trait. One example was *Restraint is also a Virtue,* a kind of protest against bombast in art, while *Portraiture, the Dying Art,* with its ominous title, was a modest effort to highlight the fact that the most searching and artistically valid images have, in the nineteenth and twentieth centuries, been painted by non-professional portraitists.

Three out-of-character deviations were prompted simply by their aesthetic appeal: one from Hong Kong with the contemporary Chinese painter Lui Shou Kwan and two other shows of Khmer and Thai sculpture. The last two came about through my friend Robert Haines to whom, in Australia, we had sent a few shows. Formerly the director of the Brisbane Museum, he had moved to Sydney where he created a splendid commercial gallery for the big firm of David Jones. Much drawn towards the art of South-East Asia, he had proposed a change of exhibitions with us, a proposition we gladly accepted. For these Khmer and Thai shows we felt that we needed to change the gallery's atmosphere as far as possible, so we transformed our walls from their habitual whiteness by hanging dark stone paper all over them. All daylight was excluded by blocking our windows and the lights were so placed that a shaft from above fell upon each individual piece of sculpture. The effect was dramatic, like a cave full of treasures. To suggest the random growth from which the fragments had been rescued before voracious vegetation completely engulfed them, we surrounded them with plants of all kinds. I enormously enjoyed our home-made improvisations which we repeated once again some years later. The occasion for this was an exhibition by the German ecclesiastical sculptor, Ulrich Henn, whose maquettes for his large commissions we showed. For him too we created a hushed retreat into an illusion of a more peaceful world.

Juan Gris, *Still Life on Round Table*, dedicated to Ozenfant. Private collection

Forain and the monograph

As exhibitions had been catalysts for me in the past, so it was our *Forain* show of 1964 that gave rise to my book on his paintings. He was widely recognized as an outstanding draughtsman but very few knew that he was also a painter who, at his best, could be remarkably good. Although the Tate possesses three of his canvases – including a *Court Scene* which belonged to Degas – only one hangs in the main galleries while the other two are in the Reserve. Since Tooth's made an exhibition some forty years before, no collection of Forain oils had been seen in London, and so with the help of museums and the few private owners, we gathered together twenty-five paintings and a smattering of drawings. The overall quality of this small group of paintings was an eye-opener, even to us; it made me feel they should be seen in more depth, and as no one was likely to make a comprehensive exhibition with works being borrowed from Europe and the States, a book was the only solution.

As it happened, the difficulties proved out of proportion to the comparatively slender importance of Forain as a painter, though I still believed that the book was worth doing as a small addition to the history of art. It also made sense from the personal angle for it fitted my corner: following my books on Degas and Sickert, a volume on Forain would complete the triangle, for like Sickert, Forain was a disciple of Degas. I had been very spoilt on former occasions by having two famous publishers agree to publish my work before seeing it, but this time I realized that would not be the case, for production had become much more costly. A volume of Forain would have a limited sale and few firms, if any, would undertake its publication.

Three monographs on the artist, long out of print, had done little more than repeat the same stories, mostly concerning his caustic *bon mots* and the prodigious number of his influential cartoons: I needed to trace his career as a painter and was therefore relying on research in the libraries, and on his granddaughter, for more factual information on his actual work of this kind. I went to see Mme Chagnaud-Forain in the old family home bordering on the park of Versailles, but although she was charming and welcomed my project, I got no further than this. She was either unable or unwilling to provide any of the pertinent insights I sought. I was rewarded instead with a family lunch and entry into the studio which remained exactly as the *maître* had left it – a typically sentimental French shrine to his memory of which I had seen several others. I was also invited to visit his grave, a 'privilege' I could scarcely refuse; so there in the churchyard we both stood in silence, our heads bowed in respect, though I am afraid that my thoughts were far from devout for by this time I only wanted to make my escape. In the Cabinet des Estampes my friend, Nicole Villa, did everything possible to help me. However, in spite of days of laborious searching I obtained only trivial facts. After much patient work I at last made some sense of Forain's development as a painter – if 'development' may be applied to an artist who, roughly halfway through his professional career, refuted the aesthetics of his modern contemporaries in favour of those of the past.

The deep social as well as political conscience, which informed all Forain's journalistic drawings, caused him to abjure his beguiling small paintings, comments upon the Paris of *la Belle Epoque*, and turn to one of the objects of his hatred, the corruption and heartlessness of the French legal system. Like Daumier, he expressed his anger through a series of court-room pictures; but the subject demanded of the painter a more sombre approach. The attraction of colour was therefore renounced and replaced by a near monochromatic palette, with an accent upon *chiaroscuro* and a rich, flowing handling of pigment, all reminiscent of the seventeenth-century Dutch, particularly of Frans Hals. That Forain's *volte face* was acceptable to Degas is endorsed by the painting he owned, although Degas is said to have remarked what a pity it was that his two disciples (Forain and Sickert) both seemed to prefer painting at night.

I quickly discovered, to my dismay, that side by side with near masterpieces, Forain could paint the most dismal failures. I know of no other artist so lacking in self-appraisal, although he is said to have destroyed much. That he was able at all to separate the cartoonist from the demands of the painter is remarkable enough in itself, but the variations in quality posed a further problem in the compilation of my book: was I to show Forain in his totality as a painter or ignore a whole body of his output? A compromise seemed the best solution, with a few of the better failures reproduced. I still believe that his successes warranted a monograph on the paintings of this brilliant and fantastically prolific cartoonist.

Since the untimely death of Keith Roberts of Phaidon who was hopeful that they would publish the book, no other firm showed any interest in Forain until I chanced to meet Paul Elek. He had published Anita Brookner's *Greuze* when her fame as a novelist was still in the future, and as she was acclaimed as one of the most perceptive and gifted of art historians whom we not only respected but enjoyed reading, I was delighted that my subject intrigued Paul Elek sufficiently for him to decide to publish it. Sadly he never saw *Forain* completed for he died whilst it was still at the printers; with his disappearance went an independent spirit, one of the few private publishers left.

Two months after *Forain the Painter* appeared, a large retrospective show of the artist's work was staged at the Musée Marmottan in Paris. As it only comprised examples gathered in France, the excellent Forains in the States and in England left a big gap in the *oeuvre*. This could, in a measure, have been rectified had my book been on show with the rest of the literature; it was not only absent but no one in the Marmottan appeared to have heard of its existence. Even Jean Lapeyre, another of my Paris friends, and Nicole Villa, both by then attached to the Louvre, had no idea that it had been published and thought I had abandoned the project. There was no other volume on the paintings of Forain so that mine was pertinent to the Marmottan exhibition. If I was annoyed, I was not surprised, as this was my second reminder of French insularity. Although *Degas Dancers* had been accepted by scholars as the definitive work on the subject, as far as I know neither it, nor *Forain*, has ever been available in any bookshop in Paris.

Change at Cork Street: the opening of Browse & Darby

After working together for some thirty years, Roland, G. and I had our first serious disagreement. The bone of contention was the gallery's future. We were all of an age and if the firm was to continue, which I earnestly hoped it would, then we had to incorporate one or two young people in order to train them in the gallery's ways. Some years before, Roland's son, Anthony, had come to us as a trial, and wishing to give him more freedom of movement, we sent him as our agent to Paris. Although gifted and dedicated, it gradually became evident to G. and myself that his talents lay in some other art enterprise, and so he left to immerse himself, first in the making, and then in the distribution of films on the pictorial arts in which area he has scored a huge success. Roland, quite naturally, was deeply disappointed for he envisaged that Tony might take over the firm. When this prospect faded his reaction was such that he lost all interest in its succession and adamantly denied entry to anyone else.

G. minded little about the gallery's future, accepting that it would close when we three retired; he did not believe it was of any importance or that its demise would cause a hiatus. So both of my partners refused even to contemplate any of the young men who approached us, and although I considered one or two had potential, my arguments fell on deaf ears. Having always been in harmony with them concerning the gallery, I could not understand their attitude: the child we had created and nourished with care was to be discarded with total indifference. Admittedly, it had fulfilled its original purpose and had provided us with a comfortable income, but surely our attachment to it went deeper than that? Over the years it had won a reputation that, in its field, was second to none. We had a staunch following of clients and art lovers who valued our taste and integrity, and equally important was our group of artists who would not so happily fit anywhere else – each gallery having its particular flavour. My partners rationalized my attitude as being sentimental – I had to agree but was not ashamed.

The last months of Roland, Browse & Delbanco were horrible as I tried to pretend that it was 'business as usual': gradually we were dispersing our remaining stock, forgoing pictures we would normally have bought and not planning exhibitions for the years ahead. For some of our artists we had found other homes, the rest stayed with us until the end. Relentlessly RBD's closure drew near, our racks were depleted and our lease was for sale; and finally we presented our ultimate show, *Our Thirty Years in Retrospect*, which closed in July 1977. This comprised the best works that the gallery had sold and which had remained in this country. No private owners re-fused to lend, while museum directors were no longer their own arbiters and needed their conservation department's consent. Modern technology has worked wonders in the restoration and preservation of art of all kinds, but when it comes to the question of drawings, I believe things have gone a little too far. It goes without saying that drawings must be protected from over-exposure to light; however it is pointless to show them if they cannot be seen, as happened a few years ago when the Leonardo sketches were on view at Burlington House. The lights were so dimmed as to prevent the close study that these rare, tiny gems demanded, and other museums follow the same procedure even when it seems to be absolutely unnecessary. When the National Galleries of Scotland presented their fine and important Degas exhibition, their rooms were so dark that instead of the excitement ex-pected on entry, one was faced with an air of gloom; and as one progressed through the rooms it was found that the ever-fresh colours of his pastels, as well as his oils, were reduced to an untruthful pallor.

Light was not so critical to our exhibition because we did not include any drawings, but when we borrowed an early O'Conor landscape back from the Tate, which a client of ours had bought from us and subsequently pre-sented to them, we were told that the loan would only be possible if one of their staff came to hang it himself. Its state was now described as 'delicate', although we had always known it as sound. Be that as it may we found the proviso comic, as we were hardly unaccustomed to the handling of paintings.

A further example of conservationist zeal was the attitude of the Birm-ingham Art Gallery which, as I have said, had bought more works from us than any other museum in the country. They actually sent a representative to London to measure the temperature and humidity of our rooms for fear that their loans might suffer deterioration during the mere four weeks of our show. The gallery, not surprisingly, did not come up to standard, neither would have any other art dealer's premises, so only a Jongkind was thought to be safe to withstand our dangerous environment.

Had it not been for its finality, this exhibition would have been a source of much pleasure; as it was I could only view it with some sense of pride in that each work, whether by a 'big' hand or a 'small' one, was of a consistently high quality. A tinge of sadness hung in the atmosphere during this our last private view, packed as it was with clients and friends, many of whom expressed their regrets in person. Others who were unable to attend wrote appreciative and even touching letters.

For a while it seemed certain that No. 19 Cork Street would no longer be used as an art gallery, and being sentimental about it as my partners had said, the thought caused me extra distress. Ever since I had first known it, which was in the 1930s, this little building had been nothing else – the oldest gallery in the street after the Redfern. But life often springs the greatest surprises and so, at the last moment, I found myself starting all over again with a new and much younger business partner.

William Darby was running a small gallery of his own on the first floor of a building near Sotheby's, in which firm he had started his career in the art world. Not seeing any future for a number of years, he had grown impatient and decided to leave and, like many of his colleagues, to branch out on his own. I knew him by sight for he often stood among the small group around the auctioneer's rostrum gaining experience by watching the sales. He had also bought a drawing from us. One day he came again to the gallery to ask if we had some other picture that he might possibly buy; in the course of a chat I happened to tell him that the lease of our building was going to be sold and was about to be put on the open market. Hearing this news he grew very excited and said he only wished that he could buy it, having always looked upon it with longing as the most charming art gallery in London.

When at home in the evening Sidney and I were exchanging the day's happenings, as was our custom, I told him about William Darby's reaction to what I had said. Sidney made no comment, but after dinner he raised the subject again. Knowing better than anyone how much I was fretting about the impending closure, he suddenly said, 'Why don't you two buy the lease together?' – an idea I had not considered. It would be a solution, but could William Darby find the necessary finance? I knew little or nothing about him, but I had taken a chance with my former partners, and I had a hunch that it might work, undoubtedly influenced as I was by his affection for the gallery. When I told Will of Sidney's suggestion he was delighted, for it was a vague hope he had not dared entertain and he could hardly believe his good fortune.

With much goodwill, a modicum of stock and nothing like enough capital behind us, the gallery was saved from extinction in times that presented far greater difficulties than those that attended its beginning. When I asked myself why I was courting this risk when in fact I had no need to do so, I found that although I was intrigued by the challenge, it was the gallery's succession that really mattered.

Less than three months after RBD's closure, Browse & Darby opened in October 1977 with a show by Euan Uglow. For a while many visitors did not notice the change as everything looked the same as before; the furniture was still in its usual place and one familiar face was there to greet them.

After two years of slow building, but with encouraging results, we were joined by Paul Thomson, Will's old friend from Sotheby's; and after another couple of years, with the knowledge that the gallery was in good hands, I thought it was time for me to retire and to leave these two men of the same generation to continue the firm on their own. Now I am in Cork Street in nothing but name; after my departure Will and Paul modernized the gallery's interior to create a new atmosphere and impress their own stamp upon it. Even without this refurbishing it had to be different, for each change of personalities sets a fresh tone, and this is exactly as it should be. Sadly a tragic event marred this happy story for after suffering for some years from a serious illness, Paul died in the winter of 1987 leaving Will to work on his own. Soon, however, his engaging wife, Letty, filled the gap as far as her experience allowed and ten years after Paul's death Charles Bradstock, a much younger man who had also served his apprenticeship at Sotheby's, became a third director of Browse & Darby.

Epilogue

I so much treasure those Cork Street years and still find myself missing the gallery life, although I realize how much the art world has changed. Apart from the pleasure of continually handling pictures, often making a good purchase and occasionally a 'find', it was fulfilling to be able to offer an exhibition to a painter who one felt had some promise. These were the days when London was the undisputed centre of the art trade and although, some twenty years ago, I resented my partners' decision to retire, thus bringing about the closure of our original gallery, I have since appreciated their foresight.

That remarkable sale in New York of 1958 carried the warning of distant thunder, and the fact that the storm has started to break is evinced by the various attractive fairs being held overseas and the few most important French sales taking place in New York. London is no longer the magnet; it is necessary to travel in the hope of buying fresh stock and of making new clients. Even in the late seventies we had an inkling that all this might happen, that we should have to travel very much more and, therefore, to some extent neglect our London gallery.

From now on this situation must only grow worse: the doubling of the already destructive VAT to be introduced soon with the threatened Droit de Suite (a form of artist's copyright) will further drive both buyers and sellers away from our capital to cities where these tolls do not apply.

While this situation adversely affects the whole country – the art trade has without doubt represented good business over an unexpectedly wide field – it might well be a hopeful sign for our living painters. For, as already said, there is today a much wider interest in art than ever before and, correspondingly, the number of galleries is growing. These dealers, mostly outside the West End where overheads are enormous, perforce handle mainly living artists, many of whom have suffered unwarranted neglect. But the signs are that not only are they beginning to be appreciated and therefore to sell but also in the States they are being sought with much interest at particular fairs.

Art auctions were originally confined to old masters. Then the Impressionists and Post-Impressionists followed with their Big Bang. Now, because of the scarcity of golden eggs, the formerly despised Pre-Raphaelites and their Victorian contemporaries are being highlighted by extravagant fully colour-plated catalogues. When this period too becomes exhausted, the sale rooms will be forced to diversify again, as they have already started to do. I believe, and hope, that the art world will then settle down to a moderate pace with artists showing in large general exhibitions as well as with their individual dealers, and all may return to sanity again.

Index

Artists and doyens of the world of ballet are noted by dates in brackets. Lillian Browse is abbreviated as LB, Roland, Browse & Delbanco as RDB. Numbers in *italics* indicate illustrations in the text, numbers in **bold** the plates, of which 1 to 8 are between pages 50 and 51, **9** to **16** between 100 and 101, and **17** to **24** between 150 and 151